Praise for *Learning JavaScript*

"Between modern web interfaces, server side technologies, and HTML5 games, JavaScript has never been a more important or versatile tool. To anyone just starting out with JavaScript or looking to deepen their knowledge of the practical core of the language, I would highly recommend *Learning JavaScript*."

—Evan Burchard, Independent Web Developer

"Although I've read a couple of books about JavaScript before, as a backend developer, I was thrilled to see Tim Wright's *Learning JavaScript*. The nuances of progressive enhancement versus graceful degradation are finally explained in a manner that someone new to front-end coding can understand. Bravo, Tim."

—Joe Devon, Cofounder, StartupDevs.com

"Tim Wright has written a delightfully practical book for the novice front-end developer who wants to learn JavaScript. This book's strength is in providing a good introduction to JavaScript while also illustrating the context of when and where it should be used."

—R. S. Doiel, Senior Software Engineer, USC Web Services

"*Learning JavaScript* is a great introduction into modern JavaScript development. From covering the history to its exciting future, Learning JavaScript equips the novice developer to practical application in the workforce. I wish this book came along when I was a novice!"

—Hillisha Haygood, Senior Web Developer, Sporting News

"Tim presents invaluable techniques for writing JavaScript with progressive enhancement at the forefront. If you are new to JavaScript then this book will prove to be a great asset in your learning. Covering all the basics and then right through to touch events, AJAX, and HTML5 APIs, the examples are clear and easy to follow. Using this book, you will learn when and how to use JavaScript to great effect."

—Tom Leadbetter, Freelance Web Designer

"*Learning JavaScript* is valuable for both new and veteran developers. It is great for new developers because it is easy to read and provides a step-by-step process to becoming great at JavaScript. Veteran developers will be reminded of many of the best practices they have already forgotten."

—Christopher Swenor, Manager of Technology, zMags

Addison-Wesley Learning Series

♦ Addison-Wesley

Visit informit.com/learningseries for a complete list of available publications.

The Addison-Wesley Learning Series is a collection of hands-on programming guides that help you quickly learn a new technology or language so you can apply what you've learned right away.

Each title comes with sample code for the application or applications built in the text. This code is fully annotated and can be reused in your own projects with no strings attached. Many chapters end with a series of exercises to encourage you to reexamine what you have just learned, and to tweak or adjust the code as a way of learning.

Titles in this series take a simple approach: they get you going right away and leave you with the ability to walk off and build your own application and apply the language or technology to whatever you are working on.

♦ Addison-Wesley   **informIT.com** | **Safari»** Books Online

ALWAYS LEARNING

PEARSON

Learning JavaScript

Learning JavaScript

A Hands-On Guide
to the Fundamentals
of Modern JavaScript

Tim Wright

✦✦Addison-Wesley

Upper Saddle River, NJ • Boston • Indianapolis • San Francisco
New York • Toronto • Montreal • London • Munich • Paris • Madrid
Cape Town • Sydney • Tokyo • Singapore • Mexico City

Many of the designations used by manufacturers and sellers to distinguish their products are claimed as trademarks. Where those designations appear in this book, and the publisher was aware of a trademark claim, the designations have been printed with initial capital letters or in all capitals.

The author and publisher have taken care in the preparation of this book, but make no expressed or implied warranty of any kind and assume no responsibility for errors or omissions. No liability is assumed for incidental or consequential damages in connection with or arising out of the use of the information or programs contained herein.

The publisher offers excellent discounts on this book when ordered in quantity for bulk purchases or special sales, which may include electronic versions and/or custom covers and content particular to your business, training goals, marketing focus, and branding interests. For more information, please contact:

U.S. Corporate and Government Sales
(800) 382-3419
corpsales@pearsontechgroup.com

For sales outside the United States, please contact:

International Sales
international@pearson.com

Visit us on the Web: informit.com/aw

Library of Congress Cataloging-in-Publication data

Wright, Tim, 1982-
  Learning JavaScript : a hands-on guide to the fundamentals of modern JavaScript / Tim Wright.
      pages cm
  Includes bibliographical references and index.
  ISBN 978-0-321-83274-0 (pbk. : alk. paper) – ISBN 0-321-83274-4 (pbk. : alk. paper)
1. JavaScript (Computer program language)–Handbooks, manuals, etc. I. Title.
  QA76.73.J38W755 2013
  005.2'762–dc23

                                    2012019351

Copyright © 2013 Pearson Education, Inc.

All rights reserved. Printed in the United States of America. This publication is protected by copyright, and permission must be obtained from the publisher prior to any prohibited reproduction, storage in a retrieval system, or transmission in any form or by any means, electronic, mechanical, photocopying, recording, or likewise. To obtain permission to use material from this work, please submit a written request to Pearson Education, Inc., Permissions Department, One Lake Street, Upper Saddle River, New Jersey 07458, or you may fax your request to (201) 236-3290.

ISBN-13: 978-0-321-83274-0
ISBN-10: 0-321-83274-4

Text printed in the United States on recycled paper at Edwards Brothers Malloy in Ann Arbor, Michigan.

First printing, August 2012

Editor-in-Chief
Mark Taub

Acquisitions Editor
Laura Lewin

Development Editor
Songlin Qiu

Managing Editor
Kristy Hart

Project Editor
Anne Goebel

Copy Editor
Barbara Hacha

Indexer
Lisa Stumpf

Proofreader
Debbie Williams

Technical Reviewers
Evan Burchard
Alex Moffat

Publishing Coordinator
Olivia Basegio

Cover Designer
Chuti Prasertsith

Compositor
Nonie Ratcliff

❖

For Ma.

❖

Contents

Table of Contents

Acknowledgments

There are a lot of people who contributed in some way to the completion of this book. First of all, I want to thank the folks at Pearson for giving me the opportunity to not only write this book, but structure it in a way that truly reflects how I believe the topic should be taught. The book would not have stayed on track without them. My technical editors were also instrumental to the process in pointing out any missteps, giving praise when needed, and making sure every detail of the book was written with accuracy and precision; I could not have done it without you (Evan Burchard and Alex Moffat). I would also like to give special thanks to my parents, friends, and family for the continued support, encouragement, and patience throughout this long process and for pulling me out of my "writing cave" for fresh air every once in a while. Without you all, nothing would have been possible.

About the Author

Tim Wright has been a Web designer and front-end developer since 2004, primarily focusing on CSS, HTML5, accessibility, user experience, and building applications with the capability to scale seamlessly from desktop to mobile device. He has worked at various universities nationwide and fostered the advancement of Web standards at each stop along the way. Tim has written many articles for popular Web design online publications, such as *Smashing Magazine*, *SitePoint*, and *Web Designer Depot*, on all facets of front-end development from HTML5 and CSS3 to user experience and advanced JavaScript techniques. He also writes many articles via his personal blog at csskarma.com. Tim holds a Bachelor's Degree in Marketing Management from Virginia Tech, with a specialization in Graphic Design.

Introduction

When I decided to write a book about JavaScript, I wanted to create it in a way that felt natural to how I learned the language. I didn't learn it from school or a book; my JavaScript knowledge comes from real-world application, trial and error, and self-motivation. I wanted to present the information in a unique way so that you could get up to speed quickly, but still develop a solid base for the language and move forward without feeling overwhelmed with too much information. I combined my teaching experience with how I felt while I was learning to create an environment that moves quickly but has built-in break points and reviews to always keep the mind focused and clear. The JavaScript language can be confusing if taken all at once. There are hundreds of way to accomplish the same task, most of which you don't need to know. I did my best throughout this book to not show too many ways to do the same thing, but rather focus on doing one thing really well.

The organization of this book is a little different from that of a normal JavaScript book. Often terms are introduced, explained in real-time, and readers can feel like they are taking in too much information at once. This can cause a loss of focus on the main task at hand. I addressed this issue by putting all the common JavaScript terms right up front in the book instead of piling them in a glossary that no one will read. As you go through them, they provide brief explanations of many core concepts in the language. This way we don't have to spend valuable time giving broad definitions of miscellaneous terms and can focus on getting you the most knowledge out of this short time we have together.

The process of learning a robust language like JavaScript may seem intimidating at first, but don't worry, it's not that bad. After you grasp some of the basic ideas, the rest is like learning a spoken language; the hard part is properly organizing it, performance tuning, and most of all, knowing when to use CSS instead. Hopefully, by the time you're finished reading this book, you will have gained the knowledge you need to effectively create a better user experience by responsibly using JavaScript.

JavaScript is a language with an amazingly rich history and an even brighter future. Throughout this book you learn the basics of the language, but at the same time you learn more advanced topics, such as HTML5 JavaScript APIs and how you create a touch-enabled interface. You can be assured that even though JavaScript is code, it's far from boring; you can create some pretty wild interfaces and have a lot of fun in the process.

I hope this book can serve you well for years to come and will act as a launching pad for your continued interest in JavaScript. If this is the first step in your journey to learning JavaScript, welcome aboard; if you already know the language, welcome back.

Target Audience for This Book

The audience for this book is anyone starting out in Web design and development who wants to learn about JavaScript. Before reading this book, you should be knowledgeable in HTML and CSS, and be familiar with the concepts behind progressive enhancement.

This book can equally serve absolute beginners and seasoned Web veterans who are expanding their knowledge into JavaScript. All the while, I hope it instills enthusiasm to learn more about this rapidly moving industry.

Code Samples for This Book

The code samples for this book are available on the book's website at http://learningjsbook.com.

Progressive Enhancement

As much as we'd like to think that people visit our sites to look at the majestically created intricate graphics, slick CSS animations, and semantic HTML, I can confidently tell you that, unfortunately, that is not true. I certainly visit some sites because of that—you may even do it as well—and it's possible that it's a topic of conversation over drinks after work, but real Internet users (we're not real users; we're developers and designers—we're "edge cases") don't notice that stuff. All they care about is how efficiently they can do what they need to do, whether it's checking email and the weather, downloading a song, or watching a movie. But that's the point: We're supposed to be designing things so well that the techniques go virtually unnoticed to an untrained eye. When they start to stand out, the overall goals tend to get blurred.

People come to your site, my site, Yahoo!, Google, or MSN for the same reason: **content**. Everyone wants the content; content is king. It's the most important aspect of any website or application. Think about it next time you visit a site. Why are you there? The answer is almost always "content." In the Web design community, we have a guiding principle that stresses the importance of content. It guides the way we approach all our projects, big and small, and it's called **progressive enhancement**.

Defining Progressive Enhancement

Progressive enhancement is the fundamental base for all front-end development. At its most basic level, it is creating a functional separation between HTML, CSS, and JavaScript. It's obviously much more than that (or there wouldn't be an entire chapter dedicated to it), but if you remember to always keep those three technologies separate, you're off to a good start.

Progressive enhancement is a layered approach to Web design, where focus is put on content, the user, and accessibility. The first step is keeping your HTML, CSS, and JavaScript separated, but we don't refer to them as HTML, CSS, and JavaScript. We refer to these three "layers" as **structure**, **presentation**, and **behavior**, probably so the methodology can be accurately applied to other areas beyond the current state of Web design. Regardless, it is a bottom-up or inside-out building model for a website or application.

You first focus on the content and mark it up with semantic and meaningful HTML. This is the first layer, "structure." After the content is properly marked up, we can move onto layer two, "presentation." On the presentation layer, we deal with CSS. The third layer of progressive enhancement, "behavior," we deal with last. This is where we will be spending a lot of time because this is where the JavaScript lives. Figure 1.1 shows the different layers of Web design.

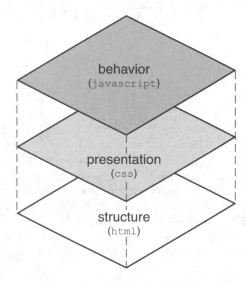

Figure 1.1 Graphical representation of progressive enhancement

The interesting thing about having these three layers is that they are never intended to touch each other, yet they're all integrated—as you move up the ladder, the next layer is dependent on the previous. JavaScript needs CSS, and CSS needs HTML. This ordering is set up so you can remove each layer from top to bottom and you never lose the most important aspect of your site: the content.

As long as you keep your layers separate, make your site work with only HTML, pretty it up with CSS, and then smooth out the behavior with JavaScript, you will make sure that your content is always accessible.

History

In 2003 in Austin, TX, at South by Southwest, a new term was coined that realigned the Web with the original path of Tim Berners-Lee; this term was announced as **progressive enhancement**, and ever since, the face of Web design has been changed. The way we build and think moved from focusing on machines (browsers) to a more friendly model, which centered around people (users). We started realizing that content was more important than decoration. We cared about users and we cared about getting them to the content they were seeking as quickly and as easily as possible.

Until this point, Web applications would either break a few browser versions back when designers stopped testing, or valuable time would be wasted trying to retrofit newer features into alternative outputs. Many things such as new devices, screen sizes, bandwidth restrictions and memory limitations would constantly crop up. Progressive enhancement was our way out of this endless cycle, and almost 10 years later, it's still working great.

To this day we are still building and finding ways to improve content and focus on user-centered design. Progressive enhancement changed the Web.

Purpose

The purpose of progressive enhancement is to put the importance on content, which makes perfect sense; it's why people visit your site. Although the main focus is on content, it also takes technology into account. Suppose you're building a site with progressive enhancement and beautiful JavaScript animations, and users visit your site with JavaScript turned off in their browser. They won't see any of the JavaScript enhancements you added in with such care, but it shouldn't matter because you can always peel back the layers and effectively get to the content.

Keeping your layers in separate files will also guarantee that if users were to visit without JavaScript, because it's in an external file, the users wouldn't have to waste the bandwidth to download all that code that they won't be using. So it addresses performance issues as well.

Accessibility

Putting so much emphasis on content makes sure that your content is always accessible, no matter what. When you hear the term **accessibility**, you probably jump right to thinking about disabled users, and you would be right to assume that, but there is more to it than that. Maybe there's a slow connection or tight bandwidth, but 9 out of 10 times the content will still be able to render because it will be meaningful and lightweight by not being bogged down with other layers.

Keeping your HTML clean, meaningful, and semantic will ensure that your content is easily consumable by everything from a constricted bandwidth to a disabled user accessing your site through screen reading software.

Reusability

Keeping all your layers separated raises the reusability factor of your code. You will be able to not only use the same code over and over throughout the same site, but as you move forward in your design career, you'll be able to reuse code from past projects. If the layer were not separated, a specific line of JavaScript or CSS would be very difficult to locate in a project and reused somewhere else, unless the development conditions were exactly the same—and they never are.

Progressive Enhancement Versus Graceful Degradation

Progressive enhancement was built off an old software development methodology called **graceful degradation**, where developers would build software for the most advanced version of a browser, but also make sure the software functioned in older browser versions. You wouldn't have all the bells and whistles, but everything would function.

It sounds familiar, doesn't it? In a lot of ways, graceful degradation is similar to progressive enhancement. Some might even say it's all in how you look at it. The main difference between the two methodologies is that progressive enhancement's main focus is content, whereas graceful degradation's main focus is the browser. Progressive enhancement also has a heavy focus on the layered separation between structure, presentation, and behavior. Next, let's take a deeper look into each layer, how they relate to each other, and how you'll build applications with this in mind.

Structure Layer

Everything has meaning and nothing has design.

The first step in progressive enhancement is to lay the content out, structured in a meaningful way with HTML. Headings are marked up as headings creating a hierarchical flow, paragraphs are wrapped in `<p>`'s, lists are marked up as lists, and we make sure that the HTML is meaningful without communicating anything about the design.

This is a harder concept to make click in someone's head than you may think. We've all been wired by what we've seen in working with word processing softwares, rich text editors, and what you see on the Web to forget what constitutes "design." Many have even forgotten the difference between what the true output for something is versus what can be changed with CSS.

Knowing CSS will make your HTML better. Knowing that just because the default behavior of `<blockquote>` is to indent text doesn't mean you should use a `<blockquote>` to indent text is a very important principle of progressive enhancement. You need to know what `<blockquote>` means (it's used for block-level quoted text) and that, for your purposes, it's irrelevant that a Web browser's default way to display that element is to indent it. HTML's default output is based on a stylesheet that the browser chose for convenience to keep unstyled content still functional and readable. When you write custom CSS for a site, you're overwriting what the browser did and creating new styles to match your design needs.

It's important to know that things like padding, indentation, **bulleted lists**, and numbered lists are no different from font size, background color, and font family, and that **a bullet list does not always mean an unordered list**. Most of the time it will, but a bullet is nothing more than a style declaration. After you wrap your head around that, you'll be ready to move on to the next area of progressive enhancement. Let's take a look at the basic HTML document in Listing 1.1.

Listing 1.1   **HTML Document**

```
<!doctype html>
<html>
<head>
    <title>Great Home Page</title>
    <meta charset="utf-8">
</head>
<body>

<div id="header ">
    <h1><a href="/">Great Home Page</a></h1>
</div>

<div id="nav ">
    <ul>
        <li><a href="/about">About</a></li>
        <li><a href="/articles">Articles</a></li>
        <li><a href="/staff">Staff</a></li>
        <li><a href="/contact">Contact</a></li>
    </ul>
</div>

<div id="main ">
[content here]
</div>

<div id="footer ">
    <p>&copy; 2012 Awesome Site</p>
</div>

</body>
</html>
```

In this example, you can see that you have a basic document with a header, navigation, content area, and footer. As far as structuring a document, this is right where you want to be, not thinking about how this HTML will render in a browser, because it doesn't matter at this point. All we want to do is make sure the most important heading on the page is a top-level heading, that the list we're using for our navigation is correct, and that our document is divided up into meaningful sections.

This content is easy to work with, clear, semantic, and most importantly, accessible. After you have the document structure nailed down, you can move on to the presentation, start applying some CSS, and work out the look and feel.

> **Note**
>
> As you're building a list of any kind, you will often need to decide whether to use an ordered or an unordered list. At this point, we generally use unordered lists for navigation and simply move on (because we've figured that out). Most of the lists you work with will probably be unordered, but what about when you need guidance for a gray area? Here's a way to make sure you're choosing the right kind of list: Ask yourself if this list would make sense if you were to shuffle all the items. If the answer is "yes," your list has no critical order; if the answer is "no," you probably have something like a ranking or a step-by-step recipe where the order truly matters (you can't stick a cake in the oven before cracking the eggs and mixing the ingredients). This can be tricky at times, so be careful when thinking about whether mixing up the order of the list items truly breaks the goal of the content. This will ensure that you have a meaningful content structure.

Adding More Meaning with HTML5

The document from Listing 1.1 is a perfectly valid and semantically marked-up document, and it is a great starting point for any project. You could take that, use it, and create a great product. However, with the influx of HTML5 recently, we can now take this basic mark up one step closer to our goal of creating HTML that contains meaning and communicates a true structure for our CSS to run with.

New elements in HTML5 such as `<header>`, `<nav>`, `<section>`, `<article>`, `<aside>`, and `<footer>` open up opportunities for designers to further describe the content within an element. Each of these new elements has special meaning and rules for its use, whereas the previously used `<div>` has very little or no semantic meaning. Let's take a look at the same document in Listing 1.1.1, now marked up with full HTML5:

Listing 1.1.1   **HTML5 Document**

```
<!doctype html>
<html>
<head>
    <title>Great Home Page in HTML5</title>
    <meta charset="utf-8">
</head>
<body>

<!-- replacing DIV with the new HEADER element -->
<header id="header" role="banner">
    <h1><a href="/">Great Home Page in HTML5</a></h1>
</header>

<!-- replacing DIV with the new NAV element -->
<nav id="nav " role="navigation ">
    <ul>
```

```
            <li><a href="/about">About</a></li>
            <li><a href="/articles">Articles</a></li>
            <li><a href="/staff">Staff</a></li>
            <li><a href="/contact">Contact</a></li>
        </ul>
</nav>

<!-- replacing DIV with the new ARTICLE element -->
<article id="main" role="main">
[content here]
</article>

<!-- replacing DIV with the new FOOTER element -->
<footer id="footer" role="contentinfo">
    <p>&copy; 2012 Awesome Site</p>
</footer>

</body>
</html>
```

HTML5 also brought with it new accessibility attributes for describing content to screen readers. In the preceding listing, you can see new "role" attributes attached to the new HTML5 elements. These are very helpful because the HTML5 elements can be used over and over inside a single document (an element that you can only use once isn't super-helpful) and by assigning a role to an element, you can more accurately describe its content. For example, the <header> in Listing 1.1.1 has a role of "banner," which lets you know that, in this case, the <header> is being used as a banner or masthead for the document. These are called **aria roles** and go slightly beyond the scope of this book, but they are a great enhancement to your HTML. Whether you're using HTML5 or not, you can still use these aria roles to create more accessible content.

Now that you have a strong understanding of document structure, you can begin adding design to the document with the second layer of progressive enhancement: CSS.

Presentation Layer

All content must be reachable without CSS.

After your document is laid out in a meaningful structure, you can start accessing that structure with CSS and applying the design. This can be the most important layer in progressive enhancement because of how flexible it is. Knowing CSS will help you write better JavaScript. For performance, you can't beat the rendering speed of CSS, especially when compared to that of JavaScript, which is notoriously slow to render in a browser.

Knowing all the capabilities of CSS and understanding the separation between presentation and behavior will allow you to offload a lot of heavy JavaScript functions to its more efficient relative, CSS. Most people are surprised when I tell them that *the key to writing great JavaScript is knowing when to use CSS instead*. However, you still need to know how to write good CSS. You can use a few ways to attach style to a document. Progressive enhancement states that you keep CSS out of your HTML (external CSS), and that is correct, but I also want to go over another method, inline CSS.

Inline CSS

Inline CSS is used with a style attribute, which is attached directly to an HTML element, and styles are applied to only that element; they cannot be cached and cannot be reused like the style applied in Listing 1.1.2.

Listing 1.1.2   **An Example of Inline CSS**

```
<nav id="nav" role="navigation" style="background:#c00;padding:10px;">
    <ul style="list-style:none;margin:0;">
        <li style="float:left;"><a href="/about">About</a></li>
        <li style="float:left;"><a href="/articles">Articles</a></li>
        <li style="float:left"><a href="/staff">Staff</a></li>
        <li style="float:left;"><a href="/contact">Contact</a></li>
    </ul>
</nav>
```

There are many reasons to not treat your CSS and HTML like this. Right off the bat, you can see that this HTML looks very cluttered, and it's hard to tell what content is buried in there. I already mentioned that it won't be cached, so you will need to rerender the styles each time the page loads unless the HTML has been cached. This way of applying styles is also very difficult to maintain and reuse on a site because everything is customized and tied to the element to which it is attached.

Inline CSS is fairly important because many of the functions that are common to JavaScript dynamically generate these style attributes in your HTML, and if all your JavaScript is doing is generating CSS, then why not just use CSS? This is what I was talking about when I mentioned how knowing CSS well will help you write better JavaScript. Generating inline CSS with JavaScript on-the-fly can be just as bad as applying them by hand in your HTML. It's certainly something to be aware of when you're building out a site.

Linking Up Your Stylesheet

Keeping your CSS in a completely separate file and linking it to your HTML document is, by a wide margin, the most desirable and best way to apply design to a site. You'll be applying styles through meaningful hooks you left in the HTML-like classes, IDs, and even normal HTML elements. In Listing 1.1.3 you can see how simple it is to link a CSS file to an HTML document.

Listing 1.1.3   **<head> Section of the HTML5 Document**

```
<head>

    <title>Great Home Page in HTML5</title>
    <meta charset="utf-8">

    <!--CSS-->
    <link rel="stylesheet" href="css/styles.css">

</head>
```

It is best to keep all your CSS in one file, even though you could, in theory, attach as many as you want. Linking any asset (CSS file, JavaScript file, image) to an HTML document fires off what is called an **HTTP request**, which just means the browser has to go get the asset and download it before it's viewable to the user. It happens all the time, and for the most part it's transparent. However, you still want to minimize the number of HTTP requests; at some point it will start to bog down the performance (load time) of a site. If you can, you should keep all CSS contained in a single file (one file = one HTTP request). Listing 1.1.4 is what your CSS file might contain to be applied to the HTML in Listing 1.1 or Listing 1.1.1.

Listing 1.1.4   **CSS Contained in the styles.css File Referenced in Listing 1.1.3**

```
#nav {
    background:#c00;
    padding:10px;
    overflow:hidden; }

#nav ul {
    list-style:none;
    margin:0;
    padding:0; }

#nav li {
    float:left; }

#nav li a {
    padding:0 10px; color:#fff; }
```

Admittedly, this is a pretty ugly design at this point, but that's okay because it illustrates the point that it is very easy to separate the structure of a document from the way it looks. As you can see in Listing 1.1.4, we are adding some light design to the navigation without touching the markup to convey it.

> **Note**
>
> You may have noticed that even though the HTML5 example has only one element, `<nav>`, we still choose to target the element by its IDs of #nav in the CSS. This is done because there can be multiple `<nav>` elements on one page that you may want to style differently, and it also allows a little flexibility in changing the HTML afterward. As long as the ID value doesn't change, you can keep your change isolated to only the HTML. It keeps your CSS that much more independent and maintainable.

Behavior Layer

Everything must be fully functional without JavaScript.

In this book, you will be spending the most time in the behavior layer. It's the basis for this book because JavaScript is the entire behavior layer, and you'll be learning JavaScript.

In many cases, JavaScript is nothing more than a luxury. You use it to smooth out interactions, make Ajax calls, slide elements around a page, and modify HTML. It really is another layer in progressive enhancement because by the time you make it to the third layer, your site or application should be fully functional. It needs to work completely before you start layering on the behavior and how you want it to act. It won't be as nice of a user experience, but if you can make it work without JavaScript, you will not only have built-in fallbacks if JavaScript fails, but you will have to write far less JavaScript to accomplish the same smooth experience for your users. Of course, less code means better performance, and better performance means a better user experience. That's what this is all about—providing the best user experience we can. If you can do that with less code, you absolutely should.

Like in CSS, with JavaScript you target elements in HTML and do stuff to them. In CSS, you apply style and in JavaScript you apply JavaScript and behavior. And also like in CSS, there are a few ways you can apply JavaScript to an HTML document. We're going to talk about three ways:

- Inline JavaScript
- Embedded JavaScript
- External JavaScript

Inline JavaScript

Inline JavaScript, like inline CSS, is when you attach JavaScript directly in the HTML. This has the same pitfalls the inline CSS has, but you still see this quite a bit, where inline CSS is all but dead in the wild. One of the most common applications of inline JavaScript is adding a click behavior to an element. "Click" is a JavaScript event that executes when a user clicks, and you can tie certain behaviors to it when adding interaction to a page. Listing 1.1.5 shows how you might apply that event with inline JavaScript.

Listing 1.1.5   **<nav> Section of the HTML5 Document with Inline JavaScript**

```
<nav>
    <ul>
        <li><a href="/about" onclick="alert('this is the thing'); ">About</a></li>
        <li><a href="/articles">Articles</a></li>
        <li><a href="/staff">Staff</a></li>
        <li><a href="/contact">Contact</a></li>
    </ul>
</nav>
```

In this example, when the user clicks "about" a JavaScript alert will pop up saying, "This is the thing" and then execute the normal link behavior of visiting the About page. It's a simple interaction, but anything could be substituted in place of the alert; any function, call or method can be executed upon clicking the element. There are ways to prevent the normal link behavior from executing, but we'll get into that a bit later in the book. If curiosity is overcoming you right now, feel free to flip to the index and look up "return false" or "preventDefault."

Using inline JavaScript is generally not a good idea, but it is a good way to illustrate interacting with the user through JavaScript events. Using JavaScript this way will clutter your HTML with unnecessary behavior, which should be sectioned off and isolated in its own layer. When JavaScript is inline to the HTML like this, we refer to it as **obtrusive JavaScript** because it's kind of in the way. Our goal is to write unobtrusive JavaScript.

Embedded JavaScript

Using embedded JavaScript is your first step toward having the language be unobtrusive to the HTML. It's not totally unobtrusive because it still sits in the HTML, but the syntax style is the same as fully unobtrusive JavaScript.

Embedded JavaScript is JavaScript that is inside an HTML document, but contained within a `<script>` element and executed only on that page.

In Listing 1.1.6, we added an ID of `"about"` to the first anchor (the first link) in the navigation. This was done because it is valid HTML, still remains semantic, and now you can easily target that link without adding any JavaScript inline to the document. This is a way to maintain the layer separation we're looking for in progressive enhancement, even if you are collapsing the layers by having JavaScript inside your HTML document. Listing 1.1.6 illustrates the same functionality as Listing 1.1.5, but in an embedded style.

Listing 1.1.6   **HTML5 Document with Embedded JavaScript**

```
<nav>
    <ul>
        <li><a href="/about" id="about">About</a></li>
        <li><a href="/articles">Articles</a></li>
        <li><a href="/staff">Staff</a></li>
```

```
        <li><a href="/contact">Contact</a></li>
    </ul>
</nav>

<script>

/*
The Function,
define the thing you want to happen
*/

function doTheThing(){
    alert('This is the thing!');
}

/*
The Variable,
get the element you want to do it on
*/
var elem = document.getElementById("about");

/*
The Event Listener,
set up something to listen for the event you want, then execute the function
*/

elem.addEventListener("click", doTheThing, false);

</script>
```

In the preceding example, you can see that there is a <script> element placed under the <nav> element, and inside the <script> three things are going on:

- Defining a function
- Defining a variable
- Setting up an Event Listener

Although this JavaScript is completely unobtrusive, it still lives in the HTML document, and that's not something progressive enhancement likes to do. Ideally, all that JavaScript should be placed in an external file. When you do that, you finally hit the goal of external and fully unobtrusive JavaScript, which means all your layers are successfully isolated based on the principles of progressive enhancement. Next, we'll take a look at how you can externalize this script.

External and Unobtrusive JavaScript

In the last layer of progressive enhancement, you will be taking the final step in removing all JavaScript from your HTML document and tightening up the separation between structure, presentation, and behavior. As mentioned previously, by the time you get to this point, your application or site should be fully functional. You're using JavaScript only to enhance the user experience and make a project more responsive to user needs, providing quick access to information.

Making a JavaScript file external isn't that different from doing the same to a CSS file. The `<script>` element you learned about in the previous section has an available attribute called `src` (source), which allows you to pull an external JavaScript file into an HTML document and execute the containing functions.

In Listing 1.1.7 you can see how to link up a JavaScript file at the bottom of an HTML document, followed by Listing 1.1.8, which is the contents of the JavaScript file.

Listing 1.1.7   **Bottom Section of Our HTML5 Document with External JavaScript**

```
<script src="js/script.js"></script>

</body>
</html>
```

> **Note**
>
> Linking your JavaScript file at the bottom of the document rather than at the top will let you control the rendering of the page a little better. It can technically be linked from anywhere in the HTML document, but because there are some pretty nasty performance problems with the way browsers render and execute JavaScript, you will want to use the bottom of the document to ensure that your JavaScript is the last item loaded. Because you used progressive enhancement, and your site is fully functional without JavaScript, this shouldn't be a problem for the user. On another note, JavaScript is a little easier to work with when the entire HTML document has already been rendered, so doing this will save you some minor headaches down the line.

Listing 1.1.8   **Contents of script.js**

```
/*
The Function,
define the thing you want to happen
*/

function doTheThing(){
    alert("This is the thing! ");
}
```

```
/*
The Variable,
get the element you want to do it on
*/
var elem = document.getElementById("about");

/*
The Event Listener,
set up something to listen for the event you want, then execute the function
*/

elem.addEventListener("click", doTheThing, false);
```

In Listing 1.1.8 you can see that the contents of script.js are the same as the code contained within the `<script>` tags from Listing 1.1.6. It functions the same, as well; the only difference is that it now lives in an external file, can be independently cached, and is easily reused throughout the entire site simply by linking the file up to any applicable HTML document.

Doing this also allows you to reuse the function and variable you defined over and over in different ways, rather than having to constantly rewrite them from scratch.

Using an event listener in your external JavaScript file is the equivalent of using the `onclick` attribute in Listing 1.1.5. They accomplish the same outcome of waiting (listening) for the user to click the link before executing the function you defined. Moving forward with this model by adding all your CSS into the CSS file you created and adding all your JavaScript into the same JavaScript file will ensure that you have a maintainable site or application that has started on a path toward a good user experience through optimal performance.

Benefits of Progressive Enhancement

Now that you have gone through the guts of progressive enhancement, you may be asking yourself what the benefits are to all this extra work? The first is that doing all this work and organization up front will save you a lot of time fixing it later. One of my personal favorites in progressive enhancement is the document design you come out with in the end. In Figure 1.2 you can see how a file structure starts to get created when you keep your layers separated. There's no guessing, for you or anyone else who may work on this project, where you would make a design change. Not only do you know it's in the CSS file, but you know that it is going to live in the "css" directory, providing a direct path to where you need to be. The same goes for behavior and structure; they're all separated in the meaningful way.

Coding mindset can also be helped with this structure—there's something to be said about opening up a JavaScript file and seeing only JavaScript; opening up an HTML document and seeing only structural markup; and cracking open your CSS file, knowing exactly what to expect. Using progressive enhancement will certainly improve your workflow. In Figure 1.2 you can see a clean and meaningful directory structure.

Figure 1.2   A beautiful and organized file structure

Some of the more obvious benefits in using this method are performance and scalability. Let's talk about those a little bit before you move on to some more intense JavaScript.

Performance

By externally linking your CSS and JavaScript files, you are allowing the browser to cache them in memory for each user. What does this mean? When someone accesses your home page, many of the assets get saved so the user doesn't have to redownload them. This betters the performance of your site from a user perspective. If all the JavaScript for the entire site gets downloaded at the first visit to a site or application, as the user navigates around, there is no need to download that asset again, hence speeding up the load time for the site and minimizing HTTP requests. The same rules apply for CSS. All the user needs to download after the assets are cached is the new, clean HTML you build for the internal pages. Because no inline CSS or JavaScript is in there, it is extremely fast to download.

Building for the Future

There are two types of scaling in progressive enhancement:

- Adding features
- Scaling to grow for the future (we're talking about mobile here)

Adding features to a website or changing the design of a site that has already been built with progressive enhancement can be as easy as cracking open the appropriate layer, making your enhancements and getting out of there. It also helps working on a team where one person can work on the JavaScript while another is playing with the CSS and design. Team members can work independently and ensure that all the work fits together in the end.

Scaling a small screen interface to grow for the future is a little further out there in terms of concepts related to progressive enhancement, but stay with me here. Listing 1.1.9 contains a CSS media query, and it goes at the bottom of your CSS file.

Listing 1.1.9 **Using a Media Query in CSS**

```
@media only screen and (max-width:480px) {

    /* do something to the design for small screens */

}
```

The job of a media query is to detect the screen or window size of the device a user is using to view your site or application. In the preceding example, you are detecting for a maximum screen size of 480px; then inside the brackets, you adjust the design (in the presentation layer) to better fit the smaller screen size. The best part is that it is device-independent, so you can activate these media queries simply by resizing your browser window down to 480px.

Unless you have to make serious structural changes to your document for a mobile version of your site, you can use these media queries to reflow the layout or make small tweaks to the design to optimize it on a smaller screen device. This lets you maintain the progressive enhancement layer stack by applying all design changes in the presentation layer.

Using a media query is a very fast and lightweight way to target a user on a smaller screen. These are great because they not only apply to mobile devices, but also to any device with a smaller screen, such as a netbook. They help a great deal in preventing horizontal scrolling, not to mention the user possibly feeling cramped when using a smaller browser window, while still presenting a usable design.

> **Note**
>
> If you loaded the example to this point up on a phone, you would notice that your media query isn't working yet. The Web page probably looks all zoomed out, and this obviously isn't what we're looking for. There is an HTML `meta` element that you need to add into the `<head>` of your document to make sure this initial zoom happens and your media queries work as expected. That element looks like:
>
> `<meta name="viewport" content="width=device-width, initial-scale=1">`

As much as we want it to, a small screen doesn't necessarily mean a touch device. Even a small screen that supports media queries may not be a touch device. So although this method may work very well for general design and layout, it basically fails to transfer over into interface design. Some user interactions, like drag and drop, work fine on a device with a small screen— as long as there's also a pointing device. With a touch-only device, drag and drop is woefully inadequate. There is also the possibility that media queries might be unsupported by a given device. Depending on your audience, you may want to explore another option.

The Touch Interface

Touch interfaces are awesome, right? They are the wave of the future. But the way we interact with a touch-enabled device is a lot different from the way we interact with a nontouch device.

When building in a touch-based environment, you lose elements like normal drag and drop or hover, and you gain access to interface delights such as pinch-zoom and swiping/gestures. If you focus on these features rather than the device, you can maintain the layer's structure and plan for these behaviors to be active. Listing 1.1.10 illustrates how to detect for touch capabilities in a site. This is something that would be in your external JavaScript file.

Listing 1.1.10   **Using Touch-based JavaScript**

```
if("ontouchstart" in window){

    /* do something only for touch devices */
    alert("You have a touch device!");

}
```

With this bit of JavaScript, you can conditionally load features into an interface that specifically target how users have access to the gestures and other features like touch activation.

Combining all these features and maintaining the guiding principles behind progressive enhancement will open up opportunities for you to create high-end, high-performance, extremely maintainable websites and applications. It's not to say that there won't be challenges along the way, and many times you'll want to divert away from full-on progressive enhancement, but if you stay the course, you'll be much happier later on when you have an application you built on a single HTML base that has the capability of being deployed on an endless amount of platforms both current and in the future.

Final Words on Progressive Enhancement

We talked about a lot of new items in this chapter that you may not fully understand at this point—specifically functions, variables, and event listeners in JavaScript. But that's okay. The most important thing to take away from this chapter is not the code samples; it's the overall concept of progressive enhancement, why we use it, and the benefits of building within the model. As you go through the rest of this book, have no fear, those knowledge gaps will be filled in and you'll have plenty of "Ah-ha" moments.

Clearly seeing the reason for a methodology like progressive enhancement and creating a solid base will save you mounds of frustration as you continue your career. By building on best practices and using them in ways that will help you avoid coding yourself into a corner (as they say), you will not waste valuable time going over and rewriting hundreds of lines of code. That's not to say that you'll *never* have to refactor code, but having a clean and solid structure with an understanding and mental path to the future will make your job a lot more fun. So keep those layers separate!

Summary

In this chapter you learned about the guiding principle behind front-end development, progressive enhancement. We talked about each of the three layers and the technology that they are directly related to. We also touched on how building sites with progressive enhancement in mind can increase your site's scalability and maintainability in the future.

You learned what the benefits of using this methodology are and how important they are to the overall goal of a site in regard to performance, accessibility, and making sure content is always available to the user no matter what. Content is king.

Exercises

1. What are the three layers of progressive enhancement?

2. What part of any website is flagged as the "most important" when we think about progressive enhancement?

3. How does using progressive enhancement benefit performance?

2

JavaScript in the Browser

In this chapter, we lay the groundwork to help you keep proper focus as you write JavaScript on any project. Just like anything in life, as you get deeper and deeper into something, you tend to stray from the path every now and then. Knowing the core reasons for each decision you make in your code will not only help you successfully defend your choices later on, but also create the best user experience possible in writing high-performance JavaScript.

Step 1 to writing good JavaScript is getting to know your environment. Well, step 1 is really knowing JavaScript (history and so forth, but we'll get to that shortly). As developers and designers, our environment is the browser. The browser is the crutch to our limping friend, JavaScript. For all intents and purposes, without a browser of some kind, there is little need for a language like this. Later on you'll find out that this isn't necessarily true, but for right now you can take it as law.

When you break down the environment even further, you find that just like in CSS it's not just "the browser," but depending on your audience, the "environment" can be anywhere from 1 browser to 10 or more browsers. In most cases, those browsers will have slight differences (quirks from Firefox on a Mac versus Firefox on a PC) or massive differences (Google Chrome versus Internet Explorer 7) in things like rendering speed and feature support.

Feature support is something that you need to test out in each browser (or read articles/books about it), but rendering speed, conventions, and best practices are global to how JavaScript interacts with any browser. Knowing those will help you make the right decisions with your code and create a top-notch user experience.

A People's History of JavaScript

What's that old George Santayana saying? "Those who cannot remember the past are condemned to repeat it." There are reasons that you're forced to take history classes in school, reasons why you value experience, or even reasons why you might ask advice from the elderly. There is knowledge and great power in knowing the origins of something before diving in head first and repeating mistakes of the past unnecessarily. *Learning history is the easiest way to plan for the future.* With that in mind, let's take a brief look at where JavaScript came from; this will also help you when you're having conversations about the language with other people. Many don't take the time to learn this stuff—hopefully, you will.

Origins

Most people will tell you that Java and JavaScript are completely unrelated. It's true that they are very different languages, but their pasts are intertwined quite a bit. Without Java, there would have been no JavaScript (or "LiveScript" as it was originally named). The original purpose fueling JavaScript was to create a language that would give easy control and access of Java Applets in the browser. We don't use Java Applets anymore, but they were basically interactive blobs in the middle of an HTML document, sometimes containing an entire application. It's like the olden-days version of Flash or HTML5's canvas element. JavaScript was intended to let designers hook into these applets without having to use a more intense language like Java. This initiative was championed by a little browser maker called Netscape in late 1995 (parent company, Mozilla), but you probably know them by their current name, Firefox.

Even though the intention of JavaScript was to work with Java Applets, we all know that users never use the things we make in the way we think they should. Designers started heavily using JavaScript to change around HTML, adding some behavior like roll-over effects to Web pages (we mostly do this with CSS now).

The language had great success because of its ease of use and its dynamic nature. You could do a lot of cool stuff relatively quickly, which is a key to the success of any product. The support was poor; there were no real tools to help test code other than the browser, and there was a growing mountain of security holes with the browser implementations of the language, but people loved it. It continued to explode despite being written off by traditional programmers as "not a real language." That attitude, to an extent, still exists among the hardcore development community, but I can assure you, JavaScript is indeed a programming language. It becomes more and more evident with every passing year and with every added feature.

With subsequent releases of supporting browsers, many of the security holes in JavaScript were planned for and blocked in various ways. This created a slightly tainted perception of JavaScript with the public. When I was first starting out, the language was thought of as easily exploited, and many people around the community made an active decision to turn off JavaScript as they browsed the Web. This attitude, although fading quickly, still exists in pockets and is the driving reason that it is best practice to be sure all your content is accessible and your applications are usable without JavaScript turned on.

For a long time Internet Explorer did not support JavaScript, but rather used a proprietary language with the same intention of providing interaction with embedding page elements (like the Java Applets). They called this JScript. We all hated it, and it launched the bad practice of browser detection (which is still around in various forms). Designers would have to check the browser for JavaScript support, write the JavaScript, then either ignore Internet Explorer, or rewrite the functionality in JScript to create a consistent user experience. It was a terrible model, but everyone followed it for lack of a better way.

This time in the front-end scripting world wasn't all for nothing, though. Through the frustration of browser compatibility problems came a desire to create some form of Web standards and a common language that would work across many browsers. This first attempt at standardization/merging of JavaScript and Jscript was called EMCAScript. This new language was more of a standardized version of JavaScript, but we still called it JavaScript, obviously, or this book would be called *Learning EMCAScript*. But it did kickstart the conversation about the Web needing some form of standardization.

This conversation also brought to light problems with how browsers were creating the outline for an HTML document, which was JavaScript's main access to the Web. The browsers' inconsistencies this created were the root problem. At this point in history we started to see the power of current-day JavaScript take its form. This agreed-upon universal document outline was eventually called the document object model (DOM). Creating a truly universal DOM led the Web back to its roots where the actual structure of the document was just that—structure, without communicating any information about presentation. This was the first step toward a true separation between structure, presentation, and behavior. As you learned in the previous chapter, it wasn't until years later that the official term for this was coined for Web and we entered the age of progressive enhancement.

In 1999, Microsoft created the earliest stage of Ajax in the form of an ActiveX control called XMLHTTP, which allowed internal content areas of an HTML document to be updated without refreshing the browser window, wasting valuable bandwidth. This feature was so popular and highly desired that other browser makers adopted it almost immediately under its current (technical) name, the **XMLHttpRequest** object. It wasn't until 2005 that the term **Ajax** was coined, but the underlying technology is still the XMLHttpRequest object in JavaScript.

All these standards, browser wars, and debates that happened throughout the years contributed to what you use today in JavaScript. It is important to know what is going on right now, but it is equally important to learn about the origins, how we got to where we are, and the evolution of the language so you can recognize times when trends seem to be circling back to old ways. Knowing the history and being able to tell when a new technology is going to fail (because something similar already failed in the past) can save you a lot of frustration in learning technologies that have shortsighted futures.

Progressive Enhancement

As mentioned in the previous chapter, progressive enhancement is the layered approach we take when building for the Web, where the main focus is placed on accessibility of content and the user, rather than the browser (that's graceful degradation). We use HTML for structure, CSS for presentation, and JavaScript for behavior. But you already knew that from Chapter 1, "Progressive Enhancement." There was lot of embedded and inline JavaScript happening throughout the Web. It made sites very difficult to maintain, and this methodology helped guide the creation of a Web that was not only more pleasant from a user standpoint, but also much more maintainable from a developer/designer standpoint. There was no more guessing where an update needed to be made in the code; you knew exactly what layer a change lived on, and it was inevitably separated out into its own cacheable file where the modifications could be isolated from the rest of the site or application.

The Behavior Layer

Most of this book will be focused on the behavior layer of progressive enhancement and tearing it apart piece by piece, so it is important to understand where the layer sits in the process, why is it there, and how to utilize its best features. Be aware that there are good features and bad features. Browser wars of the mid-90s exposed a lot of security flaws in JavaScript, and I'm sorry to say that they aren't getting fixed at the JavaScript level. With most other languages, if there is a highly publicized security hole, a version patch will come out and fix it. Because JavaScript is executed in an environment you can't control, this is very difficult to do without breaking a lot of sites. Unless you go to your grandmother's house and manually upgrade her browser (I've done that), it is almost impossible to control. Since 1995, there have been two major releases of JavaScript as an official language. The second one was very recent. With security holes never getting patched, it's more about education than anything. Knowing what not to use can be very powerful. In this book you will learn the correct methods.

Making the jump from inline functions to using unobtrusive JavaScript was a struggle for some because it was a new way of attacking interactivity. Instead of using onClick events in HTML, you had to pull that out and start using Event Listeners in an external JavaScript file. It was a new way of thinking and a large mental jump, whereas moving CSS to an external file was not, because the syntax was often very similar. You didn't have to learn anything new, but this wasn't the case with unobtrusive JavaScript. It took a little while to catch on, and it is still something we fight against. You will still see it quite often in the wild.

JavaScript as a language is far from perfect. As mentioned previously, it has a lot of security flaws and inefficiencies, and it can sometimes feel like you're trying to untangle a ball of yarn when combing through to find a bug. But when you hit that groove where you're firing on all cylinders, your behavior layer is completely abstracted from structure and presentation, and your code is flying light and fast, you will find yourself creating a user experience like no other that is a delight for your users to click around and achieve their goals. A happy user is a repeat user. Treating JavaScript as a behavioral technology will help you create a mental model for effectively constructing your next project.

Moving Past Today

The future of JavaScript obviously has not been written yet, but if you go into it with an open mind and a good understanding of its past, you will be able to remain flexible enough to mold into an industry with rapidly changing directions.

JavaScript has come a long way since it was first conceived in 1995, and it still has a long way to go. We use it to create a more pleasant experience in the browser. We use it to send data more efficiently and to store information in various ways (you'll get to that in Chapter 5, "Storing Data in JavaScript"). Many times it is overlooked that you can formulate the coolest interaction ever conceived, but if the platform can't handle it, it is of little use to the end user. Understanding the limitations of the browser environment and grasping the concept of how JavaScript travels from the code you wrote all the way to the screen is extremely important. How browsers treat JavaScript will guide a lot of your performance-based decisions.

Browser Interactions with JavaScript

As mentioned previously, JavaScript isn't like other programming languages where you can control the environment. When coding in PHP, as long as you have the correct version of PHP installed on your server, it will work, and you know it will work. The same principles can be applied for other back-end languages like Python or Ruby; if they work on the server that you control, they will work for users who visit the site or application. There really isn't even any gray area, if it works for you, it will work for everyone. JavaScript isn't like that. It's primarily a front-end language.

A front-end language doesn't get run or executed until it is rendered in a Web browser. HTML and CSS are other examples of front-end languages. This is important to note because many factors, such as feature support, connection speed, screen size, and rendering performance, are completely out of your hands. When coding with front-end languages, you have to keep all those inconsistencies in mind as you go about your build process.

You may have heard terms like client and server in your day-to-day JavaScript life. **Server** is pretty straightforward; it's the physical machine on which you execute something like PHP, Python, or Ruby, and then serve up those pages to the end user. You control the server. You can upgrade it if it's too slow or breaking down, and you can run server-side technologies on it. **Client** trips people up from time to time because its name isn't quite as clear. In a nutshell, the client is the browser and you run **client-side code** on the client. JavaScript is an example of client-side code. It's sometimes referred to as the **front-end**, as well. It is almost always true that code on the server executes faster than it does on the client, so if you can do something server-side rather than client-side, it's generally a good idea.

Figure 2.1 depicts the (high-level) process that happens each time an asset gets rendered in a browser.

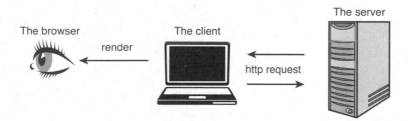

Figure 2.1   The process for accessing data on a server

In Figure 2.1 you can see the basic three-step procedure for getting assets to the user. This happens many times for each page. The process of getting assets from the server to the client, then rendering that content in a browser can be very resource intensive. A normal website can contain many assets that need to be sent to the browser, including

- Images
- HTML
- JavaScript files
- CSS files
- Multimedia content (audio/video)
- Font files

In many cases, there are more than one instance of each type of asset (multiple images on a page, for example), and each asset requires an individual and costly HTTP request to fetch it from the server and display it in the browser.

HTTP Requests

When you visit a URL, it is prefaced with http://. What's going on is that you are creating a single HTTP request for the HTML that lives at that URL. Figure 2.2 depicts a basic HTTP request for an HTML document. You're basically saying, "Hey, give me the HTML that lives at this address."

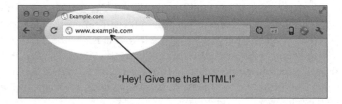

Figure 2.2   A URL example of the most basic HTTP request

Unless the server (or your Internet) is down, your browser will request the HTML for the URL. When the HTTP request is completed, the browser begins rendering the document, parsing through the HTML code and hitting requests for other resources. As it hits these other requests, it will fetch them from the server the same way it fetched the original HTML document. This will happen until all the assets have been fetched and downloaded. Listing 2.1 shows the HTML code a browser will parse through and various resources it will need to fetch throughout the document.

Listing 2.1   **A Basic HTML Document with HTTP Requests Bolded**

```
<!doctype html>
<html>
<head>
    <title>HTTP Request Example</title>

    <meta charset="utf-8">

<!-- 1 HTTP request for the favicon -->
<link rel="shortcut icon" href="images/favicon.ico">

<!-- 1 HTTP request per CSS file (2 total) -->
<link rel="stylesheet" href="css/style.css" media="screen">
<link rel="stylesheet" href="css/print.css" media="print">

</head>
<body>

<!--1 HTTP request per image file (4 total)-->
<img src="images/picture-of-allie.gif" alt="placeholder content">
<img src="images/patricks-mug.gif" alt="placeholder content">
<img src="images/clay.gif" alt="placeholder content">
<img src="images/linh-in-a-chair.gif" alt="placeholder content">

<!--1 HTTP request per JavaScript file (2 total)-->
<script src="js/plugins.js"></script>
<script src="js/script.js"></script>
</body>
</html>
```

As you can see in Listing 2.1, this is a very basic layout, but it is still firing off 10 HTTP requests to render the page (including the original request for the HTML). They pile up fast, so it's best to keep an eye on them. You may also have hidden requests if you're getting images via your CSS file (background images), which add to the total count and can bog down page performance.

By default, the average browser will fetch these assets in pairs—that is, two at a time. It can get two images, two CSS files, and so on until everything has been fetched. It can't download everything at the same time because of bandwidth constrictions, but there is a user setting in most browsers to change this setting from 2 to whatever you'd like (it is extremely rare to encounter someone who has changed this setting). It's generally kept at 2 to keep wear on the processor as low as possible to not affect anything else running on a user's machine.

Two is our magic number here. Assume that you can get the browser to download only two assets at a time. This is the exact reason that you want to do your best to keep the number of HTTP requests to an absolute minimum. There are some that you really can't control, like the number of content images in a news article; you need what you need for something like that. What you *can* control are the elements of the page that you constructed, the overall design, the CSS, HTML, and JavaScript.

HTML

Keeping HTML as lean as possible will ensure that a browser does not have to parse through unnecessary HTML elements to display content to the user. Keeping your HTML as semantic as possible while still being able to achieve your design goals is important. Don't be one of those people who throw in a bunch of meaningless div elements. From a document-parsing perspective, having too many HTML elements is just as bad (sometimes worse) than using a table-based layout. Keeping HTML to a minimum will also speed up your JavaScript, but cut back on the number of elements that might need to be parsed.

CSS

CSS is often broken apart into easy-to-use modules in a file structure and then combined later. As long as the combination happens on the server and not on the client, this is fine. You will get into performance trouble when using more than one CSS file per document because each additional file requires an extra HTTP request that could easily be removed by having all your CSS live in a single (cacheable) file on the server. If you're looking for a general rule here, anything more than one CSS file is generally unnecessary and bad for performance. There are constant battles being waged between performance and maintainability, but plenty of server-side technologies can combine and minify (remove all whitespace from) your CSS files to keep the number of HTTP requests as low as possible.

JavaScript

JavaScript follows the same HTTP rules as CSS does. The fewer requests the better. In the real world it's not uncommon to see three JavaScript files attached to a document and have it be fully justified if you're using libraries and external code extensions (plug-ins), but that's a topic we will cover in Chapter 10, "Making JavaScript Easier with Libraries."

One notable and important difference exists between the HTTP requests that assets like images and CSS and other asset types use versus the HTTP process JavaScript uses. As mentioned previously, assets get downloaded two at a time. This is true for everything other than JavaScript. JavaScript is sort of treated like the queen of the browser. When it travels via an HTTP request *everything else stops*. Nothing else can come in while JavaScript is coming in, and this poses an interesting problem in all browsers. This is what people are talking about when they say that JavaScript is blocking. The way browsers implement JavaScript makes it block everything else from being downloaded until it's finished. So, JavaScript in itself isn't blocking; it's the browser's implementation of the language that actually produces the blocking nature of the language.

Generally speaking, the code you don't see in the browser, such as `<meta>` elements, the `<title>` element, `DOCTYPE`, links to favicons, or an external CSS file, are placed in the `<head>` or at the top of the document, because you want all those assets to be downloaded first so by the time the document is rendered, your design will be all worked out and placed correctly.

If you've ever been to a Web page that has a flash of white before is it completely rendered in the browser, that is the JavaScript (placed in the `<head>`) being downloaded and blocking all the other assets in the process. It's only a second usually, but it is certainly something that can be easily fixed by moving your JavaScript reference to the bottom of the document. This will ensure that the entire document renders smoothly. If you build with progressive enhancement in mind, your website or application will still be fully functional before the JavaScript is fully downloaded and rendered; it should be a transparent process to the user, who is most likely there for content and not your cool JavaScript animations (don't worry, I'll be there for the cool animations).

While the assets are being downloaded, the last step in the process is also happening; the browser is translating the code you wrote into some form of coherent output. This is called **rendering** and all browsers do it differently.

JavaScript and Rendering Engines

A rendering engine in a browser creates what you see on a screen. There are different ones for each browser. Table 2.1 shows common browsers paired up with their associated rendering engine.

Table 2.1   **Popular Web Browsers and Their Rendering Engines**

Firefox	Gecko
Internet Explorer	Trident
Chrome	Webkit
Safari	Webkit
iOS & Android	Webkit
Opera	Presto

As you can see in Table 2.1, there are a fair number of rendering engines. When you talk about code working differently in different browsers (modern browsers), you are generally referring to the rendering engine. That's why you have very few differences in support between Chrome and Safari; they are both built on the same open source rendering engine, Webkit.

> **Note**
>
> You may notice that the rendering engine names map to vendor extensions in CSS. On certain CSS functions (like keyframe animations), prefacing a property with `-webkit-` will target all browsers that use the Webkit rendering engine.

Some rendering engines are faster than others, but this also extends to the JavaScript engine in each browser. Just as some rendering engines are better than others, the same can be said about JavaScript engines that are built into the browser. The speeds of these JavaScript engines vary greatly, and this is generally why JavaScript is so slow to execute when compared to other technologies, like CSS.

Because of the special rendering attention JavaScript demands, performance is always a large concern. You have to pay close attention to each line being executed, making sure that they are all as efficient as they should be while making the code-base maintainable. I wish I could sit here and type out the answer for this problem, but you will certainly experience it on most projects where you need to write custom code, and most of the time it's something you have to adjust on-the-fly.

This is all part of client-side performance; it is a constant weight on the mind of a front-end developer or designer. Performance is your first line of defense when trying to create the best user experience possible. If, on every project, you reduce HTTP requests to a bare minimum and master the rendering bottlenecks, you'll be well on your way to that ideal user experience.

What JavaScript Can Do

JavaScript can do almost anything; it's a very dynamic language. It can create and destroy HTML, add and remove CSS, and even inject more JavaScript into a document. It's crazy, and you certainly need to keep yourself in check or you can easily go overboard and code yourself into a corner. Hopefully you'll avoid that by first learning what you can do with JavaScript and its core capabilities and intentions. Then further that into how you *should* use it.

Being introduced to the capabilities of JavaScript can be pretty overwhelming, so right out of the gate we'll lay out the three main functions of JavaScript:

- Modifying HTML
- Communicating with the server
- Storing data

These are the three high-level topics that cover just about all the basics of JavaScript that I discuss throughout this book. It doesn't seem too overwhelming when you break it down like that, does it? There are certainly a lot of topics packed into those three items, and later on when HTML5 JavaScript comes into the picture, those topics will have to be expanded on.

But without any further ado, let's get into it.

Modifying HTML

With JavaScript, you will be doing a lot of adding to, inserting, and removing HTML. This can take the form of physically adding a block of markup into a document with JavaScript, changing style properties, or adding or removing attributes. Everything in the document is up for grabs.

It's still very important to not only know that you can change HTML at your will with JavaScript, but also be able to identify when you should and—more importantly—when you shouldn't. Again, if you follow the principles of progressive enhancement, you will often be able to catch yourself doing something that feels a little off. And when that happens you can always go back to correct something before it becomes a real problem.

Make no mistake, modifying HTML in various ways is a huge deal in JavaScript. You will be doing it quite a bit while you're striving to create that perfect user experience. Don't worry—you'll be learning the right way to do it and, even better, *when* to do it.

Communicating with the Server

Generally speaking, when you hear people talk about JavaScript communicating with the server, they're talking about Ajax. It's not *always* Ajax, but it often is. JavaScript can communicate with the server in a lot of different ways. The purpose is to improve user experience. By using JavaScript to talk to the server, you can save both yourself and the user time and energy.

Saving the user time and energy is your number one concern, and creating an environment that offers less hanging around and more real-time (not quite real-time, but close) interaction can be a breeze when you sprinkle a JavaScript communication layer into your application. The ability to refresh parts of a page on-the-fly grows more common with every passing year. Creating truly responsive, user-centered applications is a desire of every designer. It can be easily accomplished with the proper fallbacks and JavaScript.

Saving yourself some headaches is always a nice bonus of building for the user. How do JavaScript, Ajax, and client-side server communications benefit you? Being able to refresh small parts of a page will save you some bandwidth by not forcing a user to do a full-page refresh to request new data. Using less bandwidth is always better for everybody. Of course you still need to have everything work without JavaScript, so the small portion of the population that is affected will still need a page refresh, but the data and content will always be available. Using JavaScript to communicate with the server can often be more efficient than not, and with the proper fallbacks in place, there is usually little reason to not go this route. We'll get into this in a lot more depth later on in the book.

Storing Data

Another important function of JavaScript is data storage. When I mention data storage you may be thinking about databases, and you're not too far off. Data storage in JavaScript is very similar to data storage in most server-side technologies. The formats are similar, and the caching is subject to the same rules. The main difference is that accessing server-side stored data from the client takes much longer than accessing the client-side stored data from the client. And it makes perfect sense that you don't have to travel to the server and back again in a costly HTTP request, but rather access it right where you are, in the browser.

Current client-side data storage methods can range from simple variables you reference from within your JavaScript files all the way to full databases stored locally in the browser. Storing an entire database in the browser is cutting edge as of this writing, but the capabilities of storage in JavaScript are constantly growing and pushing the limits to see just how fast and responsive you can make an application.

How You Should Use JavaScript

As I mentioned before, JavaScript is a very dynamic language, and you can do almost anything with it. You can do a lot of good, but you can also do a lot of bad. It's very easy to get lost in your JavaScript code. Just because JavaScript can modify HTML and control CSS doesn't mean that it should be done there. Remember the progressive enhancement layers? It is important to stick to those layers as much as you can. There will naturally be some overlap as you go along. Maybe you have to inject an HTML snippet into the document. From time to time you will naturally run into things like that, but make sure you're not just doing it because you have the JavaScript file open at the time. Everything in your codebase should have meaning.

A good check for yourself is to turn off JavaScript in the browser every now and then and see if, as a user, you can still accomplish all your goals. If you can, great—but if you can't, something went wrong along the way and you should take a step back to examine where the problem happened. Were you relying too much on JavaScript to create your content? Or maybe it was just an oversight. Either way, it is good to build some checkpoints into your development and design process to ensure that you are not straying away from the goals of the project and that you are always keeping user experience in mind.

Improving User Experience

Most of what JavaScript does (or how we'll be using it, at least) is to improve user experience through the behavior layer. We'll be extending what already exists and adding some *pop* to it. Adding *behavior* to a site or application, making it more responsive with things like Ajax, creating local data sources to improve performance, and cutting down on lag time between user generated requests (the user clicking around) can make or break a project.

Everything you do with JavaScript should guide user experience, and as you go through this book, a path to properly using this powerful language will be exposed.

Using JavaScript Responsibly

Using JavaScript responsibly involves knowing the difference between when you need JavaScript and when you can use CSS. As mentioned earlier, JavaScript is a performance hog.

It blocks everything from loading, it's slow, and it has security holes you need to worry about. As you build out the behavior layer of your project, you need to ask yourself if you absolutely need to use JavaScript to accomplish what you're trying to do. Many times you can partner JavaScript with CSS to create the same effect by simply toggling a class on an element.

Hide/show is a very popular interaction on the Web, and it's mostly approached with JavaScript. But a simple interaction like this can be done much more efficiently with a combination of CSS and JavaScript. In Listing 2.2 you see a basic HTML layout that we're going to use to depict this concept by simply hiding some text when a user clicks a button. Note how there is no JavaScript in the HTML.

Listing 2.2   **A Basic HTML Document for a Hide Behavior Demo**

```
<!doctype html>
<html lang="en">
<head>
        <title>Click to Hide</title>

        <meta charset="utf-8">

        <!-- css -->
        <link rel="stylesheet" href="css/hide.css">
</head>
<body>

<button type="button" id="hide">Hide the text</button>

<div id="target">
<p>Lorem ipsum dolor sit amet, consectetur adipiscing elit. Morbi dolor metus,
sagittis et aliquam et, ornare et libero. Etiam eu nisi felis, ac posuere metus.
Vivamus molestie bibendum imperdiet. Etiam et faucibus metus.</p>
</div><!--/#target-->

<!-- javascript -->
<script src="js/hide.js"></script>

</body>
</html>
```

As you can see, there wasn't a whole lot going on there; the main focus was the button, which has an ID of "hide" and the block of text, which has an ID of "target" (it's our target). Next, we're going to build the CSS you might use to hide something. Listing 2.2.1 illustrates a CSS style object created for the purpose of hiding elements.

Listing 2.2.1 CSS Attached to the HTML Document in Listing 2.2

```
.hide {
    display: none;
}
```

You see objects like this in CSS a lot in the form of classes like clearfix, float-left, float-right, and so on, which are generally set up for HTML to work with. You can do the same for JavaScript. Putting a class of "hide" in the CSS allows us to use it as a behavior over and over. This is a very primitive example, but you could create any number of these types of classes with the intention of having them referenced throughout your JavaScript file. It also allows you to keep CSS out of your JavaScript and in the CSS file, where it belongs.

Listing 2.2.2 shows the JavaScript you would use to add the "hide" class to the target element when a user clicks the button.

Listing 2.2.2 JavaScript Attached to the HTML Document in Listing 2.2

```
/* save the 2 nodes to variables */
var button = document.getElementById("hide"),
    target = document.getElementById("target");

/* define what we want to do in a function */
function hide(){
    target.setAttribute("class","hide");
}

/* add the CSS class when the button is clicked */
button.addEventListener("click", hide, false);
```

All we're doing here is adding a class and letting the CSS do the rest. If you try this demo, clicking the button should hide the text. This model of using CSS whenever you can will help improve the overall performance of your site because CSS renders much faster in the browser than JavaScript does, and the CSS class should already be in the browser's cache by the time you're ready to use it.

This may seem like a small trick right now, but as your project grows over time, saved milliseconds quickly turn into saved seconds on the load time. Knowing when to use CSS and when to use JavaScript for interactions is often overlooked, but it's still very important.

Creating Fallbacks

A fallback is something you create in case your main feature doesn't work. Think of it like making backup plans for a night on the town. Creating fallbacks is a two-fold discussion. First, you already learned about progressive enhancement and making sure everything works without

JavaScript enabled. Many times, fallbacks like that need to happen on the server (if we're talking Ajax interactions), and sometimes it can be as simple as making sure a tabbed interface will display all the tab content without JavaScript. That's the first level of fallback that needs to be created, and it always comes back to the fact that, in some way, everything needs to work.

The second level of fallback creation is when you want to use a feature in JavaScript that doesn't have good browser support, but you can accomplish the same behavior with something else. This is a slightly different concept than making sure everything works without JavaScript, but bear with me here.

Suppose you want to use one of the new forms of data storage that shipped with HTML5, **localStorage**. JavaScript already has the capability of storing data. We've been using it for years; it's called **cookies**. In this case there are three levels of fallbacks. Figure 2.3 shows how you would fall back from **localStorage** to **cookies**, to a server-side storage method.

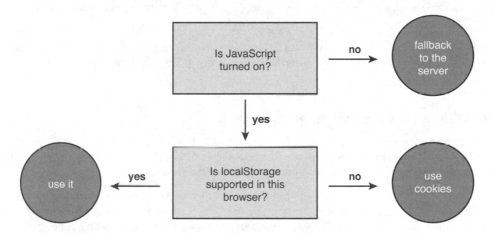

Figure 2.3   Flowchart depicting the process of using proper fallbacks in JavaScript

Using proper fallbacks allows you to use cutting-edge coding practices while still offering less-cutting-edge technologies if the user is visiting with a browser that doesn't support a certain feature. Listing 2.3 shows what the JavaScript might look like for checking a browser for support and then falling back to a lesser technology. The concept is more important than the syntax at this point.

Listing 2.3   **Using JavaScript Responsibly**

```
/* You know JavaScript is enabled at this point because none of this would apply
otherwise */

/* check if localStorage is supported */
if(typeof window.localStorage !== "undefined"){
```

```
        // use localStorage
} else {
        // use normal cookies
}
```

Tools to Help You Use JavaScript

JavaScript isn't like a server-side language where if you make a syntax error it's plainly visible because your application has crashed with a nice helpful error message. Many JavaScript errors go overlooked because, if built correctly, everything will still work fine. This can be a double-edged sword in that you want your users to be able to continue about their business like nothing is wrong, but it can also make finding a problem extremely difficult. Luckily, there are some tools built into the language and some tools on the Web that can ease your pain with JavaScript debugging.

JavaScript debugging is the process you go through when tracking down an error in your code. Don't worry, nobody's perfect. We all make syntax errors. If we didn't, none of these tools would exist.

Tools Built into the Language

The JavaScript console is a feature that can save your life as a designer or developer. The actual "console" is something that you will use in a browser, but I consider it something built into the language, so here we are, under this heading instead of the next one.

The console does some things automatically, such as monitor Ajax calls and output error codes with line numbers to help you out. You can see the URL of an Ajax request and pick apart any data that was being passed through. That can be immensely helpful for any debugging assignment.

The console can also be manually worked with from inside your JavaScript file. It can be useful for outputting data or locating points of failure in your code. Because JavaScript runs from the top of the file (generally) to the bottom, it can be very easy to pinpoint the exact spot where a script may be breaking. In Listing 2.4 you can see how to use the console to output various information.

Listing 2.4   **Utilizing the JavaScript Console**

```
/* output a basic message to the console */
console.log("hello there");

/* output a variable in the console */
var msg = "this is from a variable";

console.log(msg);
```

Every browser has a JavaScript console available; mostly it's a matter of finding it. If there is a Developer menu, it is inevitably in there. Figure 2.4 shows where the JavaScript console is for Google Chrome.

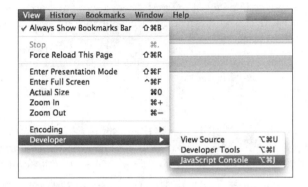

Figure 2.4   JavaScript console in Google Chrome

Entire articles have been written about using the console, but for our purposes we will be using it for debugging, monitoring errors, and Ajax interactions. The console can be your best friend when debugging.

Tools Built into the Browser

By *tools built into the browser* I mean Web applications that have been created with the sole purpose of helping you write better JavaScript. Nice, right? Browser tools can help you remove all whitespace from code to improve performance, like the YUI Compressor (www.refresh-sf.com/yui/). The compressor can greatly help the performance of your JavaScript by reducing the file size. This application can take text (pasted code), uploaded files, or remote URLs as forms of input. *Use this with caution.* The YUI compressor is a great tool, but it does make your code basically unmanageable by shrinking it all down to one line. With that in mind, if you plan to use this service, be sure to have an uncompressed version of the file that you can work in as well.

Compression applications like YUI Compressor are great, but there's another online service called JSLint (http://www.jslint.com), which will parse through your JavaScript and look for syntax and formatting problems. The slogan "JSLint will hurt your feelings" is absolutely dead on. It's always a shock to read through errors this application produces. Most are not actually errors in the browser, but JSLint will guide you toward best practices in code organization as well, helping you create even more streamlined, functional JavaScript.

Summary

In this chapter, you learned about the history of JavaScript: how it came from its inception in 1995 to the present-day version and why we deal with it the way we do. The history was then connected to the previous chapter about progressive enhancement, and we started zooming into the behavior layer with reasons for its existence while introducing some of the imperfections in JavaScript as a language.

Next, browser interactions were introduced, including how JavaScript gets rendered in the browser, what a rendering engine is, and why JavaScript is best placed at the bottom of an HTML document rather than placing it at the top with all the other "hidden" code, like meta elements and CSS.

We also talked about some of the capabilities of JavaScript to prepare you for what will be going on throughout the course of this book, including HTML modification, data storage, and communicating with the server through technologies like Ajax and the XMLHttpRequest.

We then elaborated on the capabilities of JavaScript and got into proper usage, including improved user experience, using JavaScript responsibly in a partnership with CSS, and creating proper support fallbacks while keeping performance in mind in a fragile environment.

Last, we discussed some JavaScript tools that will help not only your journey throughout this book, but also your journey as a designer. Consider these supplemental materials to the textbook.

Exercises

1. In which layer of progressive enhancement does JavaScript belong?

2. Why do you generally place JavaScript at the bottom of an HTML document?

3. What is the most widely supported method of persistent data storage in JavaScript?

3

JavaScript Terminology

In this chapter, you learn all the beginner-level JavaScript terminology you need to get the most out of this book and also feel comfortable in moving forward with the language. I've always said that the key to solving a problem is first knowing how to identify it, and a big secret of great coders is that we know how to find a solution. Sometimes it's in your head; often times it isn't, and you have to look it up somewhere. Knowing what a problem is called or a general solution that you need to expand upon will help guide you to the answer. This is why getting to know the terms you will be coming across and what they mean is vital to problem solving with JavaScript.

We go over some terms and look at general code examples, so whether you're creating JavaScript from scratch or jumping into someone else's code, you'll be able to identify what you're looking at. As you go through this book, knowing what these terms mean will help you flow through some of the examples.

Basics

You'll need to know some basic terms in JavaScript, and this section will briefly go over those topics and display some code examples where applicable. These are terms you should have a strong understanding of before moving on to the next chapter because you will be encountering them quite a bit in the course of reading this book.

JavaScript is a very flexible (some call it unstructured) language, so many of these terms may be called something else in different circumstances (like a function vs. a method—you'll get to that). But knowing the basics will help you a lot.

Document Object Model (DOM)

At its simplest level, the DOM is an outline of the HTML document you are accessing. It functions in much the same way that an outline for any document would function—a book, an article, a grocery list, anything with structure. There are top-level items, items nested under them, and items grouped in chunks (like pages in a chapter and chapters in a book). These items are called **nodes** and every node in the DOM has a relationship to its surrounding nodes. These relationships, just like in a real-life family, are

- Parent
- Child
- Sibling

Parents

A parent node is anything that contains other nodes. Is that a little too vague? For example, a `<body>` element is the parent of anything contained within it; div tags, table elements, headings, everything nested inside counts as a child. The `<body>` element can certainly contain other parents, but to the `<body>`, they will always be children.

Listing 3.1 shows a simple unordered list and keeping with the family theme, they are all members of *my* family. In this example, the `<UL>` is the parent to all the list items because they are all contained within it.

Listing 3.1   **Parent Element in HTML**

```
<!-- the <ul> is the parent element to all the list items -->
<ul>
    <li>Joan</li>
    <li>Charlie</li>
    <li>Peter</li>
    <li>Christine</li>
    <li>Anna</li>
    <li>Tim</li>
</ul>
```

Children

In the DOM, children are positioned inside parent nodes. In Listing 3.1.1 you can see that the parent `<ul>` is wrapping all children (child nodes). It's like a parent giving all the children a big hug.

Listing 3.1.1   **Children Element in HTML**

```
<!-- the <li>s are all children (child elements) of the <ul> -->
<ul>
    <li>Joan</li>
    <li>Charlie</li>
    <li>Peter</li>
    <li>Christine</li>
```

```
    <li>Anna</li>
    <li>Tim</li>
</ul>
```

Siblings

Siblings, like in real life, are on the same level (without the inherent rivalry). If a parent has multiple children, they are referred to as **siblings**. In Listing 3.1.2 you can see that all the list items underneath the parent <ul> are on the same level, making them children of the <ul>, but also siblings to each other. They can be a child, parent, and sibling all at the same time if they have children.

Listing 3.1.2   **Sibling Element in HTML**

```
<!-- each <LI> is a sibling of the other list items, because they're on the same level -->
<ul>
    <li>Joan</li>
    <li>Charlie</li>
    <li>Peter</li>
    <li>Christine</li>
    <li>Anna</li>
    <li>Tim</li>
</ul>
```

Although all the people in Listing 3.1.2 may not be siblings in real life, they are in the eyes of the document object model.

Variables

Variables in JavaScript can hold values, objects, or even functions. They can change, they can be static, and they can even be empty. I guess you could say that their function in JavaScript is variable (pun intended). The basic function of a variable is to store some information. There are a couple types of variables that you may encounter as you're learning JavaScript: **local variables** and **global variables**.

Local Variables

Local variables are defined within a function and can be used only within that function (you will learn about functions in a bit). That means that you can't declare a local variable inside function A and use it in function B because they are contained inside the function in which they were defined. Local variables are always prefaced using "var" when they're defined. Listing 3.2 shows a list of basic variables defined. These are empty variables right now, but we'll be filling them up pretty soon.

Listing 3.2   **A List of Empty Variables**

```
var familyMember1;
var familyMember2;
var familyMember3;
var familyMember4;
var familyMember5;
var familyMember6;
```

When variables are empty like this, it's called **initializing** a variable, and it is necessary from time to time, as you will see later in this chapter when you get into loops.

Global Variables

Another kind of variable you may come across is a global variable. Global variables are well named because they can be used globally throughout your JavaScript. They can be defined three different ways:

- Defining them with "`var`" outside a function

- Adding something directly to the `window` object

- Defining them anywhere without using "`var`"

Something to consider when using global variables is to keep track of the names so you don't have any duplicates. This is especially important when using a large amount of JavaScript to prevent naming collisions. Listing 3.2.1 shows you how to set up global variables. Use them sparingly.

Listing 3.2.1   **An Empty Global Variable**

```
/* with var outside a function */
var titleOfApplication;

/* attached to the window object */
window.titleOfApplication

/* global from inside a function */
titleOfApplication;
```

Global variables like this are generally used for things you know for a fact will never change or something that needs to be filtered through an entire JavaScript file, like a directory URL or a special prefix you may be using. They can be handy on smaller projects but quickly become difficult to work with as an application grows larger, so be sure to use them sparingly.

Strings

A string is a group of miscellaneous characters, basically just a *blob of whatever*, typically saved to a variable. Not everything saved to a variable is a string. In Listing 3.2.2 you can see that we have started adding some content (strings) to the variables defined in Listing 3.2. The variables are starting to make more sense now that they contain string values.

Listing 3.2.2 **Saving Data to Variables**

```
var familyMember1 = "joan";
var familyMember2 = "charlie";
var familyMember3 = "peter";
var familyMember4 = "christine";
var familyMember5 = "anna";
var familyMember6 = "tim"; /* this is me */
```

Strings are always quoted. So, if you have a number saved to a variable, JavaScript will treat it as a string rather than a number. This is important to note if you are planning to do any math with JavaScript operators.

Comments

JavaScript comments are like any comment in another language, but you can use two syntaxes. One is intended for blocks of code and the other for single-line comments, but it's really a matter of personal preference; no one will judge you if you choose to use one comment style over another. Listing 3.2.3 shows the two styles of commenting in JavaScript.

Listing 3.2.3 **JavaScript Comments**

```
// this is a single-line comment

/*
 this is a multiple
 line comment if you need to be more descriptive
 or disable a large chunk of code
*/
```

It's important to use helpful comments in your code, not only so you can go back in at a later date and easily make updates, but they can also serve as notes for other developers who may be working in the same codebase as you. It's always said that good commenting is a sign of a good developer, so comment away! Be sure to make your comments meaningful and detailed but still brief; it can serve as the front-line type of documentation for your site or application.

Operators

Operators are the symbols in JavaScript you may recognize from math class. You can add, subtract, multiply, compare, and set values. The equal sign (=) in Listing 3.2.2 is an example of an operator setting a value. Table 3.1 shows some various operators you can use and their meaning.

Table 3.1   **JavaScript Operators**

Operator	Description
+	Add or concatenate
–	Subtract
*	Multiply
/	Divide
++	Increment (count up)
––	Decrement (count down, two minus signs)
=	Set value

In Listing 3.3, you can see variables and strings being added and concatenated with the + operator.

Listing 3.3   **Adding Strings and Numbers Together with Operators**

```
/* save my name to a variable using the = operator */
var myName = "tim";

/* adding a variable to a string */
alert(myName + ", this is me");

/* adding numbers together */
alert(100 + 50); // should alert 150

/* concatenating strings together */
alert("100" + "50" + ", adding strings together"); // should alert 10050
```

> **Note**
>
> If you are using operators for any math, the values must be numbers and not strings. You can add, subtract, multiply, divide, or combine (concatenate) numbers, but the only actions of strings are combine and compare. If you have a number that JavaScript is treating as a string, it needs to be converted to an actual number to be treated as such by JavaScript operators. But it is best to start with a number if you can.

Use Strict

The "use strict" statement is something you insert into function definitions to make sure the parser uses stricter rules when executing your script; it's like using a strict doctype in the older days of (X)HTML. It's thought of as best practice now in JavaScript to prevent you from writing lazy or sloppy code (no offense). At times it can be frustrating trying to catch hard-to-find errors, but it will help you in the long run write cleaner, more scalable code. We use this method throughout the book. Listing 3.4 shows a function we use later in the chapter with the "use strict" statement at the top.

Listing 3.4   **Setting "use strict" Mode**

```
function getFamilyMemberNames() {

    "use strict";

    /* the rest of your function code goes here */
}
```

Storage

Data storage is one of the main functions of JavaScript; since the early days the community has been on a quest for the Holy Grail of client-side storage. Because of this, there are a lot of different ways to store data in JavaScript. Some are specific methods that you will get into later on in the book, but there are some terms that will help you along the way.

Cache

Cache, in regard to JavaScript, doesn't necessarily mean browser cache, although browser cache is vitally important. Caching in a JavaScript file usually refers to variables. When you declare a variable, it is cached, and you can reference it at any point. This is where you start seeing some performance implications. Using a variable over and over will perform better than redeclaring the same string over and over. You can define it once and continuously reference it.

Variables are great for organizing your code, but if you are using a string only once, it may be better for performance to not save it to a variable. This is part of the constant balancing act you will have to perform in JavaScript—between making something as high performance as possible versus making it as maintainable as possible. As far as performance goes, it's pretty minor, but still something to consider.

Arrays

In a nutshell, arrays are lists. They can get very complicated when you get deeply into them, but on the surface they are no more than a list. Lists can be simple and straightforward or complicated and nested (multidimensional arrays). Arrays are one of the most flexible data storage formats in JavaScript, and they are very common in Ajax calls because data is often stored in an array format of some kind for easy JavaScript parsing. Listing 3.5 shows an array in its most basic form.

Listing 3.5 **Saving Data to an Array**

```
/* store family member names in an array */
var family = [
    "joan", /* numbering starts at "0" */
    "charlie",
    "peter",
    "christine",
    "anna",
    "tim" /* this is me! */
];
```

Cookies

Cookies are used on both the server and the client (different kinds of cookies—think oatmeal vs. chocolate chip; sure, they're both technically cookies but they're very different monsters). They allow us to store data locally in the user's browser to be accessed at a later time. This is starting to become a dated way for storing data, but it does have full support in all major browsers. It's currently a setting that can be turned off by the user, so it's best to not rely too much on this type of storage for critical issues.

JavaScript Object Notation (JSON)

JSON is another data format that can be easily integrated with JavaScript; it's often used with external services you are consuming within your JavaScript. Generally speaking, JSON will live in its own file and often on another server completely. It is currently the most common format for API services, and it was chosen because the human eye very easily reads it. It was originally thought to be an alternative to XML in data exchanges and quickly took over.

JSON is favored heavily over XML because it's very lightweight and can be accessed across domains for easy remote Ajax calls. Although it is native to JavaScript, it is platform independent and can be used with any technology on the client or server side to transfer data.

Listing 3.5.1 shows how the array defined in Listing 3.5 would look if it were converted to JSON format.

Listing 3.5.1 **Saving Data to JSON**

```
{
    "family" : [
        "joan",
        "charlie",
        "peter",
        "christine",
        "anna",
        "tim"
    ]
}
```

Objects

Rather than saying an object is a "thing" that's made up of other things—because that isn't very helpful—let's right off the bat compare it to my grandmother. In JavaScript, my grandmother would be considered an object (not in real-life, but definitely in JavaScript) and she has traits or properties. She has a first name, a last name, and a nickname, and those are also all objects of the parent object "grandmother."

You can see my grandmother depicted in JavaScript object terms in Listing 3.5.2. Notice the parent declaration of "grandmother" and the nested objects of "first-name", "last-name", and "nickname." Everything in JavaScript is an object, and when you start aligning your code with that assumption, a lot of the concepts become more clear and easier to consume.

Listing 3.5.2 **Saving Data to an Object**

```
/* store extra information about my grandmother in an object */
var grandmother = {
    "first-name": " anna",
    "last-name": "carroll",
    "nickname": "ma"
};
```

Anything can be stored in an object; it could be a string, like "anna", or even an entire function, like getTheMail(). That is the first step in creating object-oriented JavaScript and developing a code organization pattern.

Creating Interaction

Creating an interaction layer is what JavaScript does, and this section contains the tools of the trade for doing just that. This is where all the action is.

Loops

Loops in JavaScript exist to allow you to execute a block of code a certain number of times. The block of code can be inside a function or it can be a function by itself. In the **family** array we build, there are six items; executing a loop on that code means we want to go into each item (called **looping through**) and do something. Listing 3.5.3 illustrates how to set up and use a basic `for` loop.

Listing 3.5.3   **A Basic `for` Loop Parsing Through Each Item in the Family Array**

```
/* save the array of family members to a variable, and save the length in
➥peopleCount */
var people = family,
    peopleCount = items.length,
    i;

/* checking to make sure there are people in the list */
if(peopleCount > 0){

    /* loop through each person, since i is the total number this code will loop six
➥times */
    for(i = 0; i < peopleCount; i = i + 1){

        /* this represents 1 person */
        var person = people[i];

    }
}
```

Conditionals

Conditionals are used when you want to execute different code based on certain conditions. The use of conditionals also opens up the opportunity to compare values with even more types of operators, like "===", which looks for an exact value match. This is how you write code that can make decisions.

if Statement

An `if` statement is the most common of all the conditionals. In plain English, it's as if you were saying, "If this is going on, do something." The `if` statement has three types:

- A normal `if` statement
- An `if/else` statement, which has two conditions
- An `if/ else if/ else`, which has an endless number of conditions

Listing 3.5.4 shows an example of a basic if/else statement, which checks to see if the variable "person" is an exact match for "tim."

Listing 3.5.4   **A Basic if/else Statement Checking to See if a Person Is "tim"**

```
/* looking for an exact value match for the string "tim" */
if(person === "tim") {

    alert(person + ", this is me");

} else {

    alert(person);

}
```

When comparing numbers, you can also use the following operators:

- < (less than)
- > (greater than)
- <= (less than or equal to)
- >= (greater than or equal to)
- != (not equal to)
- == (equal to)
- === (exactly equal to)
- !== (exactly not equal to)

switch Statement

A switch statement checks for a certain condition just as the if statement does. The difference is that after a condition (case) is met, the switch statement will stop, whereas the if statement will continue checking all the other conditions before moving on. switch statements are good for long conditional statements for that reason. Listing 3.5.5 shows you how to set up a switch statement that might iterate over an array of data.

Listing 3.5.5   **Example of a switch Statement Looping Through the Family Array**

```
switch (person) {

case "tim":
    alert("this is me");
    break;
```

```
case "christine":
    alert("my sister");
    break;

default:
    alert(person);


}
```

Functions

A function is a block of code that is executed through an event. The event can be a page load or a use-initiated event like `click`. You can also pass variables into functions via arguments to extend their functionality and make them even more flexible. Functions can also create or return variables that can later be passed into other functions.

Listing 3.5.6 shows the code snippet you have been working with throughout this chapter and converts it into a function you can execute at any time. This function, called `getFamilyMemberNames`, contains the "use strict" statement, the `array` of family members, the loop to run a block of code over each name, and the `if` statement checking to see if the person's name is an exact match for "tim."

Listing 3.5.6   **A Function That Will Take the Family Array, Loop, and Alert the Results**

```
function getFamilyMemberNames() {

    "use strict";

/* store family member names in an array */
var family = [
    "joan", /* numbering starts at "0" */
    "charlie",
    "peter",
    "christine",
    "anna",
    "tim" /* this is me! */
];

var peopleCount = family.length;
var i;

/* checking to make sure there are people in the list */
if(peopleCount > 0){

    for(i = 0; i < peopleCount; i = i + 1){
```

```
        var person = family[i];

        /* if the person is "tim", do something special */
        if(person === "tim") {
            alert(person + ", this is me!");
        } else {
            alert(person);
        }
    }
}
}

/* call the function */
getFamilyMemberNames();
```

Just like before, this code block should `alert` each family member's name and add the string "this is me!" to the end of "tim."

Anonymous Functions

Anonymous functions are functions that are declared as they are run, and they have no name assigned to them. Rather than writing a detailed function, like the one in Listing 3.5.6, you can use an anonymous function and have it execute immediately when it is run, instead of having it reference a function elsewhere in your document.

Anonymous functions perform better than a normally defined function because there is nothing to reference; they just execute when needed. These functions are used only once; they can't be referenced over and over. Making something an anonymous function will prevent the variable being used from slipping into the global scope (the variables are kept local to the function). In Listing 3.6, you can see that the previously defined function of `getFamilyMemberNames` has been converted to an anonymous function that is immediately executed on page load.

Listing 3.6   Converting `getFamilyMemberNames` to an Anonymous Function

```
(function () {

"use strict";

/* store family member names in an array */
var family = [
    "joan", /* numbering starts at "0" */
    "charlie",
    "peter",
    "christine",
    "anna",
```

```
    "tim" /* this is me! */
];

var peopleCount = family.length;
var i;

/* checking to make sure there are people in the list */
if(peopleCount > 0){

    for(i = 0; i < peopleCount; i = i + 1){

        var person = family[i];

        /* if the person is "tim", do something special */
        if(person === "tim"){
            alert(person + ", this is me!");
        } else {
            alert(person);
        }
    }
}
}
})();
```

Callback Functions

When a function is passed into another function as an argument, it's called a callback function. The function can be something you define, or it can be something native to JavaScript already. Functions can be very helpful in separating your logic and keeping your codebase as reusable as possible. Anonymous functions can also be callback functions. They're a little difficult to explain, so let's just jump right into Listing 3.7, which shows an example of a callback function as an anonymous function.

Listing 3.7   **An Example of a Function Calling a Function (callback)**

```
window.addEventListener("load", function (){

    alert("call back function");

    }, false });
```

The preceding callback function is attached to the native JavaScript method addEventListener and executes on the event "load." This brings us right into talking about one of the more interesting topics of JavaScript events.

Methods

First off, a method is, for all intents and purposes, a function. The difference between labeling something a function versus a method is about code organization. Earlier in the chapter, there is a section about **objects** in JavaScript, and I mentioned that anything could be saved into an object, including functions. When this happens, when a function is saved inside an object, it is referred to as a **method**. That's why things like the JavaScript method `alert()` that we have been using throughout this chapter is called a method even though it looks exactly like a function call.

Although JavaScript created the `alert()` method, you can also create methods, and it's totally contingent on how you choose to organize your code. In Chapter 9, "Code Organization," you will get into code organization in more depth, but for now it is important to note that when something is native to JavaScript or built into an external library, it's usually called a method. Listing 3.8 illustrates how you would define your own method.

Listing 3.8   **An Example of a JavaScript Method**

```
/* defining your object aka naming this group of functions */
var getInformation = {

    /* first method (function inside an object) is called "names" */
    " names": function () {

        "use strict";

        alert("get the names");
    },

    /* second method is called "checkForTim" */
    "checkForTim": function () {

        "use strict";

        alert("checking for tim");

    }
};
/* get the names on load */
window.addEventListener("load", getInformation.names, false);

/* check for Tim on click */
document.addEventListener("click", getInformation.checkForTim, false);
```

As you progress and become a JavaScript expert, you will probably catch yourself creating more and more methods. It is a very object-oriented approach to writing in any language and great for maintainability, although there are performance implications you will get into later on by nesting functions deep into other objects. This is a very popular way to make well-organized and reusable code.

Events

Events are how you elicit feedback from the user. If you want to execute any JavaScript on a page, it must happen through an event of some kind. Loading of the page, clicking a link, and submitting a form are all considered events, and you can attach functions to them all. There are a lot of events you can attach functions to in JavaScript, including

- click
- dblclick
- mousedown
- mousemove
- mouseout
- mouseover
- mouseup
- keydown
- keypress
- keyup
- blur
- focus
- submit
- load
- touchstart *
- touchmove *
- touchcancel *
- orientationchange *
- gesturestart *
- gestureend *
- gesturechange *

* New event specialized for touch interactions.

Listing 3.9 shows how you would execute the getFamilyMemberNames function upon loading of a page and then again upon clicking anywhere in the document.

Listing 3.9 Load and Click Events to Execute the `getFamilyMemberNames` Function

```
/* execute the function on load of the window*/
window.addEventListener("load", getFamilyMemberNames, false);

/* execute the function on clicking the document */
document.addEventListener("click", getFamilyMemberNames, false);
```

Ajax

Ajax is the concept of refreshing a part of an HTML document without reloading the entire page. It is extremely misused, but I assure you that you will learn the proper ways to use this technology as you read this book (Chapter 8, "Communicating with the Server Through Ajax," is all about Ajax and server communications).

Ajax is not an acronym; it does not stand for anything. Many think it stands for Asynchronous JavaScript and XML, but it doesn't; it's just a word. Ajax can be synchronous, and it doesn't have to be XML. It can be XML, JSON, or even HTML. It's all about the data you want to pass to and from the server, in almost any form you want.

Summary

In this chapter you learned the terminology that all JavaScript developers need to be familiar with to succeed. As you go through this book we will be expanding upon each of these topics in a lot more detail. We will be going over in-depth examples, real-life scenarios, and learning about situational JavaScript (when to use what thing).

We covered everything from the basics, such as the DOM, variables, and strings, to definitions of the various types of data storage options in JavaScript (there are a lot more, but that's for a later chapter), and we even delved into the more advanced topics like conditionals, loops, and functions.

If you found this chapter a little overwhelming, don't worry; we'll be breaking down each of the topics individually throughout the book and building on each one. Right now it is important to know the terms, be able to recognize them as code samples, and know their general meanings. This will aid in having a more fluid conversation about JavaScript. We can now talk about functions and loops because you know what they are.

Exercises

1. What is an anonymous function?

2. When is a function considered to be a callback function?

3. How do you elicit feedback from a user?

4

Accessing the DOM

In this chapter, we start putting into practice some of the concepts you learned about in previous chapters and begin coding some basic JavaScript. We get into the different ways to manipulate elements within a page, access HTML nodes, and learn how to move up and down the document structure. This is the basis for all JavaScript interaction; as you move forward in your JavaScript life cycle, these are skills you will be using on most days (the good ones, at least).

What Is the DOM?

When you hear people talking about JavaScript, they often mention the "DOM," or "Document Object Model." This is one of the most common and important aspects of JavaScript that you'll encounter. You will use it every time you modify a page and every time you insert data or modify an interface. In a nutshell, the DOM is a mapping layout model for your HTML and a way for JavaScript to get in there and do its thing. The DOM can be a JavaScript developer's best friend after it is mastered.

The DOM is not HTML and not JavaScript, but they are all very interconnected. It contains some very basic concepts, and as you lift up the hood to see all the possibilities, you'll notice that it's much more than a mass of HTML and text. It is the combinations of the elements you use (object), the order you choose to display them (model), and an endless offering of access points for you to add, delete, or modify any part of the overall structure (document) while navigating around with the various methods JavaScript provides.

Step one, and something that many beginners get stuck on conceptually, is that the HTML file is a document when we talk about the Document Object Model. Your document is made up of a bunch of objects (HTML elements, text, and attributes). Those objects come together in a certain order, which is considered the "model."

JavaScript is all about creating behaviors and data interactions by accessing the DOM. To create and control truly interactive experiences through interface design, you will certainly have to master and grow accustom to working in this robust environment.

The DOM Tree

Every document has some kind of structure behind it, whether it's a chapter of this book, a flier for a yard sale, a newspaper, or an HTML document. In this case, we'll obviously be talking about an HTML document, but the principle is true for most things we create.

The DOM starts with the Web browser. When you visit a website, the browser renders the HTML into a document, reads through the elements, and displays them to the user in the correct format. This process creates the initial model for the document, and it gets stored so we don't have to do all that work again to access each individual element (we just reference what the browser already has stored for the most part).

Consider the HTML structure shown in Listing 4.1.

Listing 4.1   **Basic HTML Structure to Illustrate the DOM**

```
<!DOCTYPE html>
<html>
<head>
        <meta charset= "utf-8 ">
        <title>Basic DOM example</title>
</head>
<body>
        <h1>Hello World!</h1>
        <p>While this is a <strong>very basic HTML document</strong>, it actually
serves as a detailed example of the document object model.</p>
</body>
</html>
```

At first glance this may look like an extremely basic example of an HTML document, and it is, but it's also a pretty good representation of all the items we have to deal with in the DOM.

The DOM is made up of items called **nodes**, which can have parents, children, and siblings (just like a family), and this determines its position in the tree. Children are underneath parents and siblings are at the same level as other siblings (brothers and sisters, if you will). Let's take a look at the DOM translation of this HTML document in Figure 4.1.

In Figure 4.1, you can see how we create a parent-child relationship in the DOM by moving from the top of the document all the way to the bottom as the nodes begin to create a pseudo-hierarchy in the diagram. I say "pseudo" because as we approach the bottom of the document the branches start to break off into different kinds of nodes that are represented by the circles that may technically be at the same level as others but are not considered to be relevant in the parent-child relationship to each other.

As you may have guessed, there are indeed different types of things we call nodes in the DOM. Nodes that represent HTML elements are called **element nodes**, ones that represent text are called **text nodes** and last are **attribute nodes**, which represent, you guessed it, attributes. All nodes are also children of the overall parent **document node**, represented at the top of Figure

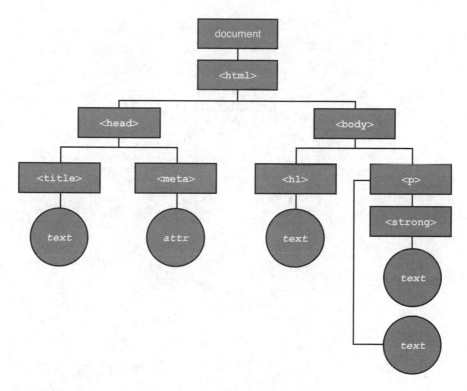

Figure 4.1   A graphical representation of the Document Object Model (DOM)

4.1. It's important to know the difference between these types of nodes because we access them differently when traveling throughout the DOM with JavaScript.

> **Note**
>
> The document node is extremely important and is often overlooked when building out the DOM's graphical representation. As you will learn later, whenever we want to access a node in the document, we first have to pass through the document node before we can step down the tree and start any sort of interaction.

Element Nodes

Element nodes will occupy the majority of your document and are the basis for how you will move around (we'll get to that in a bit). These nodes will define your structure and hold most of the data and content you will want to interact with and modify. The element nodes occupy most of the document and create the tree-like structure you see in Figure 4.1. Let's take a look at our element nodes highlighted in Figure 4.2.

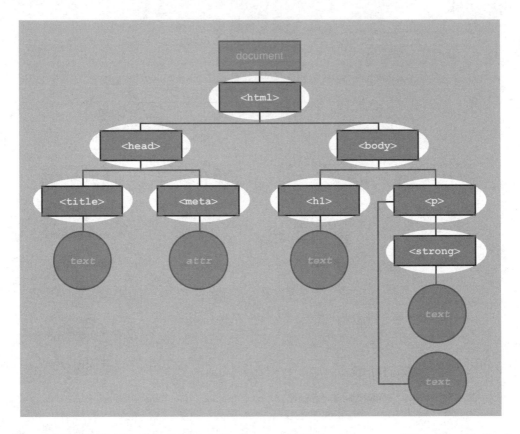

Figure 4.2   Highlighting the element nodes from our DOM. As you can see, this is the majority of our document.

Text Nodes

Text nodes are similar to the element nodes because of how they sit in the DOM and the fact that we use the same JavaScript methods to access them. Of course, some differences exist between these two types of nodes, or we wouldn't need to learn more terminology.

The most notable difference is the way they look; element nodes are contained in angled brackets (greater than and less than symbols). Text nodes are not; they are between element nodes. In Figure 4.3, you can see this depicted graphically.

One other important distinction between the two node types is that text nodes cannot have children (they've been trying for years, no luck). You can see in Figure 4.1 that the <p> element node has a text node and another element node <strong> has children. However, although the element node <strong> is technically inside the paragraph's content in the HTML structure, it is not a child of the text node. This is where we start getting into the pseudo-hierarchy mentioned earlier. Instead of nesting the tree further, we break off into a whole new branch and dead end at the text node. With that in mind, let's take a look at our text nodes highlighted in Figure 4.4.

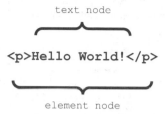

Figure 4.3   Showing the difference between an element node and a text node

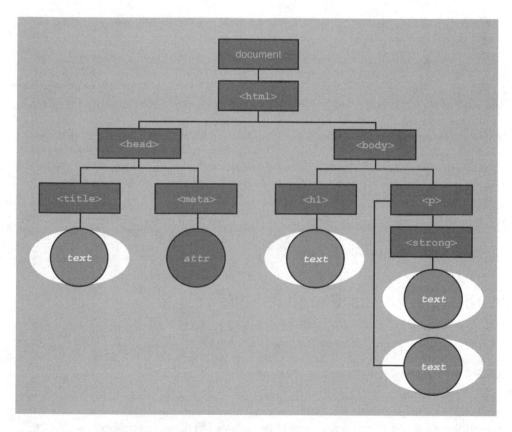

Figure 4.4   Highlighting the text nodes in our DOM. As you can see, the branches do not continue past our text nodes.

Attribute Nodes

Attribute nodes, like the document node, are easy to overlook when building your DOM because they appear to be part of the element, but they're an entirely different type of node, and are extremely important. They're also treated differently than text and element nodes are. In Figure 4.5, you can see the attribute node called out separately from the element node.

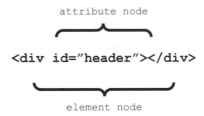

Figure 4.5   Illustrating the position of an attribute node in relation to an element node

Like text nodes, attribute nodes cannot have children (it's a sad story), but they're also not children themselves. That's right, attribute nodes are not considered to be children of their containing element; it's a little odd, but stick with me here. They sit in the DOM structure under element nodes because they're always attached to element nodes, but they are not children—they are treated and accessed differently. (Think Paul Newman in *Cool Hand Luke*.) They both do their own thing against the norm and refuse to conform. This is the reason attribute nodes have their own methods in JavaScript. We use basic JavaScript methods to get near an attribute, but after we get there we have to use special methods to get inside. This may seem a little confusing, but when you get used to it, it's actually pretty nice to have them separate.

When writing efficient JavaScript (don't worry, you will be by the time we're done here), you'll be constantly adding and removing classes from element nodes, and this is where we'll be heavily using attribute nodes. Let's take a look at our last type of node, the attribute node, highlighted in the DOM model in Figure 4.6.

Working with the Element Node

Now that we have a solid understanding of what exactly the DOM is and how parent-child relationships are built, we can start accessing it. Every node we talked about can be reached in some way. Some are easier than others, but I assure you, if something is listed in the DOM, we can grab it and store or modify it with JavaScript.

As mentioned in previous chapters, because of browser rendering weirdness, performance in JavaScript is a constant issue, especially when moving through the DOM. You always want to minimize the amount of nodes that need to be evaluated in order to get where you need to be in the document. Knowing the different ways to jump into the DOM and finding the most efficient access points may seem like a trivial thing, but every millisecond counts when we're talking about creating a good user experience, so we want to do this as fast as possible.

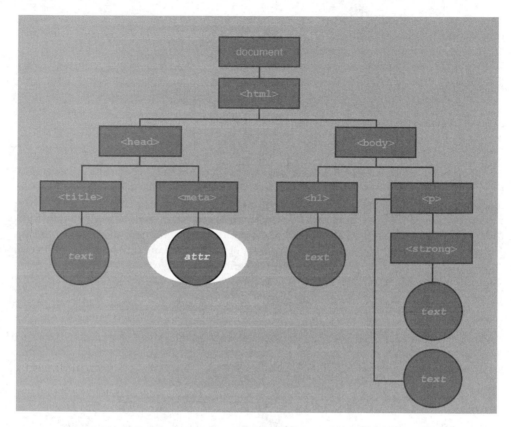

Figure 4.6   Highlighting the only attribute node in our DOM example

Targeting by ID

HTML standards state that an element's ID value must be unique to the document. In other words, there can be only one ID per page. Because of that, using an element's ID as the document access point is by far the most efficient and most desirable. We use this method whenever we can, but let's take a look at just how we would do that. Consider the following HTML snippet in Listing 4.2.

Listing 4.2   **HTML Element Labeled with an ID for Quick Access**

```
<div id="header">
        <h1><a href="/" id="homelink">Title of your site</a></h1>
</div>
```

This is a simple HTML snippet consisting of two ID values that we can use to access each element. Most times you will have natural IDs on your HTML elements (like "header" in the example) that you can use for targeting, but sometimes you do need to add in extra (or unnatu-ral) IDs (like "homelink" in the example) to gain quick access to an element node. There are other ways, but performance-wise, this is the fastest. In Listing 4.2.1 let's take a look at the JavaScript you would use to access these nodes.

Listing 4.2.1 **JavaScript Used to Access an Element by Its ID**

```
document.getElementById("header");
document.getElementById("homelink");
```

As I mentioned earlier, you have to access the document object before you can get to the node you want. After you have access to the node, you can store, modify, or retrieve extra infor-mation about the element with the plethora of methods built into JavaScript that we will be exploring throughout this entire book. It's important to remember that, although we are using the ID attribute to access the node, we are still accessing the *element node* and not the *attribute node* at this point. If we were to access the content of the ID attribute (the text "header" and "homelink"), we would be accessing the attribute node, but since we're not doing that, we're still on the element node.

Support

Support for the getElementById() method is widespread throughout all browsers, because it is one of the older and most well-used methods we have. In fact, you might even call it "retro." We all know that retro is hot right now, so use it well!

Note

Using IDs throughout your HTML is not only great for JavaScript performance but also CSS performance and specificity when applying styles. IDs can also be used for accessibly enhance-ments when creating jump or "skip to content" links for screen readers or visually impaired users.

Targeting by Tag Name

Because IDs are unique to each document, getElementById() can return only a single element. Sometimes that just doesn't fly, and we need more than one, or even a group of elements. When this is the case, we use getElementsByTagName() in a similar way.

Note

A pretty common (and frustrating) mistake in JavaScript syntax is not pluralizing the word "ele-ments" in getElementsByTagName(). Pay close attention to this and you'll save yourself some debugging time.

Targeting an element (node) by tag name is another popular method of creating an access point in the DOM. You can both target a group of elements and a single element inside of a group if you want. Suppose we have a pretty stripped-down Web page like the one shown in Listing 4.3.

Listing 4.3   **HTML Structure with Mixed and Repeating Element Nodes**

```
<!doctype html>
<html>
<head>
        <meta charset="utf-8">
        <title>getElementsByTagname Example</title>
</head>
<body>
        <h1>Using getElementsByTagname</h1>

        <p>Content paragraph</p>
        <p>Content paragraph</p>
        <p>Content paragraph</p>

</body>
</html>
```

We can grab each paragraph in Listing 4.3 with the single line of JavaScript in Listing 4.3.1.

Listing 4.3.1   **JavaScript Example of** getElementsByTagName

```
document.getElementsByTagName("p");
```

This will return a DOM object called a **NodeList**. A NodeList is a collection of nodes that maintain their source order. In other words, it's a list of elements, and those elements stay in the same order they appear on the page. The order is pretty important because if the items were randomly shuffled, they would be very difficult to access when we need them.

After we have the NodeList, we will also want to check to see how long it is. Checking its length will allow us to make sure values are available before we execute a block of script. We can do this with the length method, depicted in Listing 4.3.2.

Listing 4.3.2   **Returning the Total Number of Elements in Our NodeList**

```
document.getElementsByTagName("p").length;
// will return 3

// checking the length before executing script
if(document.getElementsByTagName("p").length > 0) {
        // it returns "3", and 3 is greater than "0", so we're good to go.
}
```

So far we have targeted a group of elements and checked their length; after that, we may want to grab an individual node to do some work on. It's pretty easy to pull an item out of the NodeList. There are two ways we can do this:

- Using the item method
- Using an array syntax

Both methods will return the same value, so it's more an issue of personal preference when you choose the way you want to access elements in a NodeList. Let's take a look at them both in Listing 4.3.3.

Listing 4.3.3   **Using `getElementsByTagName` to Target a Single Node**

```
// the first paragraph using the item method
document.getElementsByTagName("p").item(0);

// the first paragraph with array syntax
document.getElementsByTagName("p")[0];

// the second paragraph with the item method
document.getElementsByTagName("p").item(1);

// the second paragraph with array syntax
document.getElementsByTagName("p")[1];
```

Note

NodeLists and arrays start at 0, not 1. So the list looks like 0,1,2,3,4, etc. This is why we are using 0 in the preceding example to access the first element. If only a single element returns in the NodeList, you still have to use the [0] value to grab it.

When we put all this code together, you can see a functional JavaScript snippet starting to get created. So far we've targeted a NodeList, checked its length, and accessed the individual element inside the NodeList. This is a very common thing to do in JavaScript, so let's see what it looks like all put together in Listing 4.3.4.

Listing 4.3.4   **Putting It All Together**

```
// checking the length before executing script
if(document.getElementsByTagName("p").length > 0) {
        // it returns "3", and 3 is greater than "0", so we're good to go.

        // let's access some elements with the array syntax
        document.getElementsByTagName("p")[0];
```

```
document.getElementsByTagName("p")[2];

}
```

Support

Support for the `getElementsByTagname()` method is widespread enough that we can feel free to use this as much as we want without worrying.

Targeting by Class

So far the node targeting methods we've talked about have been similar to CSS selectors. In CSS you can target by both ID and TagName, and they're very commonly used. You can also target by class. JavaScript is no different; however, it has lagged behind the curve a bit.

For years now, since targeting an element by its class was active in CSS, the community wanted the feature added to JavaScript. It took a while, but we finally have it! Recently added to JavaScript was the `getElementsByClassName()` method. This method functions much the way `getElementsByTagName()` does when it comes to producing and accessing the NodeList, but we can use some interesting combinations of selectors with this method, so let's get started with the HTML in Listing 4.4.

Listing 4.4   **HTML Snippet Illustrating Element Node with Classes**

```
<!doctype html>
<html>
<head>
      <meta charset="utf-8 ">
      <title>getElementsByTagname Example</title>
</head>
<body>
      <h1>Using getElementsByTagname</h1>

      <p class="dropcap huge">Content paragraph</p>
      <p id="e" class="dropcap">Content <span class="huge">paragraph</span></p>
      <p class="dropcap">Content paragraph</p>

</body>
</html>
```

Again, we will be working with the paragraphs in the HTML. Note the classes we're using. The first element has two classes, the second has one class on the paragraph and one on the child span node, and the last element has one class. With the JavaScript in Listing 4.4.1, we can target those nodes individually.

Listing 4.4.1 **Using `getElementsByClassName`**

```
// returns all elements with a class of dropcap
document.getElementsByClassName("dropcap");

// returns all elements with both "dropcap" and "huge" classes (1 in our example)
document.getElementsByClassName("dropcap huge");

// returns all elements classed with "huge" that are inside elements ID'd with "e" (1
element in our example — the span)
document.getElementsById("e").getElementsByClassName("huge");
```

We have a little more flexibility with this than we do with some of the others, because it's much newer to JavaScript. But as you can see, this can be a very helpful method.

Support

As I mentioned, this is a pretty new addition to the JavaScript family. This is where things start to get a little dicey; I will say that support is very good right now, but not at 100%. At the time of this writing, all current browser versions support this method. When we start to step back in time a little, we notice where support begins to weaken. The browsers you'll be concerned with are most likely IE 8 and earlier, but let's take a look at the support table, Table 4.1.

Table 4.1 **Browser Support for `getElementsByClassName`**

Internet Explorer	9.0 & up
Firefox	3.0 & up
Chrome	4.0 & up
Opera	9.5 & up
Safari	3.1 & up

Because this method was so highly sought after for so long, other developers in the community have created custom functions to handle the `getElementsByClassName` method in the case of no support. Every JavaScript library/framework available right now has also addressed this issue, but in different ways. Later on in the book we will get into extending JavaScript through libraries. In cases like this where support is lacking in older browsers, a library or custom function fallback is a good way to ensure that all users will get a similar experience, regardless of how they view your site/application.

Using CSS Selectors in JavaScript to Target Nodes

The desire to use easy-to-remember CSS selectors in JavaScript came to fruition in 2009 when JavaScript guru John Resig developed the Sizzle Selector Library. Sizzle allowed us to maintain a consistent syntax in selectors between CSS and JavaScript. This caused an explosion in the JavaScript community, and all of a sudden this previously difficult-to-use language for designers became a delight to work with.

With the release of the HTML5 specification came a new flood of JavaScript APIs as well. One of the main themes with HTML5 was listening to what the community wanted to be formalized into the language. It was clear that they wanted to use CSS selectors in JavaScript, so out came two new methods: querySelector() and querySelectorAll().

Both methods can take selectors in CSS format. The difference between the two is that query-SelectorAll() will return a NodeList (the same way getElementsByClassName() and getElementsByTagname() do) and querySelector() will return only the first element that it comes across. Let's look at the following HTML in Listing 4.5.

Listing 4.5   **Basic HTML Structure with Elements, IDs, and Classes**

```
<body>
    <div id="header  >
        <h1>Using querySelector</h1>
    </div>

    <p class="dropcap huge">Content paragraph</p>
    <p class="dropcap">Content <span class="huge">paragraph</span></p>
    <p class="dropcap">Content paragraph</p>

</body>
```

We can target those elements with the following JavaScript, as shown in Listing 4.5.1.

Listing 4.5.1   **Using querySelectors**

```
// get the header ID element
document.querySelector("#header");

// get the first element with a dropcap class
document.querySelector(".dropcap");

// get all the paragraphs with a "dropcap" class — produces a nodeList
document.querySelectorAll(".dropcap");

// get all elements with a class of "dropcap" OR "huge"
document.querySelectorAll(".dropcap, .huge");

// get all paragraphs that have a class
document.querySelectorAll("p[class]");
```

`querySelector()` is an extremely flexible and powerful method in the JavaScript language. It can take multiple selectors, IDs, classes, attributes, and even advanced CSS pseudo classes to target elements. The only complaint at this time about these new methods is that the error messages are not very helpful, but hopefully this will be worked out in the browser.

Support

This is one of those things that works where you expect it to work. What do I mean by that? Many of the HTML5 features, especially the JavaScript APIs, don't have great support in older browsers, so earlier than IE 8 (IE 6 and 7) and earlier than Firefox 3.6 is generally a good support bottleneck; this is where a lot of the newer features start to fail. This is something to keep in mind as you're developing. Let's take a look at Table 4.2 for the support of this feature.

Table 4.2   **Browser Support for `querySelector` and `querySelectorAll`**

Internet Explorer	8.0 & up
Firefox	3.5 & up
Chrome	1 & up
Opera	10 & up
Safari	3.2 & up

Because selectors are such an important part of your JavaScript code, it's always very important that they function the way you want them to. For things like `querySelector()` you need to check out your own browser statistics and decide if it's something you can safely use. It's that same old story—we need to start moving people off old browsers, which can, unfortunately take some time.

Just like any of these selectors that require a small support boost, libraries are available to help you detect for feature support and use an appropriate method based on those results. These support solutions fall under the same category as the previously mentioned `getElementsByClassName()` method. Often when using a JavaScript library, you won't know for sure which method is being used because the library will figure that out for you; but it is very important to know that they exist as options.

Working with the Attribute Node

Now that we have a strong grasp of how to work with and target element nodes, we can start working within those nodes and play around with the *attribute node*. As illustrated in Figure 4.5, an attribute is contained inside an element node, but is not considered to be a child of that node, so we need some special methods to get, modify, or remove that information. Those methods are

- getAttribute()

- setAttribute()

- removeAttribute()

- hasAttribute()

In all these methods we target the attribute and return the value, so in an example of class="visible", we would be targeting "class" and returning the value "visible".

Getting and changing attributes is paramount to writing a Web application that performs well. Because many of the most common interactions we create, like hide/show, can be created more efficiently through CSS, those can be as simple as adding or removing a class. In this example we will be working with the following HTML shown in Listing 4.6.

Listing 4.6 **HTML Example for Attribute Nodes**

```
<img src="images/placeholder.png" class="show" alt="placeholder image" id="plc">
```

Getting an Attribute

Before we can get an attribute, we need to jump into the DOM at an element node (using one of the methods we just learned about), and then we can gain access to that element's attribute. This is one of the ways we gain more information about an element. The getAttribute() method takes one argument, which is the name of the attribute you want to target.

Before we target an attribute, much like we did with checking the NodeList length, we want to make sure an element contains the attribute we're looking for. This can be done with the hasAttribute() method. Suppose you want to target the image referenced in Listing 4.6 and get the class value. The JavaScript in Listing 4.6.1 will illustrate how you might accomplish that task.

Listing 4.6.1 **JavaScript Used to Get the Class Value of Our Image**

```
// first we target the element and check if it has a class on it
if(document.getElementById("plc").hasAttribute("class")) {

    // after we know a class exists, we can then get the value
    document.getElementById("plc").getAttribute("class");

    // this would return the value of "show", which is the class on our image
}
```

You may be well aware that a class exists in the area you're targeting, but using hasAttribute() is more of a best practice, just in case it doesn't exist (it happens). We don't have to waste valuable processing time executing the JavaScript for no reason.

Setting an Attribute

Setting an attribute is valuable in many instances, whether you're temporarily saving data, setting a class, or replacing an attribute with something new. This method has a built-in if statement, so we don't need to run our conditional on it unless we want to do something other than just retrieving an attribute value.

This method takes two arguments—the first is the name of the attribute you want to set, and the second is the value you want to set it to. See Listing 4.6.2.

Listing 4.6.2   **JavaScript Used to Set the Class Attribute of Our Image**

```
// replace the current class with a value of "hidden"
document.getElementById("plc").setAttribute("class", "hidden");

// add a new attribute to the image
document.getElementById("plc").setAttribute("title", "we moved this element off
screen");
```

In this example, we changed the class from "visible" to "hidden" and, for better accessibility and screen readers, we added a title attribute to let them know we're not displaying this image anymore. Because the class already existed, our new class overwrote it. The title attribute, on the other hand, was not already on the element, so it was created for us (you just dynamically created your first node in the DOM—congrats!). Changing display properties like this allows us to maintain the separation between presentation and behavior that we spoke about in Chapter 1 with progressive enhancement. With this example, you might consider the following CSS in Listing 4.6.3.

Listing 4.6.3   **CSS to Apply to Our Image**

```
/* this is the default state of the image */
.visible {
    position: static;
}

/* this is applied when our class is changed and moves the image out of view */
.hidden {
    position: absolute;
    top: -9999px;
    left: -9999px;
}
```

> **Note**
>
> It's important to not use display: none when working like this in CSS because screen readers cannot view content that is set to display: none. That is why we choose to hide content like this by simply moving it off the screen.

Removing an Attribute

Removing an attribute is as simple as getting one. We just target the element node and use the method `removeAttribute()` to get it out of there. There are no JavaScript exceptions thrown if you try to remove an attribute that doesn't exist, but it's still a best practice to use the same `hasAttribute()` method we mentioned earlier, shown in Listing 4.6.4.

Listing 4.6.4   **JavaScript Used to Remove the Class Value of Our Image**

```
// first we target the element and check if it has a class on it
if(document.getElementById("plc").hasAttribute("class")) {

    // after we know a class exists, we can then remove it
    document.getElementById("plc").removeAttribute("class");

}
```

In this example, we simply removed the class from our image.

Support

These methods have full support in all browsers and are okay for you to freely use in all browsers.

Working with the Text Node and Changing Content

Now that we have stepped through both element and attribute nodes, we can move onto our last type of node, the text node. When you're working with text nodes, most of the work you will be doing is modification of the content. There is also no traveling about inside a text node, because it can't have any children. In some aspects the way you will be interacting with these nodes is similar to the way you interact with the attribute node. You will be modifying, getting, and removing them, but using different methods to do so.

Changing content is extremely common with JavaScript. Whether it's for a button text toggle value or the Ajax loading of content, you will find yourself inserting text or HTML into the DOM from time to time. If you want to change or modify all the content in an area rather than parsing through the DOM, you can do it in one fell swoop with the JavaScript method `innerHTML`. There are a lot of benefits to this method, notably performance. It is a lot faster to wipe out a large chunk of information than it is to do the same thing on each individual DOM node you want to replace. In Listing 4.7 you will see the HTML snippet this example will be working with.

Listing 4.7   **HTML Example to Illustrate Changing Content**

```
<body>

    <div id="target-area">
        <p>This is our text.</p>
    </div>

</body>
```

In this example, we want to target the text node and change it to "hello world". This content could come from anywhere, such as an Ajax call, or it can be hard-coded in, like in the example from Listing 4.7.1.

Listing 4.7.1   **Using `innerHTML`**

```
// targeting the text node
document.getElementById("target-area").innerHTML;

// changing the content in the text node — you can jump straight to this.
document.getElementById("target-area").innerHTML = "<p>hello world</p>";
```

Moving Around the DOM

When moving around inside the DOM, we start to really use the tree structure of the DOM and benefit from knowing the layout of our HTML document and how the elements relate to each other. To this point in the chapter, we have talked about targeting all the different types of DOM nodes, but they have all been direct access via jumping into the middle of the document by ID, class, tag name, or by specific position in the NodeList. Unfortunately, in the world of writing clean, semantic HTML, we tend to not riddle our HTML with tons of classes and IDs (well, some do but let's not get off on *that* tangent right now), and sometimes you'll only be able to reasonably jump so far into the tree. From there, you will have to navigate up and down with some of the most useful methods native to JavaScript. In this section we'll be traveling around the DOM with five new methods:

- parentNode
- previousSibling
- nextSibling
- firstChild
- lastChild

Just as you can get the children of an element node, you can also get its parent (or parents), and they all have parents. Let's take a look at the HTML in Listing 4.8 and assume that we want to get the parent element for the target node and add a class of "active" to it.

Listing 4.8   **Basic HTML Example of Navigation**

```
<ul id="nav">
    <li><a href="/" id="home">Home</a></li>
    <li><a href="/about" id="about">About Us</a></li>
    <li><a href="/contact" id="contact">Contact Us</a></li>
</ul>
```

Using the JavaScript in Listing 4.8.1, you can execute the desired behavior.

Listing 4.8.1   **Targeting a `parentNode`**

```
// target the "about" link and apply a class to its parent list item
document.getElementById("about").parentNode.setAttribute("class", "active");
```

Besides moving in a parent-child relationship (up and down), you can also move side to side in the DOM and target nodes that sit next to a target node. These are called **siblings**, and two special methods allow us to target them: previousSibling and nextSibling. In our example we still want to target the About Us link, but instead of adding a class to the parent element, we want to add a class to Home (previousSibling) and Contact Us. We could use the JavaScript in Listing 4.8.2.

Listing 4.8.2   **Adding a Class to Previous and Next Sibling Nodes**

```
// get "about" parent, then its previous sibling and apply a class
document.getElementById("about").parentNode.previousSibling.setAttribute "class",
➥"previous");

// get "about" parent, then its next sibling and apply a class
document.getElementById("about").parentNode.nextSibling.setAttribute("class", "next");
```

The JavaScript from Listings 4.8.1 and 4.8.2 should generate the HTML in Listing 4.8.3.

Listing 4.8.3   **Generate HTML After Adding Classes**

```
<ul id="nav">
    <li class="previous"><a href="/" id="home">Home</a></li>
    <li class="active"><a href="/about" id="about">About Us</a></li>
    <li class="next"><a href="/contact" id="contact">Contact Us</a></li>
</ul>
```

Using these methods will help you travel around your HTML document without having to riddle it with extra markup, IDs, and classes, while keeping performance at a manageable level. However, always evaluate the load time of a page and balance it with best practices you'd like to follow. In other words, if moving up and down the DOM tree is too resource intensive for any particular case, you may want to consider adding a class or ID to jump to. (I know, sorry to be like that, but performance is always a gray area—use your best judgment.)

Accessing First and Last Child

JavaScript offers us some alternative routes to get to node information; for example, moving straight to the first or last item in a NodeList. This is sort of like the jumping around we do with getElementById and getElementsByTagname, but like parentNode and childNodes, they're at the NodeList level. So, you would target down to the NodeList and dive in from there compared to doing it from the document level. But enough of that. Let's dive back into our HTML example from Listing 4.8 and try to add classes to the first and last list items in our navigation with the JavaScript from Listing 4.8.4.

Listing 4.8.4   **Adding a Class to the First and Last Items in Our Nav**

```
// travel to the first node and add the class
document.getElementById("nav").firstChild.setAttribute("class", "first");

// travel to the last node and add a class
document.getElementById("nav").lastChild.setAttribute("class", "last");
```

And that will generate the HTML in Listing 4.8.5.

Listing 4.8.5   **Generate HTML After Adding Classes**

```
<ul id="nav">
    <li class="first"><a href="/" id="home">Home</a></li>
    <li><a href= "/about" id="about">About Us</a></li>
    <li class="last"><a href="/contact" id="contact">Contact Us</a></li>
</ul>
```

Moving up and down the DOM is something you will do a lot, so it's worth spending some time on these methods to wrap your head around what's going on when you are using them on a real project.

> **Note**
>
> These methods can be a little frustrating to work with because some browsers will insert a text node to maintain whitespace in your code. In the example we were using, this can cause a return of "#text" rather than the first node you're expecting. These examples have been ideal-ized for readability, but in some cases you will want to remove the whitespace or adjust your targeting methods, Removing whitespace is a good idea for a lot of sites in production because it will make your overall page weight smaller and improve performance.

Dynamically Adding and Removing Nodes from the DOM

Up to now, we have been accessing nodes in the DOM that already exist. Often when building an interface, you'll need to dynamically insert nodes into the DOM, create new elements, fill them with content, and drop them into the document somewhere. Luckily, we have this capability built into JavaScript. In this section, we will be introducing four new methods:

- `createElement()`
- `createTextNode()`
- `appendChild()`
- `removeChild()`

The first three methods will inevitably intertwine as you insert new elements into the DOM, so we will go over them all at once, and use the HTML from Listing 4.9.

Listing 4.9 **HTML Example to Create a New Element**

```
<body>
    <div id="target-area">

        <p id="tagline">Hello World!</p>

    </div>
</body>
```

Adding Elements to the DOM

Creating and inserting a new element is generally a three-step process:

1. Create the element.
2. Fill it with content (or leave it blank).
3. Put in the DOM.

First, we need to use the `createElement([tagname])` method to create the element. This method takes one argument, which is the tag name of the element you want to create. When I say we create the element, it doesn't actually exist anywhere until we put it in the DOM; it helps to perceive this method as thinking up an idea. The idea is floating around your head, but isn't a physical thing until you put it on paper, tell someone, or build it.

The second step is to add content to your element. You can do this right away, or you can do it later, but eventually the element will be filled with something; what good is an empty element? We use the `createTextNode()` method to do this. It takes one argument, which is a string of text that will be inserted into the element.

The last step is picking a point in the DOM to insert your new element. We do this with the appendChild() method. This method takes one argument, which is the completed element you want to insert. Then, like magic, you've created a new element.

We went over creating new nodes earlier in the chapter with the setAttribute() method because it also can dynamically create nodes in the DOM. Now let's look at an example of creating a new element; remember, we'll be using the HTML from Listing 4.9 for this exercise and applying the JavaScript from Listing 4.9.1.

Listing 4.9.1   **HTML Example to Create a New Element**

```
// store the target area to a variable to keep things neat
var targetArea = document.getElementById("target-area");

// create our <p> element
var p = document.createElement("p");

// create a text node inside the <p>, note that we're using a variable "p" here
var snippet = p.createTextNode("this was a generated paragraph");

// insert our generated paragraph into the DOM
targetArea.appendChild(snippet);
```

The generated HTML should look like Listing 4.9.2.

Listing 4.9.2   **New Element Inserted into the DOM**

```
<body>
    <div id="target-area">
        <p id="tagline">Hello World!</p>
        <p>this was a generated paragraph</p>
    </div>
</body>
```

Removing Elements from the DOM

Just as you can add elements to the document, you can also take them away. It is a similar process, but instead of needing three methods, we need only one. It takes a year to build a house, but only a few minutes to bring it down.

Using the same HTML from Listing 4.9, let's say that instead of creating a new paragraph, we want to remove the tagline. We can do this by navigating to its parent and removing the child with the removeChild() method, as shown in Listing 4.9.3.

Listing 4.9.3   **JavaScript for Removing an Element from the DOM**

```
// store the target area to a variable to keep things neat
var targetArea = document.getElementById("target-area");

// store the tagline in a variable as well
var tagline = document.getElementById("tagline");

// remove it from the DOM
targetArea.removeChild(tagline);
```

Now you are all set: you can add and remove elements from the DOM at will, and you're officially on your way to becoming a great JavaScript mind in the industry!

Summary

In this chapter, we learned about the Document Object Model, or the DOM, and the different types of nodes that construct the tree and all its branches. We went over how to map out an HTML document and talked about how the DOM related to JavaScript.

We also learned about how to navigate the DOM tree to target specific nodes or elements you want to store or modify. Besides navigating up and down the tree, we discovered many ways to jump directly to a node based on information attached to it, such as IDs, classes, and even the tag name itself.

Later on we created new DOM nodes, filling them with content and then inserting them into the document.

Exercises

1. What are the four types of DOM nodes?

2. Explain what the DOM is and how it relates to HTML and JavaScript.

3. What happens if you try to set a node attribute for an attribute that does not exist on the node already?

5

Storing Data in JavaScript

Storing data is core functionality of JavaScript. It doesn't make things swoosh around the page, slide, fade in/out, or draw the user's eye. But properly storing your data will make it well organized and easy to access later in your application, which is one of those magic pieces about creating a great user experience that the user is completely ignorant about (in a good way—they don't notice it). Quick and easy access to data, brilliant!

In this chapter, you learn the different methods of storing data within a JavaScript model. Some methods are internal to your own personal scripting file and some are consumed externally. Externally generated data can be produced by a database local to your application or an external API service (we'll get into APIs). In some form or another, you will be storing and caching data on every project, Knowing not only your options but the proper times to use them can be very valuable when you're trying to create a codebase that performs well and is reasonably easy to maintain (a constant balancing act for all front-end code).

As you progress through this chapter, you notice a pattern exposing the history and future of JavaScript. We start off with the basics, move to more complex storage methods, then hit a point where we start talking about new methods; you'll be able to see how the once very complex data storage methods (they're still around, which is why we're learning them) begin to come back around and feel more thought-out and are easier to work with. And, as usual, the old methods are important because the newer methods may not have support in your target audience. But it is a movement toward JavaScript that works better, and it's important to realize that pattern to best utilize the technology.

Variables

Variables are the most basic forms of data storage in JavaScript. They're used in all programming languages but are especially important here because they are an unavoidable aspect of writing good, high performance JavaScript. **A variable is a label that you attached to a value**. Sometimes the value changes, sometimes it doesn't. But the label will always stay the same so you can reference it throughout your code.

Variables can be used a few different ways. You can self-define static variables, you can self define dynamic variables, or you can use variables that take into account user interaction. These can be in the form of **strings**, **numbers**, or **Boolean** values. These values can then be passed into a function, checked, combined, or modified as you need throughout your program. The first step in creating a variable is called *declaring a variable,* which sets the label to what you want. Something to remember when declaring variables is that they are **case sensitive**, so uppercase versus lowercase always matters. In Listing 5.1, you can see a few basic variable declarations.

Listing 5.1   **Code Block Title**

```
/* this style is called "camelCase" */
var myFavoriteSandwich;

/* some people choose to use underscores instead of camelCase */
var MY_FAVORITE_SANDWICH;

var my_favorite_sandwich;

/* all these variables are different in the eyes of JavaScript because the case
is different, even though they all technically read the same to a human */
```

> **Note**
>
> The case-sensitive nature of variables is not an invitation to write variables with similar names. Although these variables will not collide from a technical standpoint, they can get very confusing when a human eye is trying to debug or maintain the script. So it's best to have distinct, meaningful variable names.

Strings

A string is the first type of data that can be assigned to a variable. It's nothing more than a collection of characters and can be anything from a single word to an entire paragraph or even multiple paragraphs. They're contained within quotes and are set with an equal sign (=). In Listing 5.2 you can see the variables we'll be using starting to be formed via strings.

Listing 5.2   **Saving Strings to Variables**

```
var favoriteBreakfastSandwich = "Egg, Sausage and Cheese";

var favoriteLunchSandwich = "Turkey Club";

var favoriteDinnerSandwich = "Meatball";
```

Strings can be saved to variables with either single or double quotes; they both produce the same result, and it's more a matter of personal preference. Because both single and double quotes are commonly used inside saved strings, they will often break your JavaScript and need to be **escaped**. In Listing 5.3 you can see variables saved with single quotes, double quotes, and examples of escaping them where applicable.

Listing 5.3 **Escaping Quotes in a String**

```
/* double quotes */
var favoriteBreakfastSandwich = "Egg, Sausage and Cheese";

/* single quotes */
var favoriteLunchSandwich = 'Turkey Club';

/* double quotes escaped */
var statementOnBreakfast = "I said, \"It is important\", you know that.";

/* single quotes escaped */
var statementOnLunch = 'It\'s good for your metabolism';
```

The rules for escaping quotes is that if you use single quotes, you need to escape single quotes, and if you use double quotes, you need to escape double quotes in strings. Overall, pretty easy stuff right? If you choose one quoting method over the other, make sure it's consistent throughout the JavaScript you're writing.

> **Tip**
>
> If you are saving HTML to strings a lot, single quotes may save you some time because you won't have to escape all the double-quoted attribute values in HTML.

Numbers

Numbers are exactly what they sound like: they are number values saved to variables. The tricky part with numbers is that they can also be strings. For JavaScript to consider a variable a number, it can't be a quoted value; if quoted, JavaScript will treat it as a string, and it can be difficult to work with later.

Numbers can have math preformed on them with JavaScript operators. All the basic math functions are available: addition, subtraction, multiplication, and division. It's like having a calculator built right in the JavaScript—very handy. In Listing 5.4 you see examples of numbers being saved to variables and some simple math. Numbers can be positive, negative, or even decimals. Note that none of the values are quoted, so you can add them together.

Listing 5.4   **Saving Number Values as Variables**

```
/* Storing a count of how many sandwiches were eaten */
var mondaySandwichCount = 3;

var tuesdaySandwichCount = 1.5; // Gave half my sandwich away

var wednesdaySandwichCount = 2;

var thursdaySandwichCount = -1; // got sick Thursday

var fridaySandwichCount = 6; // recovered strong on Friday

/* alert the total number of sandwiches I ate this week (11.5) */
alert(mondaySandwichCount + tuesdaySandwichCount + wednesdaySandwichCount +
thursdaySandwichCount + fridaySandwichCount);
```

Boolean

Unlike strings and numbers, which can have endless possibilities for their values, Boolean values can be only `true` or `false`. Like numbers, Boolean values are not contained within quotes. They are often used in basic yes/no situations, such as when checking for support of a certain feature in a browser. In Listing 5.5 you can see an example of a Boolean `true` value and a Boolean `false` value.

Listing 5.5   **Saving Number Values as Variables**

```
var fullStomach = true;
var stillHungry = false;
```

> **Note**
>
> Boolean values may seem limiting, but they are the basis for most programming languages and can be very valuable when conditionally executing script.

Instead of using `true` and `false`, you can use the number values 0 or 1: 0 meaning `false`, and 1 meaning `true`; these are both also considered to be Boolean values. This can be tricky if you're setting a 0 as a number value because a Boolean comparison will treat the value as `false`.

Performance in Variables

When declaring a variable, you're caching it in your JavaScript file and allowing it to be used over and over. This can be a great way to increase the performance and maintainability of your script. Rather than outputting string after string after string (the same string over and over), you can declare it once, keep it cached, and reference that variable as many times as you'd like. Because there is a very slight amount of overhead in fetching the variable, a general rule of performance is to store data in a variable if you need to use it more than once.

Arrays

Most variables can hold only a single string, a single number, or a single Boolean value. A lot of times you need more than that. If you need to store actual data in a variable, you would use what is called an **array**. They're declared in a similar way, with a var declaration, but they can contain much more information to be passed throughout your JavaScript. An array is basically just a list of stuff saved into one variable. The benefit is that you can directly access each item in the array while having them grouped together in a logical way.

In Listing 5.6 you can see the two ways you can declare an array. Initially declaring an array with the new object tells JavaScript, "Hey, I have an array coming at ya."

Listing 5.6   **Declaring an Array**

```
/* using the "new" keyword */
var favoriteSandwiches = new Array();

/* using shorthand brackets */
var favoriteSandwiches = [];
```

After declaring the array, you need to fill it with stuff. If you have the values figured out already, you could combine the processes of declaring the array with assigning it values. The list doesn't have to be complete, but you do need something in there to start building out a list. As you'll find out later, you can dynamically add items to an array, but for now, let's manually put them in. Listing 5.7 shows a combination of declaring the array and assigning it some values.

Listing 5.7   **Declaring an Array and Assigning Values in the Same Step**

```
var favoriteSandwiches = ["Egg, Sausage and Cheese", "Turkey Club", "Meatball"];
```

Like a normal variable, the values in an array can be any combination of strings, numbers, objects, other arrays, expressions, and/or Boolean values.

Basic Array

As mentioned earlier, an array is a list of stuff (usually related stuff) and Listing 5.6 depicts an array in its most basic form. When you combine the declaration of an array with the value assignment, as we did in Listing 5.6, a number gets assigned to each value. This number is called an **index**.

In Listing 5.7.1 you can see the index assignment that gets generated for the array declared in Listing 5.7. This doesn't need to be explicitly coded to be accessed.

Listing 5.7.1   **Array Value Indexes**

```
var favoriteSandwiches = ["Egg, Sausage and Cheese", "Turkey Club", "Meatball"];

/* index build automatically for you when combining array declarations and
➥assignment */

/* commented out — no need to declare
favoriteSandwiches[0] = "Egg, Sausage and Cheese";

favoriteSandwiches[1] = "Turkey Club";

favoriteSandwiches[2] = "Meatball";
*/

/* alert the second item in the array */
alert(favoriteSandwiches[1]); // Turkey Club
```

Notice that the index value starts at 0 rather than 1. This is how programming languages generally work. It is important to note and remember that because it does trip people up from time to time. The index values can also be assigned manually if you choose to do so, shown in Listing 5.8.

Listing 5.8   **Array Value Indexes**

```
/* use short hand brackets to declare the array */
var favoriteSandwiches = [];

/* manually assign values to the array and set the index */
favoriteSandwiches[0] = "Egg, Sausage and Cheese ";

favoriteSandwiches[1] = "Turkey Club";

favoriteSandwiches[2] = "Meatball";

/* alert the second item in the array */
alert(favoriteSandwiches[1]); // Turkey Club
```

They are still accessed the same way, just declared differently.

That's the basic array—just a list of items. They are very powerful, flexible methods of data storage methods. Everything from a list of DOM nodes to this static list of favorite sandwiches can be stored in an array. You will be working with them quite a bit in their various forms, and they can get pretty complicated, but nailing down these basics will help quite a bit.

At this point you may be wondering why anyone would manually set the index values for an array. It seems like extra work you don't need if you declare everything at once. Oh, you *were* thinking that? Excellent! That brings us right into the next type of array, the **associative array**.

Associative Array

If you're looking to give a little more meaning to your data, you can use an **associative array**. The difference between normal arrays and associative arrays is that in an associative array, the index value is set to be a string rather than the normal number value. Currently, it is thought of as bad practice to use this type of array. They are rarely seen in the wild, but still worth noting in case you ever run into them.

In Listing 5.9 you can see how the array is now a little more human-readable and meaningful compared to the array declared in Listing 5.8. The items are now accessed by the string value assigned to them rather than a number.

Listing 5.9   **An Example of an Associative Array**

```
/* declare the array */
var favoriteSandwiches = [];

/* manually set the values */
favoriteSandwiches["breakfast"] = "Egg, Sausage and Cheese";

favoriteSandwiches["lunch"] = "Turkey Club";

favoriteSandwiches["dinner"] = "Meatball";

/* alert lunch */
alert(favoriteSandwiches["lunch"]); // Turkey Club
```

Multidimensional Array

Multidimensional arrays are arrays of arrays. As mentioned earlier in this chapter, you can save any kind of data to an array, even other arrays.

To this point the `favoriteSandwiches` array has been pretty limiting. What happens if I have more than one favorite kind of sandwich for each meal, and I want to combine them into a single data source? This is where multidimensional comes into the mix. You would first have to split the three meals into separate arrays: breakfast, lunch, dinner; then take those three arrays (saved to variables, remember?) and add them to a fourth array. Let's take a look at this in Listing 5.10.

Listing 5.10   **Example of a Multidimensional Array**

```
/* declare breakfast normally */
var breakfast = ["Egg, Sausage and Cheese", "Egg Whites on Flatbread", "Egg and
➥Cheese"];

/* declare lunch normally */
var lunch = ["Turkey Club", "Grilled Cheese", "Peanut Butter and Jelly"];

/* declare dinner normally */
var dinner = ["Meatball", "Hamburger", "Oatmeal and banana on Rye"];

/* combine all the arrays into "favorite sandwiches"*/
var favoriteSandwiches = [breakfast, lunch, dinner];
```

This is a way to get more data crammed into `favoriteSandwiches` while keeping the structure meaningful and reusable throughout the rest of your code. Next, you're going to want to get the data out of that mess. Accessing a multidimensional array can be tricky, so let's go over it piece by piece. Listing 5.10.1 shows how to pull out various sandwich types from the array defined in Listing 5.10.

Listing 5.10.1   **Pulling Data Out of a Multidimensional Array**

```
alert(favoriteSandwiches[0][1]); // Egg Whites on Flatbread

alert(favoriteSandwiches[1][0]); // Turkey Club

alert(favoriteSandwiches[2][1]); // Hamburger
```

Let's get into what's really going on in this data call: `favoriteSandwiches[0][1]`, which returns "Egg Whites on Flatbread." This is a step-by-step process for what is going on.

1. Access the array called "`favoriteSandwiches`."

2. Go into the 1st item (breakfast); remember, arrays start at 0, not 1.

3. Inside of "breakfast" get the second item (Egg Whites on Flatbread).

4. Alert the result.

That same pattern is applied for each time the array data is accessed. You have to pass through the first array before moving onto the second.

Pushing Data into an Array

Now that you know all the different types of arrays and how to pull data from them, the next logical step is to start dynamically adding content into an array (you don't always have to do it by hand—that would be awful). There will often be times when you need to add new information to an array, either generating the information yourself or gathering it through user input—they're both equally common.

Listing 5.11 expands on the breakfast array from Listing 5.10. In this example we want to do a few things:

- Add Jalapeño Bagel & Ham to the breakfast array.
- Alert the entire array to confirm that it was added properly at the end.
- Directly access the newly added array item (Jalapeño Bagel & Ham) and alert it.

Listing 5.11   **Adding Items to an Array**

```
/* declare breakfast normally */
var breakfast = ["Egg, Sausage and Cheese", "Egg Whites on Flatbread", "Egg and
➡Cheese"];

/* add a Jalapeño bagel and ham to the breakfast array */
breakfast.push("Jalapeño Bagel & Ham");

/* alert the whole array */
alert(breakfast);

/* pull out the newest array member */
alert(breakfast[3]);
```

Working with Array Methods

Accessing and removing items from an array are all the basic interactions you will encounter, but because this type of data storage is so critical, JavaScript opens up a whole slew of methods dedicated to the purpose of interacting with arrays. Knowing that a certain method exists is half the battle to solving a problem, so I've handpicked some methods of array interaction that I personally encounter often in my day-to-day development. Someone helped me at some point to discover these terms, and now I'm going to help you. Hopefully, this will save you hours of frustration when an array just doesn't seem to work the way you want it to.

The methods we'll be going over are

- join
- slice
- shift and unshift

- pop
- concat
- sort

join

The `join` method is a way to combine all the items in an array quickly with a certain term or separator. You may have noticed in Listing 5.11 that when we alerted the breakfast array, it came out in a comma-separated list without spaces. That is the default output of an array, but it is still technically an array at that point. If you were going to output the contents of that array somewhere, you would want to clean it up a little, add some spacing, and maybe not even use a comma.

The `join` method will convert all items in an array to a string and output them in a format you specify. In Listing 5.12 you can see that we're working with the same meal-based sandwich arrays we have been using throughout the chapter.

`Join` takes one parameter, which is the string value you want to output in between each array item. In this case it is ", plus ". The result will be [array item], **plus** [array item], **plus** [array item].

Listing 5.12   **Using `join` on an Array**

```
/* define the sandwich arrays */
var breakfast = ["Egg, Sausage and Cheese", "Egg Whites on Flatbread", "Egg and
➥Cheese"];
var lunch = ["Turkey Club", "Grilled Cheese", "Peanut Butter and Jelly"];
var dinner = ["Meatball", "Hamburger", "Oatmeal and banana on Rye"];

/* clean up breakfast for output */
var joinBreakfast = breakfast.join(", plus "); // separate them with a comma,
➥spaces and the word "plus"

/* alert it */
alert('join: ' + joinBreakfast);
```

slice

`slice` has the capability to output a range of items in an array. For example, if you want to output items 1 through 4 and leave out item 0 and anything higher than 5, that is a range of values you can target with `slice`. In Listing 5.12.1 we're accessing the *lunch* array and outputting values 1 & 2 (Grilled Cheese, Peanut Butter and Jelly) and joining them with an ampersand (&). The slice method takes two parameters, the first is your starting position and the second is your ending position in the array. The start parameter is required, the end is optional. If it's omitted, the slice will just continue to the end of the array.

Listing 5.12.1   **Slicing an Array**

```
/* slice lunch, start at 1 and end at 3 (doesn't include 3) */
var sliceLunch = lunch.slice(1, 3);

/* clean and alert lunch */
var joinLunch = sliceLunch.join(" & ");

alert("slice/join: " + joinLunch); // Grilled Cheese & Peanut Butter and Jelly
```

shift and unshift

shift and unshift are methods used to add and remove items to/from the beginning of a
specified array. In Listing 5.12.2 the shift method is set to remove the array item "meatball"
from the dinner array defined in Listing 5.12. The unshift method will then add the array
item of "Nacho Cheese-wich" to the beginning of the same array. You can then see the result-
ing array with "meatball" removed and "Nacho Cheese-wich" added for an extra-delicious
dinner sandwich array.

Listing 5.12.2   **Remove and Add Items to the Beginning of an Array**

```
/*
    SHIFT
*/

/* remove the first element of dinner */
var shiftDinner = dinner.shift();

/* alert it */
alert(" shift: " + shiftDinner) // meatball

/*
    UNSHIFT
*/

/* add an item to the beginning of the array */
var unshiftDinner = dinner.unshift("Nacho Cheese-wich");

/* alert it */
alert("unShift: " + dinner) // meatball
```

pop

pop is a method reserved for removing and returning the last item in an array. In Listing 5.12.3 you can see an example of how to remove the last item from the dinner array that was defined in Listing 5.12 to return an Oatmeal and Banana Sandwich on Rye bread.

Listing 5.12.3   **An Example of Array Popping**

```
/* remove an item from the end of the array */
var popDinner = dinner.pop();

/* alert it */
alert("pop: " + popDinner) // Oatmeal and banana on Rye
```

> **Note**
>
> Using shift(), unshift() and pop() will all change the physical length of the array if you ever need to access it again.

concat

concat is short for "concatenate." It's a method of **copying and combining** multiple arrays into a single array. The original array still exists because the combined array is only a copy. In Listing 5.12.4 you can see that the breakfast, lunch, and dinner arrays are all being concatenated into the new "favoriteSandwiches" array.

Listing 5.12.4   **Joining All the Arrays into a Single Array**

```
/* concatenate all arrays in one */
var favoriteSandwiches = breakfast.concat(lunch, dinner);

/* save HTML body element to a variable */
var target = document.getElementsByTagName("body")[0];

/* output the array values in the HTML */
target.innerHTML = favoriteSandwiches.join("<br>");
```

This example is a little different because we're not just alerting the result; we are using the DOM node "body" and outputting the content to the page with innerHTML. This is much more likely to happen in real life than alerting a value. Often you will alert a value while trying to debug or test code as you write it.

sort

sort is an interesting method; it can output alphabetical or custom sorting of array items. It takes one optional argument, which is a custom sorting function you would have to write. Otherwise, it will use basic alphabetical sorting. Something to note is that that numbers will not be sorted correctly; 30 will be considered lower than 4 because sort does not take into account true numerical sorting.

In Listing 5.12.5 we are using the sort method on the favoriteSandwiches array and outputting the alphabetical listing of all combined array items.

Listing 5.12.5   **Sorting the New Concatenated Array Alphabetically**

```
/* sort the concatenated array alphabetically */
var sortFavorites = favoriteSandwiches.sort();

/* overwrite the original outputted list with a sorted one */
target.innerHTML = sortFavorites.join("<br>");
```

Objects

When data starts to get overly complex and difficult to consume, I often find myself turning from arrays to objects. You can still save arrays to objects, but rather than piling them into complex, multidimensional arrays, you can create a more human-readable format (in my opinion) with objects.

In Listing 5.13 you can see how you might save all the favorite sandwich data into an object, and then access an individual item in each array.

Listing 5.13   **Saving Data in an Object**

```
/* saving all sandwiches to an object */

var favoriteSandwiches = {

    breakfast : ["Egg, Sausage and Cheese", "Egg Whites on Flatbread", "Egg and
➥Cheese"],
    lunch : ["Turkey Club", "Grilled Cheese", "Peanut Butter and Jelly"],
    dinner : ["Meatball", "Hamburger", "Oatmeal and banana on Rye"],

};

alert(favoriteSandwiches.dinner[0]); // Meatball
```

Objects, of course, don't have to contain arrays like that; they can also contain strings, numbers, Boolean values, or even entire functions. They are very flexible and are often the coding method of choice on larger projects where consistency is a high-level concern.

Listing 5.13.1 shows a basic array of meatball sandwich ingredients and how to access an individual item. It kind of reminds you of an associative array, doesn't it?

Listing 5.13.1   **Saving Data in an Object**

```
/* save meatball sandwich ingredients to another object */

var meatball = {

    bread: "Kaiser Roll",
    meat: "Beef",
    cheese: "Mozzarella"

}

/* alert the type of bread */
alert(meatball.bread); // Kaiser Roll
```

Performance in Objects

The objects you've seen so far have been only a single level deep, but the possibilities are limitless in how deep you can nest an object. They are great for organization and making your code more modular, but this is part of the constant balancing act you will encounter when weighing the benefits of performance versus maintainability.

For example, in Listing 5.13.1, accessing the meatball object has the following process:

- Access "meatball"
- Access "bread"
- Alert the value "Kaiser Roll"

That three-step process takes more processing time than if you were to use the string "Kaiser Roll" directly, but if you needed to use it over and over, your code would start to become a tangled mess. Instead of doing that, it will be cached in an object and referenced over and over. Only traveling one level deep to retrieve a string isn't much of a problem, but when you start getting 3, 4, or 5 levels deep in your nesting, you may hit some performance problems.

> **Note**
>
> Although object-oriented programming works well on the server, where you can control the processing speed, it sometimes fails on the client. This is where an experienced front-end developer will know when to use an object-oriented approach to development versus a non-object-oriented approach to avoid performance bottlenecks.

JSON

JSON is one of the newer data storage methods in JavaScript; it has been heavily used only in the past few years. It stands for JavaScript Object Notation and is a very lightweight format for exchanging data both on the server and on the client. It is not only easy to read and write for humans, but it is also easy to read and write for machines, so you get the best of both worlds. All modern programming languages support JSON in some way, which makes it great when you have to integrate with other systems that may not be running on the same platform as you.

Listing 5.14 shows some of the sandwich information you've been working with saved to the JSON object `favoriteSandwiches`.

Listing 5.14   **Data Saved to a JSON Object**

```
var favoriteSandwiches = {

    "breakfast" : [
        {
            "name": "Egg, Sausage and Cheese",
            "bread": "English Muffin"
        },
        {
            "name": "Egg Whites on Flatbread",
            "bread": "Flatbread"
        }
    ],
    "lunch" : [
        {
            "name": "Turkey Club",
            "bread": "Wheat Bread"
        },
        {
            "name": "Grilled Cheese",
            "bread": "White Bread"
```

```
        }
    ],
    "dinner" : [
        {
            "name": "Meatball",
            "bread": "Kaiser Roll"
        },
        {
            "name": "Hamburger",
            "bread": "Hamburger Roll"
        }
    ]
};

/* go to dinner and get the name of the first item */
alert(favoriteSandwiches.dinner[0].name); // meatball
```

Benefits of Using JSON

There are a lot of data formats in JavaScript; why would you choose JSON over something else? Right off the bat you can tell that JSON is pretty human-readable, which is a huge benefit when you have to comb around someone else's code and try to see what's going on.

JSON is used with a lot of external services to transfer data because it can be consumed cross-domain. Before JSON was popular, XML was the data format of choice if you needed to consume data from an outside source (like RSS), but you weren't able to directly access XML cross-domain with JavaScript without passing it through a local proxy. That's where JSON comes in. It's fast, lightweight, and can easily travel from one domain to another. It's great for Ajax, and it's great for general data storage. JSON also matches data models from other programming languages, whereas XML does not.

Because JSON has cross-domain capabilities (and it's really just JavaScript) it is important to use JSON only from a trusted source to guard against any sort of malicious behavior.

Using an API

API stands for Application Programming Interface. Many professional services will offer an API to developers to build and expand on their codebase. Flickr has an API for you to pull images and content onto your own site, and Netflix has the same for movies. Many other sites also function in a similar away. For right now, it isn't too important to understand exactly how an API works, but know that it is a way for a site (like Flickr or Netflix) to safely give you access to information they store in their databases for your own personal use.

When you make a request to the Netflix API, you would say (in JavaScript) something like, "give me a list of movies with 'dog' in the title," and the Netflix API would respond with a list of movies with "dog" in the title, the same as if you were doing a normal search from their website. Instead of the search results coming back in a pretty, well-designed search result inter-face, the API results in a JSON format for you to parse through.

Most modern-day APIs work this way. You make a call and you get back data in JSON format. The JSON format makes it consumable by any code base. So if you're using JavaScript, Python, PHP, Ruby, and so on, the data format never has to change (which is really nice). APIs are prob-ably the most common use of JSON today, and we live on the Web in an API-based economy, so being familiar with the data format both internally and externally to JavaScript is very important.

Web Storage in HTML5

Up to this point in the chapter, we have been talking about data storage from the developer's side (your side). User interactions are what we do with JavaScript—it creates a behavior layer (you know this). With that in mind, the next step in your JavaScript data storage progression is to start using storage as a way to interact with the user.

In the past we've used cookies to save user-generated data, but let me be the first (one of the millions actually) to say that cookies are hacky, a pain to deal with, and insecure. We've known it for years, and yet we continue to use them. The main problem with cookies is that they got such a bad rap for being riddled with tracking information and malware that people often browse with them turned off. Luckily, there's a better way and it's built right into the language.

The fine folks over at the W3C also noticed how hacky setting, getting, and deleting browser cookies was, so a new standard for Web storage was created in HTML5: `localStorage` and `sessionStorage`. These two new kids on the block (pun intended) are already changing the way we interact with user-initiated stored data. Let's take a look at them.

localStorage and sessionStorage

As mentioned, storing information locally in a user's browser dates back to the early days of the Web and cookies. Sometimes it's just a mark saying, "I've been here before." Sometimes it is actual data (name, address, and so on) triggered by some event. Either way, it's a powerful tool for creating a better and more personalized user experience in the browser.

In HTML5 you have access to two new storage objects: `localStorage` and `sessionStorage`. These objects are paired with three methods: `setItem`, `getItem`, and `removeItem`. Let's take a look at them individually.

setItem

The `setItem` method takes two arguments. The first is the equivalent of a variable label, or what you want to call the data being stored. The second argument is the data itself, which must be a string. Calling `setItem` with `local/sessionStorage` will store the data locally with the user.

Listing 5.15 shows how you would manually save a `localStorage` object called "`favoriteSandwich`" with a value of "Meatball".

Listing 5.15   **Saving Data with `localStorage`**

```
/* set localStorage */
localStorage.setItem("favoriteSandwich", "Meatball");
```

getItem

After setting an item, it's only natural that you would want, at some point, to retrieve that same item. Otherwise, why would you have set it in the first place? For this you use the `getItem` method. It takes a single argument, which is the name of the item you previously set. Listing 5.15.1 shows how to retrieve the `favoriteSandwich` data that was set in Listing 5.15 by using `getItem`.

Listing 5.15.1   **Getting Data from `localStorage`**

```
/* retrieve stored data */
var sandwich = localStorage.getItem("favoriteSandwich"); // returns "Meatball"

/* prove it was set */
alert(sandwich);
```

removeItem

My mom always taught me to clean up after myself, and I try to keep this in my head while designing and developing applications. The W3C, for mothers everywhere, added a method in Web storage to help you clean up after yourself; it is called "`removeItem`". This method will delete the item stored locally with the user. It takes one argument, just like its companion method, `getItem`. Listing 5.15.2 depicts how to remove a locally stored item.

Listing 5.15.2   **Cleaning Up After Yourself**

```
/* delete stored data */
localStorage.removeItem("favoriteSandwich"); // returns a happy mom :-)
```

Both `localStorage` and `sessionStorage` use the same syntax and methods. The only difference between the two objects is that `localStorage` will remain active until explicitly removed by you (the developer) or the user, via the browser preferences; it's actually pretty difficult for a user to clear. `sessionStorage` acts differently because it is a session-based storage method, which means it will remove itself at the end of each browser session (when the browser is closed).

Storing Chunks of Data with JSON

Web storage currently can take only strings for data. This can be problematic when you need to store multiple items. You can get around this limitation by storing your data in a JSON object and then using the JSON.stringify method to convert the entire object to a string that can be stored using Web storage.

Listing 5.16 shows how you might take the entire favoriteSandwiches JSON object that was created in Listing 5.14 and save it locally with Web storage.

Listing 5.16   Using **JSON.stringify** to Store Data

```
/* stringify the JSON object first */
var stringObject = JSON.stringify(favoriteSandwiches);

/* add the string object to localStorage */
localStorage.setItem("favoriteSandwiches", stringObject);
```

Because this JSON object is now a string, and the individual items in the object can't be accessed efficiently, when you access this item it needs to be reconverted from a string, back into a JSON object. Listing 5.16.1 shows you how to use JSON.parse to convert the string back into a workable JSON format.

Listing 5.16.1   Using **JSON.parse** to Get Data

```
/* get the locally stored data */
var storedItem = localStorage.getItem("favoriteSandwiches");

/* convert it from a string, back into a JSON object */
var convertObject = JSON.parse(storedItem);

/* prove it worked */
alert(convertObject.breakfast[0].name); // Egg, Sausage and Cheese
```

You can see that the returned value in Listing 5.16.1 is the same value as the first breakfast sandwich in the main array, but it is now pulled from Web storage rather than from the original array.

Support

Because this type of storage is new with HTML5, you have to be concerned with the support levels within your target audience. If you're targeting only high-end devices and browsers, it's probably not an issue, but for the rest of us it is important to be aware of. Table 5.1 shows the browser support for HTML5 Web storage in the popular browsers.

Table 5.1   Browser Support for `localStorage` and `sessionStorage`

Internet Explorer	8.0 and up
Firefox	3.5 and up
Chrome	4.0 and up
Opera	10.5 and up
Safari	4.0 and up

Using Web Storage Responsibly

As you can see from Table 5.1, Web storage is not supported everywhere yet. This, coupled with a general desire to create a fluid user experience no matter what browser a user is in, brings us back to something called **feature detection**, which was briefly covered in an earlier chapter. It will be a main theme whenever we're coding for these new standards brought forth by HTML5.

The main idea is that `localStorage` and `sessionStorage` are features of advanced browsers. You can detect for the presence of that feature and code for or against it. If the feature doesn't exist, you can use an alternative method that may be a little older or that might not perform as well, but it still gets the job done. Listing 5.17 shows you how you might use feature detection with `localStorage`.

Listing 5.17   Checking for `localStorage` Support Before Moving Forward

```
/* check for localStorage support */
if(typeof(localStorage) === "undefined"){

    // localStorage is not supported, maybe use cookies?

} else {

    // localStorage is supported, use it and be well.
    // add your localStorage code in here
}
```

Using this method of feature detection will make sure your users are using the latest and greatest options available to create the best possible experience. Using the `if` statement will also ensure that a browser that doesn't support `localStorage` won't have to waste valuable processor time parsing code it won't understand anyway—or even worse, throw an error, which prevents the rest of your JavaScript from executing.

Summary

In this chapter, you learned all the different methods of storing data in JavaScript and how to interact with each of them. First, we went over all the different types of data that can be stored in a variable or array. We also talked about the different kinds of arrays you will come across when working with data in JavaScript: basic, associative, and multidimensional. You also learned the cases where each may apply and how to recognize and work with them to manipulate data, along with how to dynamically add and remove items. We also got into using detailed objects instead of arrays when data starts to get more complex.

Last, we went through examples of user based data-storage methods, touched on the more advanced methods built into HTML5, such as `localStorage` and `sessionStorage`. We also talked about how to responsibly use these new features by detecting for support beforehand to conditionally load the right tool for the job.

Exercises

1. What are the three data types you can use with a variable?

2. What is an associative array?

3. What is a multidimensional array?

6

Variables, Functions, and Loops

This is one of the more important chapters in the book because you learn some of the core features in JavaScript. We expand on the variables that were mentioned in the previous chapter, then move on to creating functions, and last, we go over how to loop through data to autoexecute the same code block over and over. Using variables, functions, and loops are often the only thing a person knows how to do in JavaScript, and they usually get along just fine. You're already past that part and on your way to becoming an elite JavaScript developer, so no worries there. You'll be coding while all the others are looking up how to do something.

Now that you have a solid base in how to work with a lot of the common things in JavaScript, you can start building an application and producing something tangible. Up to this point in the book, the examples have been pretty specific, but also a little abstract. You've been manipulating content and data, then alerting or observing the result. In this chapter we expand on what you've learned already and begin building a simple JavaScript application that will get more robust as you step through the subsequent chapters.

As you progress though this chapter, you notice that an address book application should be starting to form. Some of the methods that we go over repeat in their core functionality but have very different use-cases. Although they may not necessarily all live in the same application, this is the chapter where you start building that tangible knowledge that can be directly transferred into a project.

Defining Variables

For the most part, you learned about variables within the context of data storage, but they also have an integral part in your application when it comes to functionality.

When considering variable and function naming, it's best to make them meaningful and speak to their contents or purpose. For example, using a variable name of "myBestFriend" would be much more helpful than something like, "`firstVariableName`." Something else to consider when naming variables is that they can't start with a number. They can *contain* numbers, such as "`dogs3`" or "`catsStink4Eva`," but they can't begin with a number, such as "`3dogs`."

Grouping Variables

When you're writing an application, it's best to try to group all variables at the top of your JavaScript file or function (when possible) so they can all be immediately cached for later reference. Some people find this method a little unnatural because functions are defined throughout the document, and it's a little easier to maintain when variables are right there with the function they belong to; but grouping variables at the top is one of those small performance boosts you can give to your application. It helps to think of it as one large file containing JavaScript for an application versus thinking of the file as a collection of one-off actions that get executed. When thinking of it as a single unit, it feels a little better (to me) when I'm grouping all variables together at the top.

You can group variables in your document in two ways. Up to this point we have been using a new `var` declaration for each variable; a lot of people prefer this method, and it's perfectly fine to use. An alternative method is to use a single `var` declaration, using commas to separate the individual variables and a semicolon at the very end. Listing 6.1 shows an example of grouping variables with a single `var` declaration. Note the commas at the end of each line.

Listing 6.1   **Grouping Variables with a Single `var` Declaration**

```
var highSchool = "Hill",
    college = "Paul",
    gradSchool = "Vishaal";
```

There's no difference in the way you access these variables compared to how you access variables declared with individual `var` declarations. At the variable level, it's purely a way to group. It isn't good or bad at this point—it's only personal preference. You'll see both methods in looking through JavaScript others have written, so it's good to know what's going on.

You see this style of variable declaration a lot more when getting into objects, methods, and grouping functions together. I prefer it because it feels cleaner and a little more consistent, but as you progress you will settle on a preference of your own. Both are certainly valid methods.

Reserved Terms

JavaScript contains a lot of core functionality. We've been over quite a bit of it so far. Beyond that core functionality you will be defining a lot of your own custom code. If the names of your custom JavaScript match up with anything built into the language, it can cause collisions and throw errors. It's the same as if you're writing a large JavaScript file—you want to make sure all the function and variable names are as unique as possible to prevent problems and confusion while parsing the information. If you have two functions with the same name, it's difficult to tell the browser which one to use, so it's just not allowed.

To prevent these issues with native JavaScript, there are some reserved words (keywords) that you can't use when defining variables, functions, methods, or identifiers within your code. Following is a list of the reserved words:

- break
- case
- catch
- continue
- debugger
- default
- delete
- do
- else
- finally
- for
- function
- if
- implements
- in
- instanceof
- interface
- new
- package
- private
- protected
- public
- return
- static
- switch
- this
- throw
- try
- typeof
- var
- void
- while
- with

Most of these are no-brainers, like `function` and `var`, and under normal circumstances you probably would never come across a situation where something like "`implements`" would be a reasonable name for a variable or function. If you end up using any of these terms in your code, the console will throw an error and let you know that you're using a reserved word. With that in mind, I think the value in this list is not so much memorizing it, but rather recognizing that these words map to native actions in the language. It will help you write better code and also aid in learning more advanced JavaScript down the road if you choose to research some of those terms that are beyond the scope of this book, such as public, private, and protected.

Functions

Functions in any programming language are ways to write code that can be used later. At its most basic form, this is also true for JavaScript. You can write a chunk of custom code and not only execute it at will, but you can also execute it over and over, which can help streamline your application by increasing its maintainability (declaring a chunk of code one time and referencing it, rather than rewriting what it does). It's like keeping all your CSS in the same file or why you keep all JavaScript in the same file—you know exactly where it is when you need to change or add something.

You've been using functions already in earlier chapters when you pass data into an `alert()`. "Alert" is technically called a `method` but for all intents and purposes, it's the same as a function.

Basic Functions

The chance of creating a JavaScript application without having to write your own functions is pretty low. It's something that you'll be doing on every project, and it's very easy to do using the function keyword (remember the reserved words list? This is what `function` is for).

Using the function keyword is like saying, "Hey, I'm building something over here that should be treated as a function." Listing 6.2 shows a basic function declaration.

Listing 6.2   **Writing a Basic Function**

```
function sayHello() {

    alert("hey there! ");

}
```

Calling a Function

Calling a function is very simple. You type out the name, and then parentheses and the function will be executed. The parentheses tell the browser that you want to execute the function and to use any data (arguments) contained within the parentheses within the function. Listing 6.2.1 shows how to call the function we declared in Listing 6.2. It should alert the text, "hey there!"

Listing 6.2.1   **Calling a Basic Function**

```
sayHello(); // hey there
```

Arguments

Arguments are a way to pass information or data into a function. As previously mentioned, up to this point you've been using the `alert()` method. We've also been passing it arguments. The alert method is designed in native JavaScript to take arguments and display them in the form of a pop-up box in the browser.

Functions can take any number of arguments. They can be any type of information; strings, variables, large data sets, and anything else you can think of can be passed into a function through an argument. As you're defining your functions, you will be assigning names to the arguments, sort of like the way you assign names to a variable. After that argument is named in the function, it becomes a variable you'll be using inside that function.

In Listing 6.2.2 you can see that the sayHello() function now has a single argument called "message." Inside, the function "message" is used as a variable that gets passed into the JavaScript alert() method.

Listing 6.2.2   **Passing a Function Variable Through Arguments**

```
/* declare the function */
function sayHello(message){

    alert(message); // "message" is also an argument in the "alert" method

}

/* call it a couple times with different messages */
sayHello("Hey there, you stink!");

sayHello("I feel bad I just said that.");
```

When this function is called, we're setting the string argument to "Hey there, you stink!" and then quickly apologizing with another alert, because frankly it was kind of rude. This is a very real-life way arguments are used in functions. The string can either be declared upon calling the function (like we're doing in Listing 6.2.2) or it can be declared immediately in the function declaration. (Instead of using the message variable, you could insert the string.) Calling it the way we did is much more common in the real world, though.

Anonymous Functions

Anonymous functions are functions that have no name (obviously—they're anonymous). They execute immediately and can contain any number of other functions. The syntax for declaring an anonymous function is a little different. They are dynamic in nature because they are executed at runtime rather than waiting to be called.

Anonymous functions perform very well in the browser because there is no reference to them in another part of the document. This comes with pluses and minuses. So as you write your JavaScript, it is always good to note that if you have to rewrite an anonymous function over and over, it's probably best to pull it out into a normal function to cut down on maintenance and repetitive code.

There is often a little confusion as to the purpose of anonymous functions. If you want something to execute at runtime, why wouldn't you just dump the code right into your JavaScript file? Why even bother wrapping it in an anonymous function? Well, this is a good place to bring up a term you may hear a lot: **scope**.

Scope

Scope is a programming concept that exists to reduce the amount of variable and function collisions in your code. It controls how far information can travel throughout your JavaScript document. Earlier on, we briefly mentioned `global variables`. "Global" is a type of scope; the global scope for a variable means that the variable can be accessed and used anywhere in the document. Global variables are generally a bad thing, especially in larger files where naming collisions are more likely. Try to keep things out of the global scope if possible. Listing 6.3 shows how to declare a basic anonymous function and keep variables out of the global scope.

Listing 6.3   **Defining an Anonymous Function**

```
/* set up your anonymous function */
(function () {

    /* define a variable inside the function */
    var greeting = "Hello Tim";

    /* access the variable inside the function */
    alert("in scope: " + greeting);

})(); // end anonymous function
```

For the most part, you will be dealing in function-level scope. This means that any variable defined inside a function cannot be used outside that function. This is a great benefit of using anonymous functions. If you wrap a code block in an anonymous function, the contents of that function, which would normally default to the global scope, will now be contained within the scope of that anonymous function.

Listing 6.3.1 defines a variable inside an anonymous function, alerts the variable, and then tries to alert the variable again, outside the function (it won't end well).

Listing 6.3.1   **Showing Scope Inside an Anonymous Function**

```
/* set up your anonymous function */
(function () {

    /* define a variable inside the function */
    var greeting = "Hello Tim";
```

```
    /* access the variable inside the function */
    alert("in scope: " + greeting);

})(); // end anonymous function

/* try and access that variable outside the function scope */
alert("out of scope: " + typeof(greeting)); // alerts "undefined"
```

As you can see, the variable `alert` is undefined, even though you can see it's clearly defined within the anonymous function. This is because the function scope will not allow the variable to leave the function.

> ### Note
>
> In the second alert of Listing 6.3.1 we're using the JavaScript method `typeof()`, which alerts the variable type "undefined." If we didn't do this, the file would throw an error, and you wouldn't see the second alert at all. The JavaScript console would display the error, "greeting is undefined."

Calling a Function with a Function

When you have a function that calls another function, the second function is referred to as a **callback**. The callback function is defined as a normal function with all the others but is executed inside another function. They're a little different because instead of *you* having to do something to execute the function, another function does something. It's like having robots that are built by other robots—total madness, I know.

Callback functions are a great way to separate out the levels of functionality in your code and make parts more reusable. Often you will see callback functions passed as arguments to other functions. We'll get more into that in the next chapter when we talk about JavaScript events, and they're especially important when dealing with server communications like Ajax. Listing 6.3.2 shows our `sayHello()` function being defined and then called inside the anonymous function. In this case, `sayHello()` is a callback function (calling it twice).

Listing 6.3.2   **Using a Callback Function**

```
function sayHello(message) {
    alert(message);
}

(function (){

    var greeting = "Welcome",
        exitStatement = "ok, please leave.";
```

```
        sayHello(greeting);
        sayHello(exitStatement);

})();
```

Returning Data

Every function you create will not result in a direct output. Up to this point you've been creating functions that do something tangible, usually alerting a piece of data into the browser. You won't always want to do that, though; from time to time you will want to create a function that returns information for another function to use. This will make your functions a little smaller, and if the function that gathers information is general enough, you can reuse it to pass the same (or different) information into multiple functions.

Being able to return data and pass it into another function is a powerful feature of JavaScript.

Returning a Single Value

Going back to the sayHello() function that was defined in Listing 6.2, we're going to remove the alert() action that was previously being executed when the function was called, and we'll replace it with a return statement. This is depicted in Listing 6.3.3.

Listing 6.3.3   **Returning Data with a Function**

```
function sayHello(message){
    return message + "!"; // add some emotion too
}
```

You'll probably notice that the sayHello() function doesn't do anything in the browser anymore. That's a good thing (unless you're getting an error—that's a bad thing). It means the function is now returning the data but it's just sitting there waiting to be used by another function.

Returning Multiple Values

Sometimes returning a single value isn't enough for what you're trying to accomplish. In that case you can return multiple values and pass them in an array format to other functions. Remember how I mentioned that arrays are really important? They creep up a lot when dealing in data storage and flow in JavaScript. In Listing 6.3.4 you can see the sayHello() function taking two arguments. Those arguments get changed slightly and are resaved to variables; then they are returned in an array format to be accessed later.

Listing 6.3.4   **Returning Multiple Data Values with a Function**

```
function sayHello(greeting, exitStatement){

    /* add some passion to these dry arguments */
    var newGreeting = greeting + "!",
        newExitStatement = exitStatement + "!!";

    /* return the arguments in an array */
    return [newGreeting, newExitStatement];

}
```

Passing Returned Values to Another Function

Now that you're returning variables, the next step is to pass those variables into another function so they can actually be used. Listing 6.3.5 shows the sayHello() function from Listing 6.3.1 returning an array of information and a new function called startle(), taking two arguments, passing them through the original sayHello() function, and alerting the results.

Listing 6.3.5   **Using Returned Function Values Passed into Another Function**

```
function sayHello(greeting, exitStatement){

    /* add some passion to these dry arguments */
    var newGreeting = greeting + "!",
        newExitStatement = exitStatement + "!!";

    /* return the arguments in an array */
    return [newGreeting, newExitStatement];

}

function startle(polite, rude){

     /* call the sayHello function, with arguments and same each response to a
▶variable */
    var greeting = sayHello(polite, rude)[0],
        exit = sayHello(polite, rude)[1];

    /* alert the variables that have been passed through each function */
    alert(greeting + " -- " + exit);

}

/* call the function with our arguments defined */
startle("thank you", "you stink");
```

A Function as a Method

Just as you can group variables and data into objects, you can also do it with functions. When you group functions into objects, they're not called functions anymore; they're called "methods."

When I first started out with JavaScript, I came in from a design background rather than as a developer. This meant that I wasn't familiar with common programming terms such as object, function, method, loop, and so on. I quickly learned what a function was and how to work with them through a lot of Googling. But I would hear people talk about the `alert()` method and other methods native to JavaScript, and I wouldn't really get it because they look the same as functions. Why isn't it the "alert function"? I had no idea. This comes up a lot when you're dealing with JavaScript libraries as well (we get into that later in the book); everything is a method and nothing is a function, even though they all look and act the same.

Here's what's going on. In Chapter 5, "Storing Data in JavaScript," you learned about storing information in objects. I mentioned that you could also store functions in objects. When you do that, they're called methods instead of functions, but they work the same way. It's weird, I know, and it's not even an important distinction while you're coding. It's more about organizing your functions in groups to make them easier to maintain. The `alert()` method lives inside a global object (you never see it), which is why it's called a method.

Now that we're past that ordeal, organizing your functions into meaningful objects can clean up a lot of your code, especially on larger projects where you need the code organization help to keep your sanity. Listing 6.4 should look a little familiar; it shows how to organize our two functions (`sayHello` and `startle`) inside an object called "addressBookMethods." If we were building a large-scale application with many features, this would be a great way to section off the functionality meant only for the address book feature.

Listing 6.4   **Grouping Similar Functions**

```
var addressBookMethods = {

    sayHello: function(message){

        return message;

    },
    startle: function(){

        alert(addressBookMethods.sayHello("hey there, called from a method"));

    }

}

/* call the function */
addressBookMethods.startle();
```

Calling a method is a little different from calling a function. You'll notice in Listing 6.4 that instead of calling `startle()` by itself, you have to call `addressBookMethods.startle()`. This is because before you can access the method, you have to access the object and drill down to the method.

Performance Considerations

Nesting functions in objects has the same performance implications that we spoke of when nesting variables in objects. The deeper a function is nested inside an object (`addressBookMethods`), the more resources it takes to extract. This is another place in your code where you will have to balance performance with maintainability. We're not talking a ton of time here—maybe a few milliseconds difference—but it can add up. Most of the time it won't matter, but if you find yourself needing a performance boost, function objects would be a place to look for a bottleneck. I probably wouldn't go more than a few levels deep when creating these objects. Listing 6.4 goes only one level deep, which is a nice balance between performance and maintainability.

Loops

A loop will execute a block of code over and over until you tell it to stop. It can iterate through data or HTML. For our purposes we'll mostly be looping through data. Much the way a function is a chunk of JavaScript code, a loop can make that function execute over and over—like a little buddy you have to do your repetitive tasks for you. And they're built right into the language!

For this one, we need some data to loop through. We'll be using contact information for the data and saving it to a JSON object called "contacts." Listing 6.5 shows a small sample of the contact information we'll be looping through. I find it easier to work with data that represents people, because when something goes wrong with one of the items it's more difficult to get angry at someone you know than it is at anything else. Feel free to substitute your own friends or family in the data so you don't get frustrated if something goes wrong.

Listing 6.5 Creating Data in a JSON Object

```
var contacts = {
    "addressBook" : [
        {
            "name": "hillisha",
            "email": "hill@example.com",
        },
        {
            "name": "paul",
            "email": "cleveland@example.com",
        },
        {
```

```
        "name": "vishaal",
        "email": "vish@example.com",
    },
    {
        "name": "mike",
        "email": "grady@example.com",
    },
    {
        "name": "jamie",
        "email": "dusted@example.com",
    }
    ]
};
```

for Loop

There are few different types of loops in JavaScript, a while loop, a do-while loop, and a for loop. Most of them are perfectly fine; I would avoid the foreach loop because it's known to be a performance hog, but the others are fine to use. A while loop and a for loop are basically the same thing, but the for loop is a little more direct, to the point, and it's the most common kind of loop you're going to find in the wild. In all the years I've been writing JavaScript, it's been 99% for loops. With that in mind, we're going to go over the for loop in this book.

Listing 6.5.1 will show you a basic for loop, and then we'll go over what's happening.

Listing 6.5.1   **A for Loop Integrating Address Book Data**

```
/* cache some initial variables */
var object = contacts.addressBook,
    contactsCount = object.length,
    i;

/* loop through each JSON object item until you hit #5, then stop */
for (i = 0; i < contactsCount; i = i + 1) {

    // code you want to execute over and over again

} // end for loop
```

Right away, you can see that we're saving some information to variables. The first variable "object" is saving the JSON object we create to a variable so it's a little easier to work with. The second variable, "contactsCount", looks through the JSON object and counts the number of items in there. This will let us know how many times to loop through the data. The third variable, "i", is just a way to declare the counting variable for our loop. Later on we'll be setting the value.

Inside the `for` you can see three statements. The first statement is setting the counter variable (i) to its initial value of 0 (we start at 0). The second statement is the condition in which you run the loop. As long as the "i" value is less than the overall count of items in the data, it should execute the code contained inside the loop brackets { }. The last statement takes the "i" value and adds 1 to it each time the loop executes until it's no longer less than the overall count. In our case, this loop will execute 5 times because there are five people in the address book.

Listing 6.5.2 will show the actual loop to iterate through the address book data saved to the JSON object, and then, using the `innerHTML` DOM method, output the result into the document's <body> element. Besides the output, a main difference to note in Listing 6.5.2 is that we're now running a check on the `contactsCount` variable to make sure it's greater than 0 before continuing onto the loop. This is a general best practice to prevent unnecessary code from executing should there be an error with the data.

Listing 6.5.2   **A `for` Loop Integrating Address Book Data**

```
/* cache some initial variables */
var object = contacts.addressBook, // save the data object
    contactsCount = object.length, // how many items in the JSON object? "5"
    target = document.getElementsByTagName("body")[0], // where you're outputting the
➥data
    i; // declare the "i" variable for later use in the loop

/* before doing anything make sure there are contacts to loop through */
if(contactsCount > 0) {

    /* loop through each JSON object item until you hit #5, then stop */
    for (i = 0; i < contactsCount; i = i + 1) {

        /* inside the loop "i" is the array index */
        var item = object[i],
            name = item.name,
            email = item.email;

        /* insert each person's name & mailto link in the HTML */
        target.innerHTML += '<p><a href="mailto:'+ email +'">' + name + '</a></p>';

    }
}
```

It's nice to be rid of that annoying alert box, isn't it? Rather than alerting each value, we are now choosing a target within the HTML document (<body> element) and outputting the data there. This is more along the lines of what you'll be doing in the real world, so we'll be doing that now instead of using the `alert()` method.

Performance Considerations

As mentioned in an earlier chapter, JavaScript, by nature, is blocking. That means it will stop the download of other objects on the page until it is finished with its business. This can be very evident when dealing with loops. The data we're dealing with here is only five items in length, so there isn't a problem executing this block of code 5 times. However, as the number of elements you're looping through increases, so will the time it takes to iterate over them. This is important to note when you're looping through a lot of items because it can really bog down the loading time of a page.

Any variable that doesn't change and can be defined outside the loop *should* be defined outside the loop. You'll notice in our loop that there is a variable called `contactsCount`; it is defined outside the loop and then referenced within. We can do this because the length of the data never changes while the information is being looped through. If it were inside the loop, the length would have to be recalculated each time the loop ran, which can get very resource intensive. Little things like that can help you conserve resources when you're working with loops.

Conditionals

Conditionals are how you let your program make decisions for you. Decisions can be based on the data presented (decisions you make) or based on user input, like one of those choose-your-own adventure books. It's a way to inject some logic into your JavaScript.

Conditionals can be used for everything from outputting different information into the DOM to loading a completely different JavaScript file. They're very powerful things to have in your JavaScript toolkit.

if Statement

By far, the most common type of conditional is the `if` statement. An `if` statement checks a certain condition, and if true, executes a block of code. The `if` statement is contained within two curly brackets {   }, just like the loops we were talking about earlier and the functions before that.

This is best described through a coding sample so let's move right to it. In Listing 6.5.3 you can see a basic `if` statement that is being applied inside the loop of our JSON object in Listing 6.5.2. Inside the loop, if the person's name is "hillisha" the name and mailto link with an exclamation point at the end will be outputting into the document. This output should only be Hillisha's `mailto` link without any other names.

Listing 6.5.3   **Basic `if` Statement**

```
/* if "hillisha comes up, add an exclamation point to the end" */

if(name === "hillisha"){

    target.innerHTML += '<p><a href="mailto:' + email + '">' + name + '</a>!</p>';

}
```

> **Note**
>
> Note that we're using "===" in the conditional to check if the names match what we're looking for. This triple equal sign operator signifies an *exact* match. There is also a double equal sign (==) you can use that means "match." It's best practice to use === rather than == because it's more specific, and when dealing in Boolean values it can get confusing because true = 1 and false = 0. Therefore if you're looking for a "false" Boolean value, using a double equal sign would not only return what you're looking for, but a "0" would do the same. In a nutshell, **use the === operator and not the == operator** and you won't hit that weird gray area of false versus 0 and true versus 1 when dealing with Booleans.

if/else Statement

In Listing 6.5.3 the output was only a single person's name because the condition was set to handle only that one instance of `name === "hillisha"`. Normally you will want do something for the rest of the people in your address book as they are outputted. The `if/else` statement is for just that purpose.

The `if/else` statement gives you the capability to create multiple conditions and then a fallback condition for any items that don't meet the conditions' criteria. In Listing 6.5.4 you can see that we are still looping through the address book JSON object, but this time we're setting three conditions:

- if name is hillisha
- if name is paul
- everyone else

Listing 6.5.4   **`if/else` Statement**

```
if(name === "hillisha"){

    /* if "hillisha comes up, add an exclamation point to the end" */
    target.innerHTML += '<p><a href="mailto:'+ email +'">' + name + '</a>!</p>';
```

```
} else if (name === "paul") { // line 5

    /* if "paul" comes up, add a question mark */
    target.innerHTML += '<p><a href="mailto:' + email + '">' + name + '</a>?</p>';

/* otherwise, output the person as normal*/
} else {

    target.innerHTML += '<p><a href="mailto:'+ email +'">' + name + '</a></p>';


}
```

On line 5 in Listing 6.5.4, you can see that you can combine the two types of statements into else if to create a flow of conditional statements. Using this method, there is no limit to the amount of conditionals you can write. When you get to a large number of conditionals like this, you may consider changing from an if/else statement to a slightly more efficient switch statement.

switch Statement

A switch statement, on the surface, functions almost exactly like an if/else statement. In a switch statement, you first have to set a switch value (the thing you're going to check for); in this example, we have been checking for name, so that's the switch value. You then set up cases to test against. We checked for "hillisha" once and also "paul"; those would be the cases used. Last, there is a default state if none of the cases return as true.

The switch statement in Listing 6.5.5 creates the same output as the if/else statement in Listing 6.5.4, but under the hood and in syntax they are pretty different. Let's take a look at this switch statement.

Listing 6.5.5   **Basic switch Statement**

```
switch(name){
    case "hillisha":

        /* if "hillisha comes up, add an exclamation point to the end" */
        target.innerHTML += '<p><a href="mailto:'+ email +'">' + name + '</a>!</p>';

        /* break out of the statement */
        break;

    case "paul":

        /* if "paul" comes up, add a question mark */
        target.innerHTML += '<p><a href="mailto:'+ email +'">' + name + '</a>?</p>';
```

```
        /* break out of the statement */
        break;

    default:

        /* otherwise, output the people as normal*/
        target.innerHTML += '<p><a href="mailto:'+ email +'">' + name + '</a></p>';

} // end switch statement
```

if versus switch

Besides syntax there is one major difference in how an if/else statement functions when compared to a switch statement. First, the else in an if/else isn't required; you can just run an if statement like we did in Listing 6.5.3. In a switch statement, the default option is required.

The iteration mechanism is also different. In the if/else statement in Listing 6.5.4, it still runs the same process over each item in the JSON object. For example, the first person listed is "Hillisha," so when the conditional statement is executed on that item, it asks three questions:

- Does this name equal "hillisha?" – true
- Does this name equal "paul?" – false, it's "hillisha"
- Does it equal something else – false

Even if the first condition is true, the statement continues checking against the other conditions. If you have a lot of conditions, this can be very resource intensive. This is where the switch statement really shines.

In the switch statement, after a condition is found to be true, it breaks out of the cases so there are no more checks made. In the switch statement in Listing 6.5.5, the second condition of looking for the name "paul" would look something like this:

- Does this name equal "paul?" – false, it's "hillisha"
- Does this name equal "paul?" – true, found it!
- Stop asking questions you know the answer to.

Many people like using if/else because it feels more natural, but after you get to a certain conditional count, you should consider moving over to the switch statement for a little better performance in your JavaScript.

Putting It All Together

Up to this point in the chapter, you have been building a simple address book and outputting the data.

Listing 6.6 is a cumulative dump of the code you've been putting together. It contains the JSON object with contact information, an anonymous function, and a loop with a conditional statement to check the JSON object length.

Listing 6.6   **Application Code**

```
/* create some data in the form of a JSON object you can consume and loop through */

var contacts = {
    "addressBook" : [
        {
            "name": "hillisha",
            "email": "hill@example.com",
        },
        {
            "name": "paul",
            "email": "cleveland@example.com",
        },
        {
            "name": "vishaal",
            "email": "vish@example.com",
        },
        {
            "name": "mike",
            "email": "grady@example.com",
        },
        {
            "name": "jamie",
            "email": "dusted@example.com",
        }
    ]
};

/* wrap everything in an anonymous function to contain the variables */
(function () {

/* cache some initial variables */

var object = contacts.addressBook, // save the JSON object
    contactsCount = object.length, // how many items in the JSON object? "5"
    target = document.getElementsByTagName("body")[0], // where you're outputting the
➥data
```

```
    i; // declare the "i" variable for later use in the loop

/* before doing anything make sure there are contacts to loop through */

if(contactsCount > 0) {

    /* loop through each JSON object item until you hit #5, then stop */

    for (i = 0; i < contactsCount; i = i + 1) {

        /* inside the loop "i" is the array index */

        var item = object[i],
            name = item.name,
            email = item.email;

        target.innerHTML += '<p><a href="mailto:'+ email +'">' + name + '</a></p>';

    } // end for loop

} // end count check

})(); // end anonymous function
```

There's the address book application as it stands right now. You've created the contact information for our five friends and inserted them into a JSON object. After storing the JSON object, you're looping through each item (person) and outputting them individually into the <body> element, one after another. You're also creating HTML fragments that are paragraphs and mailto links for each person.

The processes of looping through data, storing the items as variables, and outputting them into the DOM is, by far, the most common looping method you will see as you build more applications with JavaScript. This code will not only serve as a base for our application, but as a good reference point for your future JavaScript development.

Summary

In this chapter, we started off by diving a little deeper into variables. You learned the different grouping options when declaring variables, along with some best practice considerations like why you should declare variables at the top of your JavaScript document. We also went over the list of reserved terms you should consider when naming functions and variables to help prevent collisions in your scripting file.

After that, we elaborated on the different types of functions, how they differ from each other, and discussed different case scenarios for when you might want to use each type of function.

We talked about basic functions, anonymous functions, callback functions, and functions in objects, along with how to get your functions working together by returning and passing data to one another, returning both single and multiple values.

Before this chapter, we were accessing items directly when working with data. This chapter showed how to execute the same code over and over for each data item in the form of a loop. We learned about the `for` loop specifically and talked about performance considerations and why the loop is assembled in the way it is.

After loops, we got into conditionals in the form of `if/else` and `switch` statements. They appear similar on the surface, but we also talked about why they're different and the scenarios where you may want to use one style over the other.

This chapter was the first step in building a real JavaScript application (an address book). In the next chapter, we start to bring users into the mix when we talk about events, how we might apply user interactions to this application, and learn some general information about events in JavaScript.

Exercises

1. Why is it best to position all variables at the top of your JavaScript file?

2. Why are some words reserved in JavaScript?

3. How are anonymous functions different from basic functions?

7

Interacting with the User Through Events

In this chapter, you learn how to interact with users by creating and executing events. Up to this point, you (as the developer) have been in full control over all the conditions in which your functions get executed. You've learned how to create functions, build loops, store data, and travel around the DOM. All the interaction controls have been right at your fingertips. A lot of the behind-the-scenes part of an application works this way, but it's only half the battle. You won't always have control over when certain functions get executed. You'll often need to let the user decide when it's best to utilize a certain function. These are called **events**.

Events are triggered in the browser when something happens (obviously); users do not always initiate them, but they often do. For example, "load" is an event that fires when a page is first loaded; although the user *did* technically do something to make the page load, it's more indirect than, for instance, a user clicking a link. Click is another event, which happens when a user clicks something (it doesn't matter what it is, but we'll get into that in a bit).

These events need to be attached to DOM elements to be executed. The statement "click a link" means that the event "click" is being attached to a "link," and then a function is executed. Whether that function is designed to open a URL from an href attribute, to hide/show content, or maybe even load someone's contact information from a beautifully designed JSON object from a previous chapter (hint, hint), the same model applies:

1. Get a DOM node.

2. Attach an event to it.

3. Execute a specific function when the event is triggered.

You may hear this model referred to as **event-driven JavaScript**. Just like some back-end technologies are best at a class-heavy object-oriented model, JavaScript is best at dealing with an event-driven model. This means that you write code, something happens (an event), and then it gets executed (a function/method). There are constant debates over the best way to format JavaScript: whether to let it go wild, whether to use a back-end model-view-controller method, how object-oriented you should get, or whether to use an event-driven model. Some technologies are strong in a certain area and are meant for a very object-oriented model. One of my favorite parts of JavaScript is its freedom in design; it has no real implied structure, and you can do whatever is best for you, your team, and your users. Personally, I like an event-driven model because it feels more natural to the language and the idea of creating user-centered designs. Event-driven models also allow you to code in any style you want, and, depending on the situation, you can use normal functions, methods, objects, or anonymous functions when attaching an event to a DOM element.

Attaching an Event

Now that you are thinking about events, we can talk about attaching them to DOM elements. Events and functions are great; they create human-readable statements like "alert a warning message on click." That's all well and good, but by itself that statement means very little; JavaScript needs more information to complete the task at hand. You need to tell the browser exactly *what* to do when something is clicked. So statements like "alert a warning message on click of the button" or "validate this form when it is submitted" are a lot more meaningful to a program.

Attaching an event to a DOM element is one of the most important places to keep the methodologies behind progressive enhancement in mind; it's very easy to create events that (for example) communicate to the server or a data set and overlook the fact that there is no server-side fallback being created in case JavaScript is turned off. As previously mentioned, coding this way will not only ensure that your content is available to all users, but it will also cut down on the amount of JavaScript you'll need to write. This will result in better performance and a smoother user experience.

There are a lot of ways to attach an event to a DOM element. Some are just flat out wrong (using inline JavaScript in your HTML), some are less wrong, and some are much better. We'll be going over two methods:

- Event handlers
- Event listeners

Event Handlers

Event handlers are what I refer to as the "less wrong" way of attaching an event to a DOM element. That may have been a little dramatic—there's nothing technically wrong with using an event handler. The method just has some drawbacks, which are fixed by using other methods.

Event handlers are very simple to use because they're very human-readable. In Listing 7.1 you can see that we're using a button element with an id value of "btn" and attaching a click event to it in the form of "onclick"; then we set that equal to an anonymous function, which will alert the text "clicked the button."

Listing 7.1   **Adding a Basic `onClick` Event Through an Event Handler**

```
/* wrap it in an anonymous function to contain the variables */

(function(){

    // HTML: <button type="button" id="btn">a button</button>

    // save the button to a variable
    var btn = document.getElementById("btn");

    // Use an event handler to attach the "onclick" event
    btn.onclick = function(){

        // alert inside this anonymous callback function
        alert('clicked the button');

    }

})();
```

When using event handlers, the normal event you would attach is always prefaced with the word "on." That's why we're using "onclick" rather than just "click." This pattern is applied to all events: onsubmit, onchange, onfocus, onblur, onmouseover, onmouseout, ontouchstart, ongesturestart, and so on. You get the point; every event is on<event> when using event handlers.

For the most part, event handlers are fine; they have great browser support and actually predate the DOM standard. The one issue with handlers is that you can attach only a single function to a specific event of a DOM node. Basically, that means you can't attach two click functions to the same button. You might be thinking, "So what?" It's true that you probably won't be attaching two functions to the same event on the same DOM node, but there are cases where it does apply—for example, wanting to validate all the inputs in a form on submit, and then using Ajax to submit the form. I won't tell you to never use event handlers, because a lot of the time it's fine, and I do use them from time to time. Knowing the limitations of the method is important, and if you want to get in the habit of using a method that doesn't have that limitation so you never have to think about it, I highly recommend using an **event listener** instead of an event handler. What a great segue!

Event Listeners

Event listeners have a similar function to that of event handlers in that you still need a DOM element to attach them to, you still need to identify the event, and you still need a function to call. The difference is that you don't have the limitation of the handler when assigning multiple functions to the same DOM element and event. It unties your hands a little as a developer, and I personally prefer working with them a little more than I do handlers.

The syntax of an event listener is a little different from a handler—most notably, the lack of an equal sign and the fact that it looks more like a native method. Let's crack one open and look at each part of an event listener. Listing 7.2 shows an example of an event listener using an anonymous function.

Listing 7.2   **Anatomy of an Event Listener**

```
// event listener with an anonymous function
element.addeventListenter("event", function(){

    // stuff you want the function to do

}, false);
```

An event listener is made up of four parts:

- The DOM element ("element" in Listing 7.2)
- The event type ("event" in Listing 7.2)
- The eventListener, aka the function (anonymous function in Listing 7.2)
- A Boolean value used to initiate something called "capture" (set to false in Listing 7.2)

Other than initiating capture, most arguments in the addEventListener() method are pretty straightforward, so let's go over capture very briefly.

You will be setting this capture option to false 99% of the time. Setting it to true is like getting on a megaphone and announcing to all the parent DOM nodes that an event is firing on a particular node. Setting to false prevents this behavior because, for the most part, it is unnecessary. It's officially called "event propagation." There is a very detailed and confusing explanation in the W3C DOM specification, but as I said, 99% of the time just set it to false and move on.

In Listing 7.2.1 you will see a more real-world example of a basic event listener being set on a button, which has an ID value of "btn." We're using the getElementById() method to save it to a variable and add the event listener to it. The event is defined as "click," and we're executing an anonymous function to alert a message and setting the capture Boolean to false.

Listing 7.2.1   **Adding a Basic Click Event Through a Listener**

```
/* wrap it in an anonymous function to contain the variables */

(function(){

    /* HTML: <button type="button" id="btn">a button</button> */

    // save the button to a variable
```

```
    var btn = document.getElementById("btn");

    // attach a "click" listener to the button
    btn.addEventListener("click", function(){

        // alert inside this anonymous callback function
        alert('clicked the button');

    }, false);

})();
```

Browser Support

Support is a small caveat of using the addEventListener() method. It's one of the instances where "it works where you expect it to work." **Internet Explorer 8 and earlier do not support** addEventListener(), but there is something that functions in almost the same way. The method used in IE8 and earlier is called attachEvent(); the most obvious difference between the two methods is that attachEvent() takes only two arguments. It excludes the capture Boolean value because before Internet Explorer 9, there was no event propagation model available in IE. So it makes sense why the value didn't exist.

Because there is no overlap in support of the two methods, it either exists or it doesn't; you don't need to detect the browser version (which is bad, anyway), you can detect for the presence of addEventListener() and modify your script with an if statement accordingly. If the method exists, use it; if not, use attachEvent().

Listing 7.2.2 shows how to use an if statement to detect for the presence of addEventListener and conditionally let the browser decide which method to use.

Listing 7.2.2 **IE Fallback Code for Listeners**

```
var btn = document.getElementById("btn");

if(btn.addEventListener){

    /* if eventListener is supported do this */
    btn.addEventListener("click", function(){

        // alert inside this anonymous callback function
        alert("clicked the button");

    }, false);
```

```
    } else {
        /* if it's not supported do this (for IE8 and below) */
        element.attachEvent("click", function(){

            // alert inside this anonymous callback function
            alert("Clicked the button");

        });
    }
```

The method of detection in Listing 7.2.2 works because in an unsupported browser, `btn.addEventListener` will return as undefined and the `if` statement will continue onto the else portion of the statement.

Binding Events

When binding (attaching) events to DOM elements, there are a few weird things to note. Remember that when a function is nested inside an object, it's actually called a method? Well, something similar is going on with event listeners and event binding.

When a function is inside an `addEventListener()` method, it's called an event listener. It's still a function when it's outside the `addEventListener()` method, but when it's in the context of that particular method it's referred to as an event listener. It's the listener you're adding to the event.

There is one other strange thing about calling functions inside the `addEventListener()` method. They don't have parentheses like they've had up to this point in the book. Because the parentheses mean "call this now" and we don't want to do that in a listener, you leave them off. Listing 7.3 shows how to use a predefined function as a listener by dropping the parentheses off. If the parentheses were to be left on, the function would execute immediately on load of the page, even if it's inside the `addEventListener()` method.

Listing 7.3   Binding an Event to a DOM Element

```
// save the DOM element you want to attach an event to
var btn = document.getElementByID("btn");

// define your function normally
function alertMessage(){
    alert("clicked the button");
}

// or use a predefined function (event handler), "alertMessage"
btn.addEventListener("click", alertMessage, false);
```

In previous chapters, we spoke about adding a dynamic nature to functions by passing arguments through them. With no parentheses, you can't pass any arguments into the function, can you? No, but that's okay.

In order to pass arguments into a function while using `addEventListener()`, you need to use the function as a callback instead by nesting it inside an anonymous function. This may sound a little confusing, but Listing 7.3.1 shows you how to use an anonymous function and a callback function to achieve this goal.

Listing 7.3.1   **Calling a Listener with Arguments**

```
// save the DOM element you want to attach an event to
var btn = document.getElementByID("btn");

// define your function normally
function alertMessage(message) {
    alert(message);
}

// or use a predefined function (event handler), "alertMessage"
btn.addEventListener("click", function() {

    // callback function!
    alertMessage("clicked the button");

}, false);
```

As you can see, Listing 7.3.1 is very similar to Listing 7.3, but instead of simply calling a function, you can pass parameters into it.

Unbinding Events

Just like how you want to bind (attach) events to DOM elements, sometimes you want to unbind (detach) events from DOM nodes. Most of the time you'll probably attach an event and leave it alone, but if you want to clean up after yourself, you can certainly remove the listener just as easily as you can add it. Internet Explorer version 8 and earlier have their own methods for removing events (detaching events). Listing 7.3.2 shows an example of how to remove and detach an event similar to the way they are added.

Listing 7.3.2   **Removing an Event Listener**

```
if(btn.removeEventListener){

    // if removeEventListener is supported
    btn.removeEventListener("click", alertMessage, false);
```

```
} else {

    // if removeEventListener isn't supported (IE8 and below)
    btn.detachEvent("click", alertMessage);

}
```

Mouse and Keyboard Events

The most common events, other than load, that you will use are most likely mouse and keyboard-based events. What are mouse and keyboard-based events? Events such as

- click

- focus

- blur

- change

- mouseover (hover part 1)

- mouseout (hover part 2)

- submit (form submit)

There are a lot of events in JavaScript. Some you'll probably never use, like double-click. The previous list contains the popular mouse and keyboard events that I personally use very often and I imagine you will as well.

To properly go through the following example of these events, you'll first need some HTML to work with. We'll be jumping back into the address book application that we've been building off of for this chapter. The HTML will consist of a simple search form to type in the name of a contact and have the contact show up on the page. Listing 7.4 shows the basic HTML search form you'll use to build this functionality. Ideally, this form should be hooked up to a back-end technology (PHP, Python, Ruby, and the like) via the form action to process the user's request upon submitting the form so it is accessible without JavaScript. It functions in a similar manner to a normal search form, but instead of searching millions of websites this form searches through the JSON object of contacts you made.

Listing 7.4   **Basic HTML Search Form**

```
<!doctype html>
<html>
<head>

    <meta charset="utf-8">
    <title>Address Book</title>
```

```
    <style>
        .active { background: #ddd; }
        .hovering { background: #eee; }
        form > div { padding: 10px; }
    </style>
</head>
<body>

<h1>Address Book</h1>

<!-- ideally you would have this hooked up to a PHP (any backend) processing page so
➥it works without JavaScript as well, but we won't get into that -->

<form action="" method="get" id="search-form">

    <div class="section">
        <label for="q">Search address book</label>
        <input type="search" id="q" name="q" required placeholder="type a name">
    </div><!--/.section-->

    <div class="button-group">
        <button type="submit" id="btn-search">search</button>
        <button type="button" id="get-all">get all contacts</button>
    </div><!--/.button-group-->

</form>

<div id="output"></div><!--/#output-->

<!-- Keeping JS at the bottom, because we rock at performance -->
<script src="js/addressbook.js"></script>

</body>
</html>
```

You can see in the HTML that we've prepped the interface a little, so it's ready for our JavaScript functionality by adding an empty div with an ID of "output" to accept our data, and there is also a secondary button to get all the contacts into the address book.

There are a lot of active debates over inserting HTML like that into DOM; some people don't like doing it because it isn't semantic. The alternative is adding it through the JavaScript file. Adding it via the JavaScript file violates the progressive enhancement methodology of not putting HTML in your JavaScript, so we'll be leaving it in the HTML, but you should know that both methods are perfectly acceptable.

Listing 7.4.1 shows the JSON object created to hold contact information. It is the same object from previous chapters, but you should feel free to add some new people to freshen things up.

Listing 7.4.1   **Address Book Data**

```
var contacts = {
    "addressBook" : [
        {
            "name": "hillisha",
            "email": "hill@example.com",
        },
        {
            "name": "paul",
            "email": "cleveland@example.com",
        },
        {
            "name": "vishaal",
            "email": "vish@example.com",
        },
        {
            "name": "mike",
            "email": "grady@example.com",
        },
        {
            "name": "jamie",
            "email": "dusted@example.com",
        }
    ]
};
```

click

click is the most common of all the native events you will encounter. It can be applied to any element. You want to be sure that the element you're binding a click event to is indeed a click-able element. There are two ways to tell if an element if clickable. The first is to turn off all CSS and JavaScript in the browser and click it; if something happens, you have a clickable element. If not, you don't. The second is to tab through an interface and press Enter/Return when you get to that element. You will notice in your address book form that you should be able to tab through the interface and press your Return/Enter key to submit the form.

A lot of elements are clickable. A heading (H1), for example, is technically clickable, but because you can't execute that click with anything but a mouse (you can't tab to it and press Return/Enter), you should not attach a click event to it no matter how easy it would be.

All the previous event examples in the chapter have been based on the click event, so I won't spend a lot of time rehashing the same information. We can jump right into the address book application you've been building. This functionality is going to be tied to the Get All Contacts button. You can probably guess what we're going to build.

In Listing 7.4.2 the first step is to define an object to hold all our methods (aka functions). We're going to call it "adr" and the first method will be "getAllContacts". Inside that method will be the function loop you defined in the previous chapter to parse through all the contacts in your JSON object and output them in the page.

Listing 7.4.2 **Method to Get All Contacts from JSON Object**

```
/* define the adr object to hold your methods (aka functions) */
var adr = {

    getAllContacts : function(){

        /* save the DOM element we're putting the output in */
        var target = document.getElementById("output");

        /* save the contacts JSON object to a variable */
        var book = contacts.addressBook;

        /* save the length to a variable outside the loop for performance */
        var count = book.length;

        /* ready the loop! */
        var i;

        /* clear the contents of #output just in case there's something in there */
        target.innterHTML = "";

        /* as usual, check the count before looping */
        if(count > 0){
            /* loop through the contacts */
            for(i = 0; i < count; i = i + 1){

                var obj = book[i],

                target.innerHTML += '<p>' + obj.name + ', <a href="mailto:' + obj.
➥email + '">'+ obj.email +'</a><p>';

            } // end for loop
        } // end if count
    } // end method
} // end object
```

```
// save the button to a variable
var btn = document.getElementById("get-all");

// activate the click event on your button
btn.addEventListener("click", adr.getAllContacts, false);
```

The only difference between this example and the loop you created in the previous chapter is that this one is nested inside a method, which is inside an object. Toward the end you can see that we're saving the button to a variable and then binding a click event to it. If you try this in the browser now, it should output all your contacts inside the "output" <div> we created in the HTML.

focus and blur

Besides `click`, using `focus` and `blur` are the most common types of events when building a JavaScript application. The Web is made up of a bunch of links and forms, and link and forms are what work the best with the `focus` and `blur` events. A good example of a `focus`/`blur` action is activating a search form input field. Either by clicking in the field or using the Tab key to navigate to it would be a "focus," and whenever you deactivate the search box input field (such as clicking off of it), that is a blur event.

Think of `focus` and `blur` like click and unclick (if you could unclick something). They are opposite behaviors that mostly relate to forms and form elements, but they also can be applied to links. Because some elements work well with `focus` and `blur` and some don't, you first need to know whether an element is focusable before you attach this event to it. How do you tell if an element is focusable? Tab through a page; if you can reach the element you want, then it is focusable. If you're looking for a general rule, link and form input elements (text inputs, radios, check boxes, buttons) are all focusable elements.

In the search form you've been building we're going to use focus and blur to do something called **context highlighting**. Context highlighting is a method of bringing attention to a certain area of a form by changing background color. In this example, whenever a user focuses on the search field, we are going to add a class of "active" on the parent element (<div>), which we have already added CSS for to set a background color of gray. Listing 7.4.3 extends adr object to add two new methods that will be executed on focus and blur, respectively. After the methods are defined, you will see the focus and blur event listeners declared.

Listing 7.4.3   **Adding `focus` and `blur` Methods to the Search Box**

```
/* use the same adr method */
var adr = {

    /* ...previously defined methods go here... */

    // define the method (aka the function)
    addActiveSection : function() {
```

```
        // add a class of "active" to the wrapping div
        this.parentNode.setAttribute("class", "active");

    }, // end method, note the comma
    removeActiveSection: function() {

        // remove the class from the wrapping div
        this.parentNode.removeAttribute("class");

    }

} // end adr object

// save the search box to a variable
var searchField = document.getElementById(" q");

// activate the focus event on the search box
searchField.addEventListenter("focus", adr.addActiveSection, false);

// activate the blur event on the search box
searchField.addEventListenter("blur", adr.removeActiveSection, false);
```

Accessibility

There is an important characteristic associated with the focus event and how it relates to accessibility. You may notice that the listener in Listing 7.4.3 will also execute if you click the search box. This happened because clicking the search box also triggers a focus event. The reason you would use focus when dealing with forms is because, although a click event can be triggered only by clicking the form input directly, a focus event is triggered whenever the form input is activated. There are three ways to activate this search box:

- Click it.
- Click the label next to it (assuming the for attribute matches the input's ID).
- Use the Tab key to navigate to it.

Keeping these three access options open will ensure that your form is as accessible as it can be while still focusing on user experience and performance.

change

A change event is applied to form elements such as select menus, radios buttons, and check boxes. In radios and check boxes, a change value is triggered when the box/button is checked. This can happen in ways similar to how an element can get focus: clicking the box/button directly, click the associated label, and using the Tab key to navigate to it and pressing

Enter/Return. In a `select` menu, the `change` event is triggered when a new value or `option` is selected by clicking or by keyboard navigation.

Our address book doesn't have any use for the change event, but it is extremely useful to have in your toolkit, and is attached in the same way all the other events are attached—via listeners.

mouseover and mouseout (hovering)

The `mouseover` event triggers when a user positions a cursor over an element. `mouseout` triggers in the opposite case, when the user removes the mouse cursor from the same element. The combination of these two events creates a complete hover effect.

Let's go back to our address book application and create a simple event behavior of adding a class of "hovering" to the form on `mouseover` and removing that class on `mouseout`. You can see in the HTML snippet in Listing 7.4 that we have already reserved some CSS for this class. Listing 7.4.4 shows how to add this hover behavior to the search form.

Listing 7.4.4   **Adding a Hover Behavior to the Form**

```
// save the element to a variable
var searchForm = document.getElementById("search-form");

/* use the same adr method */
var adr = {

    /* ...previously defined methods go here... */

    addHoverClass : function(){

        // add a class of "hovering" to the wrapping div
        searchForm.setAttribute("class", "hovering");

    }, // end method, note the comma
    removeHoverClass: function(){

        // remove all classes from the wrapping div
        searchForm.removeAttribute("class");

    } // end method

} // end object

// activate the focus event on the search box
searchForm.addEventListenter("mouseover", adr.addHoverClass, false);

// activate the blur event on the search box
searchForm.addEventListenter("mouseout", adr.removeHoverClass, false);
```

Listing 7.4.4 is an example of how to re-create a hover effect with JavaScript to add a class to our search form. This can be done with a small amount of CSS (`form:hover{ /* css code */ })`, and probably should be. Often, developers do use JavaScript where CSS would be a better option. It's important to recognize instances like this. Although this example was just created to show how to execute the hover behavior, if you were to use this in the real world, you would want to make sure that the behavior you're trying to accomplish can't be done better with CSS.

This method is also often used for creating fallbacks if a browser doesn't support `:hover` on nonlinks (IE 6 does not support `:hover` on nonlinks). It's becoming more and more rare as the older browsers slowly die off.

submit

The `submit` event is triggered when a form is submitted, either by clicking a Submit button, tabbing to the Submit button and pressing Enter/Return, or sometimes just by pressing Enter/Return while a form element is in focus. Any way you can submit a form, this event gets triggered.

In your address book, the `submit` event will be triggered to search for a name or string and return results. Normally, this search would be done on the server, but because the address book data is a JSON object inside the JavaScript file (and we haven't made it to the Ajax chapter yet), we're going to want to use JavaScript to parse through the JSON object, search for the string entered in the search field, and return the results in the output area. Listing 7.4.5 contains a loop of the data very similar to the loop you've been using all along, but instead of spitting out all the data, we're using the `indexOf()` method in JavaScript to search for a specific string. For example, if you were to type the letter "i" into the search box and submit the form, every contact that contains that letter should be returned. The `indexOf()` method will either return a match or the number -1, so all you have to do is check for -1 and return the others.

Listing 7.4.5 **Adding a Listener to a Form `submit` Event**

```
/* use the same adr method */
var adr = {

    /* ...previously defined methods go here... */

    // define the method (aka the function)
    search : function(event){

        /* prevent the default behavior */
        event.preventDefault();

        /* save the DOM element we're putting the output in */
        var target = document.getElementById("output");
```

```
/* save the contacts JSON object to a variable */
var book = contacts.addressBook;

/* save the length to a variable outside the loop for performance */
var count = book.length;

/* ready the loop! */
var i;

// clear the target area just in case there's something in it.
target.innerHTML = "";

// check the count, of course and check to see if the value isn't empty
if(count > 0 && searchValue !== ""){

    // loop through the contacts
    for(i = 0; i < count; i = i + 1) {

        // look through the name value to see if it contains the searchterm
➥string
        var obj = contacts.addressBook[i],
            isItFound = obj.name.indexOf(searchValue);

        // anything other than -1 means we found a match
        if(isItFound !== -1) {
            target.innerHTML += '<p>' + obj.name + ', <a href="mailto:' +
➥obj.email + '">'+ obj.email +'</a><p>';
        } // end if

    } // end for loop
  } // end count check
 } // end method
} // end adr object

// save search field to a variable
var searchForm = document.getElementById("search-form");

// activate autocomplete on submit
searchField.addEventListener("submit", addr.search, false)
```

Something important to note from the search method in Listing 7.4.5 is that the form no longer submits per its default behavior when the search button is clicked. This is deliberate; if the form were to submit, you wouldn't be able to execute the JavaScript and update the page (it would have refreshed). You can stop a form submission by using the preventDefault() method.

Preventing Default Behavior

Preventing default behavior is something you often need to do when executing JavaScript on DOM elements that have another behavior attached to them. For example, a link with an `href` value wants to go to another page, or in our case, a form that wants to submit somewhere to do a search query.

Preventing default behavior is done inside the method. You first need to pass the event (form submit in our case) as an argument into the method. Then attach the `preventDefault()` method to it. This is depicted in Listing 7.4.5, but also zoomed in for Listing 7.4.6.

Listing 7.4.6   **A Zoomed-In Version of `preventDefault`**

```
var adr = {

    search : function(event){

        event.preventDefault();

        /* continue the rest of the method here */

    }

}
```

keydown, keypress, and keyup

keydown, keypress, and keyup refer to the user pressing the keys on the keyboard. Keydown is the initial press, keyup is when the finger is lifted, and keypress is somewhere in the middle. Keyup is the most popular of the three events. For example: a person, inside a search box holding down the letter "u," a keydown event would return only a single "u," whereas a keyup event would create a behavior that is akin to using the string: "uuuuuuuuuuuuuuu." The keyup event tends to be more accurate in getting text input values, so it's more widely used. These events are often used to perform an autocomplete action on a search form. That is also how we will be using it on the address book application.

Because an autocomplete action is nothing more than a basic search with fewer letters, the search method defined in Listing 7.4.5 will be 100% reusable for this purpose. The only modification that needs to be made is at the listener level. Instead of using the submit event, you need to use a keyup event. The event trigger order of key events is as follows:

- keydown
- keypress
- keyup (you want to be right here)

Listing 7.4.7 shows how you would repurpose the search method in Listing 7.4.5 to function as an autocomplete function simply by changing the event trigger. This is one of the great advantages to event-driven JavaScript.

Listing 7.4.7   **An Autocomplete, `keyup` Event Listener**

```
// activate autocomplete on keyup
searchField.addEventListener("keyup", addr.search, false);
```

Putting It All Together

Throughout this chapter, you have been building on top of the functionality you've created in previous chapters. You may have noticed in the example that a lot of variable definitions were repeated; this was to show them all in one place. However, in a real-world application you wouldn't want to redefine variables like that, but rather define them once and refer back to them. For this reason I thought it would be helpful to see all the JavaScript in once place. Listing 7.4.8 shows all the JavaScript to this point in this chapter, optimized and cleaned up with the variables properly defined and grouped together at the top of the document.

Listing 7.4.8   **Complete and Cleaned JavaScript to This Point in the Chapter**

```
/* wrap everything in an anonymous function to contain the variables */

(function() {

/* create address book data */

var contacts = {
    "addressBook" : [
        {
            "name": "hillisha",
            "email": "hill@example.com",
        },
        {
            "name": "paul",
            "email": "cleveland@example.com",
        },
        {
            "name": "vishaal",
            "email": "vish@example.com",
        },
        {
            "name": "mike",
            "email": "grady@example.com",
        },
```

```
                {
                    "name": "jamie",
                    "email": "dusted@example.com",
                }
            ]
};
        /* define the DOM elements and common variables you'll need */
        var searchForm = document.getElementById("search-form"),
            searchField = document.getElementById("q"),
            getAllButton = document.getElementById("get-all"),
            count = contacts.addressBook.length,
            target = document.getElementById("output");

    /* define address book methods */
    var addr = {

        search : function(event) {

            // save the input value, contacts length and i to variables
            var searchValue = searchField.value,
                i;

            // stop the default behavior
            event.preventDefault();

            // clear the target area just in case there's something in it.
            target.innerHTML = "";

            // check the count, of course
            if(count > 0 && searchValue !== "") {

                // loop through the contacts
                for(i = 0; i < count; i = i + 1) {

                    // look through the name value to see if it contains the searchterm
➥string
                    var obj = contacts.addressBook[i],
                        isItFound = obj.name.indexOf(searchValue);

                    // anything other than -1 means we found a match
                    if(isItFound !== -1) {

                        target.innerHTML += '<p>' + obj.name + ', <a href="mailto:' +
➥obj.email + '">'+ obj.email +'</a><p>';

                    } // end if
                } // end for loop
```

```
        } // end count check
    },
    getAllContacts : function () {

        var i;

        // clear the target area just in case there's something in it.
        target.innerHTML = "";

        // check the count, of course
        if(count > 0){

            // loop through the contacts
            for(i = 0; i < count; i = i + 1) {

                var obj = contacts.addressBook[i];

                target.innerHTML += '<p>' + obj.name + ', <a href="mailto:' +
➥obj.email + '">'+ obj.email +'</a><p>';
            } // end for loop

        } // end count check
    },
    setActiveSection : function(){

        // add a class of "active" to the wrapping div
        this.parentNode.setAttribute("class", "active");

    },
    removeActiveSection : function(){

        // remove the class from the wrapping div
        this.parentNode.removeAttribute("class");
    },
    addHoverClass : function(){

        // add the class to the wrapping div
        searchForm.setAttribute("class", "hovering");
    },
    removeHoverClass : function(){

        // remove the class from the wrapping div
        searchForm.removeAttribute("class");
    }
} // end addr object
```

```
/* activate the event listeners */
searchField.addEventListener("keyup", addr.search, false);
searchField.addEventListener("focus", addr.setActiveSection, false);
searchField.addEventListener("blur", addr.removeActiveSection, false);
getAllButton.addEventListener("click", addr.getAllContacts, false);
searchForm.addEventListener("mouseover", addr.addHoverClass, false);
searchForm.addEventListener("mouseout", addr.removeHoverClass, false);
searchForm.addEventListener("submit", addr.search, false);

})(); // end anonymous function
```

Touch and Orientation Events

Touch and orientation events can be a little intimidating because they're relatively new additions to the language, but they are really new events that get attached the same way you've been attaching all the nontouch events like click and focus. In some cases, they can even use the same functions.

Because the address book application is getting to a pretty stable point, for the touch event examples we're going to use a new, blank HTML file. Listing 7.5 shows this blank file. Note that there is a min-height set on the <body>; because it's empty we want to give it some height so there is a surface available to touch.

Listing 7.5   **Using a touch Event**

```
<!doctype html>
<html lang="en">
<head>
    <title>Touch Events</title>
    <meta charset="utf-8">

    <style>
        body { min-height:600px;background:#ddd; }
    </style>

</head>
<body>

<h1>Touch Events Demo</h1>

<!-- JS at the bottom, because we still rock at performance -->
<script src="js/script.js"></script>

</body>
</html>
```

touchstart and touchend

The paring of the `touchstart` and `touchend` are very common because they mark opposite events. The `touchstart` event is triggered when a user touches the screen, and the `touchend` event is triggered with the opposite action of untouching the screen (removing whatever you touched the screen with from the screen; if you touched the screen with your nose, it would execute when you removed your nose from the screen).

In Listing 7.5.1 we're declaring a new object to contain the touch-based events and creating two methods intended to be executed on the `touchstart` and `touchend` events by inserting some text into the document's body element.

Listing 7.5.1   **Using a touch Event**

```
/* Anonymous function wrapper again! */
(function(){

    var body = document.getElementsByTagName("body")[0];

    // declare an object to hold touch controls
    var touchControls = {

        pokeTheScreen : function(){

            // output a message to the body
            body.innerHTML += "you just poked me, how rude!<br>";

        }, stopPokingTheScreen: function(){

            // output another message to the body
            body.innerHTML += "please do not do that again.<br><br>";
        }

    } // end object

    // add event listeners to the body
    body.addEventListener("touchstart", touchControls.pokeTheScreen, false);
    body.addEventListener("touchend", touchControls.stopPokingTheScreen, false);

})();
```

If you implement the methods in Listing 7.5.1 and view them in a browser on a touch-capable device, you will see the text "you just poked me, how rude" inserted into the body when you touch the screen and the text "please do not do that again" inserted when you lift your finger off the screen. You can repeat this behavior over and over with the same result.

touchmove

The touchmove event is triggered when the user moves their finger on the screen. It is always preceded by the touchstart event. Naturally, you have to touch the screen before you can move your finger. This is often used to create swipe gestures or to move objects around the screen.

In Listing 7.5.2 we're creating a method inside the touchControls object that will output the text "moving!!" into the body while the touchmove event is being triggered. The event will trigger repeatedly until the movement stops. You can see this by moving your finger around the screen and observing the output (it should say "moving!!" a bunch of times).

Listing 7.5.2   **Using a touchmove Event**

```
/* Anonymous function wrapper again! */

(function(){

    // the same body variable, no need to redeclare it.
    var body = document.getElementsByTagName("body")[0];

    // declare an object to hold touch controls
    var touchControls = {

        /* previously defined methods here */

        showMovement : function(){

            // output a message to the body
            body.innerHTML += "moving!!<br>";

        } // end method
    } // end object

    // add event listeners to the body
    body.addEventListener("touchmove", touchControls.showMovement, false);

})();
```

orientationchange

orientationchange is the only event related to touch that really isn't a touch event. As I mentioned earlier, this is the event that relies on the presence of an accelerometer in a device. An accelerometer is what allows the screen on your phone or tablet to rotate when you rotate the device. It also allows high-end gaming because it can return how many degrees the user is turning a device in one direction or another.

There are orientation settings for portrait, landscape, upside-down portrait, and upside-down landscape, which can be returned with some work, but we're only interested in triggering the event that tells us that the device orientation has changed.

In Listing 7.5.3 you will see the method "changedOrientation" added to the touchControls object. This new method is set up to clear the contents of the body when the orientationchange event is triggered. If you add this method into the object, do some touching and dragging around; you should be able to clear the screen by rotating it to either portrait or landscape (depending on how you started off).

Listing 7.5.3   **Executing a Method on `orientationchange`**

```
/* Anonymous function wrapper again! */

(function(){

    // the same body variable, no need to redeclare it.
    var body = document.getElementsByTagName("body")[0];

    // declare an object to hold touch controls
    var touchControls = {

        /* previously defined methods here */

        changedOrientation : function(){

            // clear out the body content
            body.innerHTML = "";

        } // end method
    } // end object

    // add event listeners to the body
    body.addEventListener("orientationchange", touchControls.changedOrientation,
false);

})();
```

Support for Touch Events

Support for touch events is surprisingly good among touch devices. The touch-based events will execute only on a device that supports touch (phone, tablet, and so on), and orientation events will be supported in any device that has an accelerometer. At first glance, these seem like the same thing, but some laptops ship with accelerometers in them, even if they're never used.

These events can be used to create a native app-like experience in the browser. They are the basis for all swipe and gesture behaviors you experience on a touch device, even if they are just a simple event. For example, a drag-and-drop function for a nontouch device could easily be reused to create a touch/drag functionality on a touch-based device.

Putting It All Together

Again, I thought it might be helpful to have the entire touch event base JavaScript together. Listing 7.5.4 shows all the methods and listeners laid out together.

Listing 7.5.4   **All the Touch Methods Together**

```
/* Anonymous function wrapper again! */

(function(){

    // the same body variable, no need to redeclare it.
    var body = document.getElementsByTagName("body")[0];

    // declare an object to hold touch controls
    var touchControls = {

        pokeTheScreen : function() {

            // output a message to the body
            body.innerHTML += "you just poked me, how rude!<br>";

        }, stopPokingTheScreen: function(){

            // output another message to the body
             body.innerHTML += "please do not do that again.<br><br>";
        },
        showMovement : function(){

            // output a message to the body
            body.innerHTML += "moving!!<br>";

        }, // end method
        changedOrientation : function(){

            // clear out the body content
            body.innerHTML = "";

        } // end method
    } // end object
```

```
    // add event listeners to the body
    body.addEventListener("touchstart", touchControls.pokeTheScreen, false);
    body.addEventListener("touchend", touchControls.stopPokingTheScreen, false);
    body.addEventListener("touchmove", touchControls.showMovement, false);
    body.addEventListener("orientationchange", touchControls.changedOrientation,
➥false);

})();
```

Summary

In this chapter, we went over one of the most important concepts in JavaScript development, events. We talked about the different ways that you can tell the browser to call a function when an event occurs. We talked about the differences between event handlers and event listeners and also how to create a cross-browser supported version of event listeners. We also went over a few of the more popular events you will come across, such as `click`, `focus`, `blur`, `change`, `keyup`, `keydown`, `keypress`, `mouseover`, and `mouseout`. We then took many of those events and directly applied them to our address book application.

The address book should now contain three features: get all contacts, basic search, and autocomplete.

Last, we branched off a bit and got into touch events, giving you some information about when and how they are executed along with some basic examples of how they work in the real world.

In the next chapter we'll begin to explore Ajax and learn how removing the data from your JavaScript file will help you create a more scalable and maintainable application, which will have the capability to fall back in non-JavaScript environments.

Exercises

1. What is the difference between an event handler and an event listener?

2. What method is used for fallback support of event listeners in IE8 and earlier?

3. What is the purpose of the `preventDefault()` method?

Communicating with the Server Through Ajax

In this chapter, we take a step into the world of Ajax. We extend code from previous chapters and take that codebase to the next level by interlacing it with a server communication layer to retrieve the data. More specifically, we take the JSON object you've been working with and move it to an external data file. Then we pull it in with a combination of user events (just like before) and Ajax calls to create another layer of separation where the data source is external to our normal stack of structure, presentation, and behavior. The data layer can be in almost any form from JSON (which is what we're using) to a fully functional database.

In previous chapters, we mentioned Ajax briefly, but in this chapter you learn exactly how to create and execute an Ajax call. You break down the anatomy of each action and discover some new core JavaScript methods in the process. Although the functionality of our autocomplete contact search form won't change, the JavaScript file will be a little smaller without the JSON object in there, and by moving the data to an external source it will become much easier to add more contacts to the data set (scaling).

Something to note about the Ajax demos in this chapter is that because Ajax is a server communication technology, you will need a running server to see the effects of the Ajax we implement. Otherwise they will appear to be broken. If you don't have a server to run the demos on, setting up a local server is very easy. If you are on a Windows machine, there is a prepackaged server-setup application called WAMP; the Mac version is called MAMP. Both are as close to single-click server installs as you're going to get. They will install a local apache server, the latest version of PHP, and a fully functional MySQL database on your local machine. They can easily be turned on and off, so don't worry about having a server running all the time sucking up your battery life. It is also just a good idea to have a server available to you as a general best practice because you're already on your way to becoming an industry all-star!

Ajax History

Ajax is the concept of refreshing a part of an HTML document without reloading the entire page. In Chapter 2, "JavaScript in the Browser," we briefly touched on Ajax while going over the history of JavaScript and mentioned how the origins of client-server communications started in 1999 when Microsoft created the XMLHttp object.

Microsoft initially brought forward the XMLHttp object to fulfill a need in its mail client, Web Access 2000. They wanted a way for the client to be able to communicate with the server. It was first implemented in Internet Explorer 5 as an ActiveX object.

ActiveX was (and still is) a proprietary Microsoft product made for embedding objects in HTML. It was very powerful, but riddled with security holes. Because Microsoft was taking hold of the XMLHttp object and a very powerful technology that would later be called "Ajax," a little company called Mozilla stepped into the same path, developed the XMLHttpRequest object, made it native to the browser (no need for the ActiveX plug-in) and released it to the world in its first Web browser, Mozilla 1.0.

This has to be one of the greatest examples in the Web industry of a company giving information away for free and watching it change the world, which turned out to be a brilliant strategy. Support rocketed in other browsers. Everyone from Safari to Opera Mini supported the new object, and it quickly became the standard, leaving the XMLHttp object from Microsoft in its wake. It was so widely adopted that even Microsoft decided to adopt the object by version 7 of Internet Explorer.

The XMLHttpRequest forever changed the Web as we know it. It is a large part of the reason JavaScript is where it is today, and it's the reason I'm writing this chapter right now. The impact of the XMLHttpRequest has surely echoed through the entire world, even though everyone knows it by its "marketing" name: **Ajax**.

The term Ajax was coined in 2005 by Jesse James Garrett in an article titled *Ajax: A New Approach to Web Applications*. It's ranked pretty high in Google and is easy to find. I highly recommend giving it a once-over for a detailed description of the Ajax concept and how it redefined client/server communications. Since this article came out, Ajax has been on the tip of every developer's tongue and is a must-learn for anyone in the industry.

The term "Ajax" itself has evolved as well; initially it was AJAX, an acronym meaning: Asynchronous JavaScript and XML. This was quickly (in a matter of days) changed when people realized two important flaws in that statement:

- Ajax can be synchronous *or* asynchronous.
- Ajax can use XML, JSON, plain text, or HTML as a data source.

Rather than changing the acronym entirely, they stuck with it and stopped calling it an acronym, settling on "Ajax." I don't care what it says on Wikipedia, Ajax doesn't stand for anything (you heard it here); it's merely a term that represents a collection of technologies that fosters client and server communication.

Server Communication

Server communication is at the core of the Ajax technology. The goal has always been to be able to send and receive information from the client to the server and create a better user experience in the process. Until Ajax came along, all server communication happened on the server, and redrawing portions of a page required either an iframe (iframes are awful) or a full-page refresh. Neither method provided what I would call a good user experience.

Ajax offers us two types of server communication:

- Synchronous
- Asynchronous

Synchronous

Synchronous Ajax is not very common, but it is perfectly valid. You probably won't use it, but just in case you hit a situation where you need to, it's good to know what it is.

Synchronous Ajax means that the Ajax call happens at the same time as all the other requests in your application. There are positives and negatives to this. Making your Ajax calls synchronous will block the download of other assets until the request completes, which can create a weird user experience because of some extra-heavy lifting that needs to happen before a page is completely rendered in the browser. Many people skip the synchronous Ajax model and parse the data server-side to pick up some speed. This is why it isn't used often. Generally speaking, if you can process something on the server, it will be significantly faster than on the client, and you should take advantage of that.

On a more positive note, if you can find a way around the slowness, using synchronous Ajax calls opens up the opportunity to store Ajax data into an object and play around with the timing of certain functions being executed. If an Ajax call is processing something critical for the user to the point that you need to block them from doing something while the request is going on, a synchronous Ajax call may be what you need.

Asynchronous

Asynchronous Ajax is much more common. You'll probably use this 99 out of 100 times you write an Ajax call. (Yes, you'll write that many Ajax calls.) Asynchronous means that the Ajax is not firing at the same time as everything else; it's fairly independent and separated from the rest of the assets in a page or Web application. These Ajax interactions happen behind the scenes and don't really block anything from downloading. Even if you're executing an Ajax call with the `onload` event, the timing of that is usually slightly after the normal page load. Asynchronous calls can happen at any point and be triggered by any event (`click`, `focus`, `blur`, `touchstart`, and so on). The point of them is that they don't happen in one large chunk bundled together with the rest of the `HTTP` requests on a page.

Using an asynchronous call removes the blocking nature of the synchronous call because the user can continue to interact with the page in other ways while the request is being processed.

Many asynchronous Ajax calls go on constantly without the user even knowing that something is happening. Don't believe me? Visit your favorite email app in a Web browser and open up the JavaScript debug console. You will be able to see each Ajax request get executed and note how most people never even notice something happened in the background, aka asynchronously.

The XMLHttpRequest

The XMLHttpRequest object is the heart of any Ajax call. We just went over the origins of this object a few paragraphs ago, so I won't get into that again. Next, we will be cracking open the contacts search form that you have been building throughout the course of the book and adding Ajax functionality into the autocomplete feature.

Creating an instance of the XMLHttpRequest is the first step in making an Ajax call, and it's pretty easy. In Listing 8.1 you can see that we're grabbing an instance of the object and saving it to the xhr variable so we can use it later.

Listing 8.1   **Creating an Instance of the XMLHttpRequest**

```
var xhr = new XMLHttpRequest();
```

Cross-Browser Issues

Remember, from earlier in this chapter, that Microsoft first invented the XMLHttp object that later became the more popular XMLHttpRequest. This does cause a bit of an issue because the XMLHttp object is the only Ajax object supported in Internet Explorer 5 and Internet Explorer 6. No one supports IE 5 anymore, so we'll ignore that. Even though support for IE 6 is falling fast, it's worth addressing that problem up front.

If someone were to visit your Ajax enabled application with IE 6, it wouldn't support the normal XMLHttpRequest object, but rather the older XMLHttp object. It's a little bit of a pain, but if you don't personally support IE 6 in your development process anymore, don't worry about it. It's pretty easy to do a quick support check for the XMLHttpRequest and move on from there, just in case someone from that rapidly falling market share were to stumble upon your application.

In Listing 8.1.1 you can see the steps to check for support. All we're doing is running a simple if statement to check for the presence of either the XMLHttpRequest or the ActiveXObject and then setting the proper Ajax object to the xhr variable. This is a form of feature detection. Rather than targeting IE 6 directly (because that's very specific), we are instead casting a blanket over a possibly wider audience of ActiveX supporters. Again, if you don't support IE 6 at all, you don't have to worry about this step.

Listing 8.1.1 **If Statement to Check for Support of the XMLHttpRequest**

```
if ( window.XMLHttpRequest ) { // check for support

    // if it's supported, use it because it's better
    xhr = new XMLHttpRequest();

} else if ( window.ActiveXObject ) { // check for the IE 6 version

    // save it to the xhr variable
    xhr = new ActiveXObject("Msxml2.XMLHTTP");

}
```

Because this is a very common bit of functionality to have with any Ajax call and will probably be reused over and over, it is best to save it to a function. You will find similar functions all over the Web with XMLHttpRequest feature detection.

The goal of this function is to detect for the correct Ajax object and return it for use wherever you need it. Because this is a function that passes information into another function, the first step is to initialize the variable, then run the normal if statement and return the variable so it can be passed into another function. In Listing 8.1.2 you can see the complete function called getHTTPObject() and the return value of xhr at the end.

Listing 8.1.2 **Function to Return the Correct Ajax Object**

```
function getHTTPObject() {

    // initialize the variable
    var xhr;

    if (window.XMLHttpRequest) { // check for support

        // if it's supported, use it because it's better
        xhr = new XMLHttpRequest();

    } else if (window.ActiveXObject) { // check for the IE 6 Ajax

        // save it to the xhr variable
        xhr = new ActiveXObject("Msxml2.XMLHTTP");

    }

    // spit out the correct one so we can use it
    return xhr;
}
```

Creating an Ajax Call

Creating the Ajax object instance is a separate step from creating the actual Ajax call. All we've done so far is say, "Hey, we're getting ready to work with some Ajax goodness."

For our application there needs to be a little preparation to convert it for use with Ajax. The biggest change will be the data source. Previously, the data has been stored inside a JSON object within the main JavaScript file. Having the data right there with the rest of your JavaScript will provide the shortest response time but will prevent your application from scaling from the five contacts we've been using to something like a more real-world address book containing hundreds of people. Your main JavaScript file will quickly become difficult to manage. It is also pretty rare to have all your data on hand like that; it is generally hosted somewhere else.

To create a more accurate situation, we're going to move all the contacts' JSON data into an external file called contacts.json. The .json file extension isn't required, but it is best practice to use file extensions that describe the file's contents. Because you already have a valid JSON format for the data, it's a pretty easy copy and paste into the external file. The only difference is that you'll be removing the var statement. Listing 8.2 shows you what the contents of your contacts.json file should look like.

Listing 8.2   **Contents of contacts.json Data File**

```
{
"addressBook" : [
    {
        "name": "hillisha",
        "email": "hill@example.com"
    },
    {
        "name": "paul",
        "email": "cleveland@example.com"
    },
    {
        "name": "vishaal",
        "email": "vish@example.com"
    },
    {
        "name": "mike",
        "email": "grady@example.com"
    },
    {
        "name": "jamie",
        "email": "dusted@example.com"
    }
]
}
```

The examples throughout this chapter will assume the contacts.json is in a directory called "data." Just to make sure we're all on the same page, Figure 8.1 shows what your directory structure for the application should currently look like.

Figure 8.1   Current directory structure for the contacts search form application

Sending a Request to the Server

Ajax talks to the server, the server doesn't talk to Ajax. Because of this, Ajax does two things:

- Sends a request to the server
- Processes the data returned from the server

The first thing you should do after you have created an instance of the Ajax object to work with is to send a request. Sending an Ajax request opens up a new property for you to monitor called readyState, which we will get into in a bit.

GET versus POST and Performance

Ajax calls can be in the form of a GET or a POST. You don't use one over the other like using a GET when you're getting information and a POST when you're putting information. They work more like a normal HTML form method.

When you're creating a search form in HTML, there is an attribute in the form's markup called method; you can set that method to GET or POST. What it does is on the search results page—all the data is exposed in the URL. It's very common because the data isn't sensitive at all. The downside of using a GET is that there is a (pretty large) character limit for the data being passed.

Not all form methods are set to GET, though; some are set to POST because the data is more sensitive, such as a username and password. The same principles are applied to Ajax GET and POST methods. If you have sensitive data you're sending through an Ajax call, it should be sent via a POST, but if you're working with nonsensitive data (like we are right now), it's best to use a GET.

You may be thinking, why not just use a POST all the time for Ajax because the URL isn't ever exposed? The answer is that a GET request performs better than a POST in most situations. Because the data in a GET is exposed, less processing is involved, which speeds up the performance of the request.

open()

The open() method is the second step in getting your Ajax call started. Think of it like a configuration file for the Ajax call. It doesn't do any actual work, but what it does is prepare the statement to be executed by gathering all the necessary information. It's like having an administrative assistant for your Ajax call.

Listing 8.3 shows the Ajax object function we created being saved to a variable called request and then the open() method being attached to it, taking three arguments.

Listing 8.3   **Prepping the Ajax Call**

```
var request = getHTTPObject();

/* Get all the information ready to go */

request.open("GET", "data/contacts.json", true);
```

The three arguments in the open() method of Listing 8.3 are

- The method
- The file or URL to get
- A Boolean flag for asynchronous script

There are also two other optional arguments:

- Username
- Password

Method

The first argument in the open() method is the method you want to use for your Ajax call. This can be set to either GET or POST.

File or URL

The file or URL argument is a place for the file path or full HTTP URL of the data source you will be pulling in via the Ajax call. If it's a local file, like ours is, the path is relative to the HTML document you're using it in, not the JavaScript file. This is why ours is set to data/contacts.json and not ../data/contacts.json.

Asynchronous or Synchronous

The third argument in the open() method is a flag to tell the Ajax call whether it will be executed as a synchronous call or an asynchronous call. As mentioned earlier, this will be set to true almost all the time, because asynchronous Ajax calls usually provide a much better user experience when compared to synchronous calls.

Sending Credentials

The last two arguments in the open() method are reserved for a username and a password. You would use these arguments when implementing an Ajax call on a sign-in or registration form (for example). Whenever you send password information with this method, it is important to make sure the data is encrypted for better security. Even though you would use a POST method and the URL wouldn't be exposed publicly, encryption is equally as important as it is when coding on the server.

send()

After all the data for your Ajax call has been properly prepared in the open() method, you can use the send() method to ship off the data and request and begin waiting for the readyState property to let you know when the Ajax call data is ready to be used.

In Listing 8.3.1 you can see the Ajax call getting built out. We now have the Ajax object, the open() method gathering the data, and finally the send() method firing off the actual call.

Listing 8.3.1   **Sending the Actual Data**

```
var request = getHTTPObject();

/* Get all the information ready to go */
request.open("GET", "data/contacts.json", true);

/* initiate actual call */
request.send(null);

/* OR - initiate the call with some data */
request.send("hello data");
```

You may have noticed that we're passing null into the send object, which means that we're not sending any extra data with the Ajax call. We just want the file.

If you were using any back-end processing on the data URL, you can pass the extra filtering information through the send() method. Listing 8.3.2 shows what something like that may look like for a search result.

Listing 8.3.2   **Sending Extra Data for Server-Side Filtering**

```
var request = getHTTPObject();

/* Get all the information ready to go */
request.open("GET", "search.php", true);

/* initiate actual call and filter by the term "hill" */
request.send("searchterm=hill");
```

The request in Listing 8.3.2 would produce the same data as if you were to visit the URL `search.php?searchterm=hill`, a normal search results page. In our example we are doing the search processing with JavaScript, because this is a JavaScript book.

Receiving Data Back from the Server

After the request is sent, the call will return from the server, hopefully with the data you requested. As I mentioned a little earlier in the chapter, Ajax opens up a new property called `readystate`, which is tied to an event called `readystatechange`, which constantly monitors the progress of every Ajax call and reports back to you so you know when the data is available to parse.

readystate

`readyState` is the property in an Ajax call that reports back the status that corresponds with a checkpoint in the processing of that Ajax call. Five values get reported back:

- 0 – The open method hasn't been called (uninitialized)
- 1 – The open method has been called, but the send method has not (loading)
- 2 – The send method has been called and the request is being sent (loaded)
- 3 – The response has started to come back (interacting)
- 4 – The request is complete (complete)

Each time a `readyState` value changes, the `readystatechange` event is triggered. Knowing this, you can attach an event handler to this new event and wait for the "4" status to be reached before executing something on the returned data.

It is possible to listen for each step in the process if you want to provide very detailed feedback to the user, but generally speaking, it's easier to wait for the request to complete by looking for the "complete" value.

In Listing 8.4 you can see our Ajax object followed by the event handler for `onreadystatechange`, and then an `if` statement checking the `readyState` value. Not so tough, right? It looks like a normal function. And it is just a function with an `if` statement.

Listing 8.4   **Checking the Ajax Request State**

```
var request = getHTTPObject();

request.onreadystatechange = function(){

    // check if the request is ready
    if( request.readyState === 4 ) {

        // do something

    }
```

By checking the readyState value like this, you can be sure you're not executing code before you have data available to parse.

Server Status

The readystate property is great, but it only tells you what the step-by-step process of an Ajax call is. It doesn't give you any information on whether the request was successful.

The Ajax object also returns a property called status, which correlates to the server status codes you would normally find on a Web server, like 404, 200, 304, 500, and so on. An Ajax call can, in theory, go out to the server and successfully come back, but encounter some sort of failure on the server that prevented the data from being returned. Some of the more common codes you can check for are

- 404 – Page not found
- 304 – Not modified
- 500 – Internal server error
- 200 – All is well on the server

You can write conditional code for each of these statuses, but for our purposes, we are going to focus on the success status of 200 and combine that with our readyState of 4.

In Listing 8.4.1 you can see the addition to the if statement, which now not only checks for a complete Ajax call, but also for a successful server status code to be returned.

Listing 8.4.1 **Checking the Server Status**

```
var request = getHTTPObject();

request.onreadystatechange = function(){

    // check if the request is ready and that it was successful
    if( request.readyState === 4 && request.status === 200 ) {

        // do something

    }
}

/* Get all the information ready to go */

request.open("GET", "data/contacts.json", true);

/* make the actual call */

request.send(null);
```

The Server Response

Inside the onreadystatechange event handler, and after you check to make sure the request is complete and successful, you can finally get the data that was returned from the Ajax call.

In addition to readyState and status, the Ajax object also returns your data as a property. It will either be returned in the form of a string or as XML, depending on which data format you choose to interact with.

As a String

If your data response in is the form of a string, it will return as responseText. This is just a string of data that needs to either output as it is returned or be parsed with some of the native objects available in JavaScript. This is the most common form of Ajax response data.

This format is the most common format because it can contain anything from plain text, to HTML, to JSON (hint, hint), and then be parsed accordingly. To access this data inside our Ajax call, you access the Ajax object, then the responseText like this: request.responseText;

As XML

If you are returning XML data, the response will be in the form of responseXML. Everything is pretty much the same besides that.

Listing 8.4.2 shows how you would spit out the retuned data into the JavaScript console to observe the contents of the response.

Listing 8.4.2   **Outputting the Returned Data**

```
var request = getHTTPObject();

request.onreadystatechange = function(){

    // check if the request is ready and that it was successful
    if( request.readyState === 4 && request.status === 200 ) {

        // spit out the data that comes back
        console.log(request.responseText);

    }
}

/* Get all the information ready to go */

request.open("GET", "data/contacts.json", true);

/* make the actual call */

request.send(null);
```

Getting It into a Function

Now that you have a working Ajax call, you will probably want to use it more than once in your application. In fact, we do want to use it more than once. Once for the autocomplete functionality and another time to get all the contacts in a single call.

To make the function a little easier to reuse, we're going to take what we already have and put it into a function, with one small change.

To be certain that this function can be reused within the context of this application and retrieve the contacts.json file, we are going to pull the reference to data/contacts.json out of the function and instead use an argument that will be passed when it is called. Listing 8.5 shows our complete Ajax function with a dataURL argument being passed into it.

Listing 8.5   **Reusable Ajax Function**

```
/* define the Ajax call function */

function ajaxCall(dataUrl) {

    /* use our function to get the correct Ajax object based on support */
    var request = getHTTPObject();

    request.onreadystatechange = function() {

        // check to see if the Ajax call went through
        if ( request.readyState === 4 && request.status === 200 ) {

            // spit out the data that comes back
            console.log(request.responseText);

        } // end ajax status check

    } // end onreadystatechange

    request.open("GET", dataUrl, true);
    request.send(null);

}
```

With the function listed in Listing 8.5, it would now be called with the data source as an argument like this: ajaxCall("data/contacts.json"). Calling the function like this lets us easily reuse it with other data sources, either within the same project or on any number of other projects, so you don't have to keep writing the same function over and over to accomplish the same outcome of a simple Ajax call. This is how you begin building your own JavaScript function library.

Currently, it will only output the returned data into the JavaScript console, but we want to be able to return and use that data in various ways.

Returning the Data

Right now the data is stuck inside the onreadystatechange event handler. This obviously isn't what we want. If we were using this function only once, we could add all the data parsing and output right inside the event handler. You could build out all your functionality right there inside the ajaxCall() function. That would be perfectly fine—a little difficult to integrate into our current codebase, but there's nothing wrong with that.

Lucky for you, we're not going to settle for "just fine." We can make this function a lot more reusable by finding a way to work with the data it's returning while still remaining inside the context of the onreadystatechange event handler. To accomplish this goal, we need to find a way to call the ajaxCall() function and allow it to take an extra argument that is a function. This does get a little tricky, but a function that calls another function isn't a foreign concept at this point. Remember? A function that calls another function is called a **callback function**. With that in mind, what we need to do is allow the ajaxCall() function to accept a callback function.

The first step to doing this is to save the responseText to a variable so we can work with it more easily. Listing 8.5.1 introduces a new argument called callback, which will represent the function we will be passing through to access the data response. So we will have two arguments; one will be a string, and the other will be a function.

Because the data is saved to a variable (contacts), it is easy to pass that data into the callback function.

Listing 8.5.1   **Accepting a Callback Function**

```
function ajaxCall(dataUrl, callback) {

    /* use our function to get the correct Ajax object based on support */
    var request = getHTTPObject();

    request.onreadystatechange = function() {

        // check to see if the Ajax call went through
        if ( request.readyState === 4 && request.status === 200 ) {

            // save the ajax response to a variable
            var contacts = JSON.parse(request.responseText);

            // make sure the callback is indeed a function before executing it
            if(typeof callback === "function"){

                callback(contacts);
```

```
        } // end function check

    } // end ajax status check

} // end onreadystatechange

request.open("GET", dataUrl, true);
request.send(null);
```

```
}
```

In the bolded code toward the end of the Ajax status-checking-if-statement in Listing 8.5.1, you can see another if statement wrapping the callback function. This is using the JavaScript operator typeof, which can return the type of object you are dealing with. It can return things like string, number, Boolean, undefined, and in this case we are looking for it to return "function" before moving forward. This is a kind of check and balance we use when programming JavaScript just to make sure everything goes as planned.

Something else odd you may have noticed about this function is that the responseText is wrapped in a method called JSON.parse(). As I mentioned before, the response can come back as either a string or as XML; in this case, it came back as a string but to be able to work with the data in the way we did while it was an embedded JSON object, it needs to be converted (parsed) back into its JSON format. Using JSON.parse() does just that; it's a real life saver for something like JSON parsing.

Listing 8.5.2   **Using Callback Function Functionality**

```
ajaxCall("data/contacts.json", function(data){

    /*
    these are the contents of the callback function
    the "data" argument is the contact list in JSON format
    this is where you would loop through the data
    */

});
```

Making Repeat Ajax Calls

Creating the illusion of real-time data (that's right, it's an illusion) is something JavaScript, and particularly Ajax are both very good at. We already learned how to create and execute an Ajax call once, based on either the load of a page or a user-initiated event. But you can also create a system that can automatically make Ajax calls over and over.

This is a useful method when you're trying to create the real-time updating illusion. I say "illusion" because it's not truly a 1 to 1 relationship when data is returned. You can use the JavaScript object `setInterval()` to execute a block of code over and over with a set time in between each call. Listing 8.6 shows how you would use this method to execute a JavaScript alert every 5 seconds. The `setInterval()` method takes two arguments. The first is whatever function you'd like to repeat, and the second is how much time, in milliseconds, you want to pass in between each call.

Listing 8.6   **Using `setInterval`**

```
/* alert a message every 3 seconds */

setInterval('alert("fire off an Ajax call', 5000); // alert something every 5 seconds
```

The same pattern can be applied to our `ajaxCall()` function to fire the call off every 5 seconds. This process of constantly hitting the server to check for new information is called **polling**. If we were pulling data that was being constantly updated, it would be very valuable to poll the server to refresh the data onscreen every so often. Listing 8.6.1 shows how using `setInternal()` with the `ajaxCall()` function might look. We don't have a lot of use for something like this for the autocomplete form, but it is a very powerful and frequently used method when returning data from a server.

Listing 8.6.1   **Using `setInterval` with Ajax**

```
/* make this Ajax call every 5 seconds */

setInterval('ajaxCall("data/contacts.json",

        function(){

            console.log("made a call");

    })', 5000); // 5000 milliseconds = 5 seconds
```

Be careful when polling a server this way; although you want to make sure the illusion of real-time data is believable, hitting a server from a high traffic website in too-short intervals can easily bring a server to its knees.

Ajax Data Formats

Because the X in Ajax doesn't stand for anything (especially not XML), Ajax can take more than one data format. Most commonly, you will be dealing with three specific data formats: XML, HTML and JSON. Each has positive aspects and negative aspects; knowing the difference will help you choose the right tool for the job.

XML

XML stands for eXtensible Markup Language. It is a very flexible data format and immensely popular for use in application data. It is very similar to HTML in its anatomy, containing a DOCTYPE, elements, tags, and attributes. It even adheres to the same document object model as HTML.

Listing 8.7 depicts how the contacts.json data file would look if it were converted into XML format.

Listing 8.7   Example Data in XML Format

```xml
<?xml version="1.0" encoding="utf-8"?>
<addressBook>

    <person>
        <name>hillisha</name>
        <email>hill@exmaple.com</email>
    </person>

    <person>
        <name>paul</name>
        <email>cleveland@example.com</email>
    </person>

    <person>
        <name>vishaal</name>
        <email>vish@example.com</email>
    </person>

    <person>
        <name>mike</name>
        <email>grady@example.com</email>
    </person>

    <person>
        <name>jamie</name>
        <email>dusted@example.com</email>
    </person>

</addressBook>
```

Positives

Being an extensible format is a huge plus for XML. You're not locked into any predefined data structure because you can define it as you go, as long as it is kept consistent throughout the file. Adhering to the DOM standard is another positive aspect of XML. After pulling the data in through an Ajax call, it is parsed the same as a normal HTML document with methods like `getElementsByTagName()`, `getAttribute()`, `parentNode`, `firstChild`, and `lastChild`. Not having to relearn any new methods to parse XML makes it a very attractive option.

Negatives

Because XML is so similar to HTML and uses the same DOM standards, it can take a lot of code to parse through and build the output.

One pretty big drawback of using XML is that it cannot be used cross-domain with Ajax. All Ajax calls to an XML data file must come from the same domain or the request will fail. For this reason, you don't see a lot of public data sources in XML format. If they were, you would need to create a server-side proxy to pull in the XML and have the Ajax call reference the data by way of the proxy.

HTML

Working with Ajax and HTML snippets couldn't be more straightforward. You have an HTML file and you consume its contents in full with an Ajax call. Listing 8.8 shows our JSON data in the form of HTML.

Listing 8.8   **Example Data in HTML Format**

```
<ul>
    <li><a href="mailto:hill@example.com">hillisha</a></li>
    <li><a href="mailto:cleveland@example.com">paul</a></li>
    <li><a href="mailto:vish@example.com">vishaal</a></li>
    <li><a href="mailto:grady@example.com">mike</a></li>
    <li><a href="mailto:dusted@example.com">jamie</a></li>
</ul>
```

Positives

Speed is an important reason to use this method. Unlike the other data formats, no client-side parsing is needed because you're grabbing an entire snippet of HTML and outputting it into the DOM. Not having to write a lot of extra JavaScript to parse the incoming HTML will not only save you time as a developer, but it will save processing time for the user.

Negatives

Using HTML as a data source works very well if you are asynchronously updating a single block of content in a document, but it doesn't get you the fine-grained control that XML or JSON will give you.

Unless you're literally updating an HTML document with a static block of content, which would be a little odd and, frankly, pretty rare, you're going to have to do some server-side processing to get the data you want. This is generally the fastest way to do it, but if you like working in server-side code, that might be something to consider as a downside of using HTML as a data format.

JSON

Ahhhh, the wonderful world of JSON; we have been using JSON as a data format for most of the book, so you should be pretty familiar with it at this point. It's a very human-readable and machine-readable format, which has no structural limitations. Each item in a JSON data format can be different from all the others. In our data file, we are using a consistent structure of name and email, but it doesn't have to be like that because JSON doesn't force any real consistency in its format.

Listing 8.9 shows the current JSON data we have been working with so you can compare it to the XML and HTML versions in previous listings.

Listing 8.9   **Example Data in JSON Format**

```
{
"addressBook" : [
    {
        "name": "hillisha",
        "email": "hill@example.com"
    },
    {
        "name": "paul",
        "email": "cleveland@example.com"
    },
    {
        "name": "vishaal",
        "email": "vish@example.com"
    },
    {
        "name": "mike",
        "email": "grady@example.com"
    },
    {
        "name": "jamie",
        "email": "dusted@example.com"
    }
]
}
```

Positives

JSON is my personal favorite because it is native to JavaScript, very fast, flexible, and platform agnostic—meaning almost any programming language plays nice with JSON.

Unlike XML, JSON can be consumed cross-domain very easily; it has no native domain limitations because it is just a JavaScript data format. This makes it the ideal candidate for API structures. Because it is such a flexible format, you will find that the majority of Web services offered are in JSON format.

Negatives

Although the data format of JSON is very flexible, the syntax is not (but this goes with any data format). Every comma, quotation mark, and colon needs to be in the right place for the data to be parsed correctly.

Some security concerns also exist with using JSON from any third-party Web service, because at its core, it's just JavaScript, and it's very easy to remotely inject malicious scripting through a JSON object. This can be protected against, but in general you should consume JSON data only from trusted sources.

Ajax Accessibility

One often overlooked portion in Ajax development is accessibility. We go through a lot of work to make a website accessible to disabled users and yet often fall short when Ajax functionality is layered on. When the DOM is initially rendered, a sighted user is able to easily click and see the feedback of a certain region of the page when it's updated, but we tend to forget that there are ways to flag a region with attributes to let visually impaired users know that a portion of the page is going to be updated without a full page refresh so they can come back periodically and check the content of that area.

This method is called Accessible Rich Internet Applications (ARIA), and it is something you should be familiar with before diving too far into the dirty world of Ajax. Accessibility is extremely important. Think of it as usability for disabled users. The goal of creating a top-notch user experience shouldn't be derailed because a user has trouble seeing or hearing, or any form of disability. We create one Web, and that Web should be accessible to everyone, no matter what.

Live Regions and ARIA

Live regions in HTML exist to indicate to assistive technologies (screen readers) that a certain area in the document might possibly change without focus or a page refresh.

ARIA regions have been around for a few years now, living independently from the rest of the W3C specifications, but it is now getting a lot more attention. There are currently four types of live region attributes for ARIA:

- `aria-atomic`
- `aria-busy`
- `aria-live`
- `aria-relevant`

aria-atomic

`aria-atomic` indicates whether a screen reader should present all or parts of a live region based on the change notifications. This attribute takes Boolean values, either `true` or `false`.

aria-busy

`aria-busy` is a state reported to a screen reader, which reports back whether a live region is currently being updated. Just like `aria-atomic`, this attribute also takes either a `true` or `false` value. Because this attribute changes based on update status, it needs to be set and updated in the Ajax call.

aria-live

`aria-live` is a way to report how important live changes in the document are. It can take one of three values: `off`, `polite`, or `assertive`.

Setting the `aria-live` attribute to `off` prevents updates from bubbling up unless the user is directly focused on the element. The `polite` value will be sure to update the user only when it is courteous to do so. In other words, it will not interrupt the user if something more important is going on, but will update the user at the next convenient moment. The last option, `assertive`, sets changes to the highest priority and will notify the user immediately of any changes, no matter what. Because this option can be disorienting to a user, it should be used only when absolutely necessary.

aria-relevant

`aria-relevant` will notify the atomic regions as to what type of change has occurred. There are four options for this attribute: `additions`, `removals`, `text`, and `all`.

The most common values for this attribute are additions and removals; this means that the region contains items and are both removed and added to. Our autocomplete form does this. In contrast, a `text` value to this attribute means that text has been added to a DOM node within the region. Last, the `all` value means everything is going on and rather than listing `additions`, `removals`, and `text`, you can use the `all` value.

Listing 8.10 shows how we are going to apply ARIA live regions to the HTML in our auto-complete form by using atomic, live, and relevant.

Listing 8.10   **ARIA Accessibility for the Contacts Ajax Output Area**

```
<!-- adding aria to the HTML output -->
<div id="output" aria-atomic="true" aria-live="polite" aria-relevant="additions
➥removals"></div><!--/#output-->
```

Using ARIA like this will ensure that your application is as accessible to disabled users as it is to nondisabled users. As designers and developers, there isn't a whole lot we can do to help our disabled audience, so it's always nice to do little things like this that can go a long way to improve the overall user experience.

Common Ajax Mistakes

The number one mistake developers make with Ajax is using it because they think it's cool. Ajax is not always the answer. In fact, it is often not the answer at all. Use it responsibly and with caution; there is nothing worse than trying to debug an application that piles up its Ajax calls as if they were strings in a ball of yarn.

Most in-browser problems can be traced back to a JavaScript or an Ajax origin, and you will avoid a lot of headaches if you put serious up-front thought into whether you need to or even should use Ajax to accomplish a certain goal.

Providing Feedback

At this point in our application, there isn't any indication to the user that we're fetching data to be pulled in, and it's really not much of a problem because the data is so close by and small that the Ajax call executes and completes almost immediately. This won't always be the case. Sometimes the server will be sluggish, the data will be large, or the Internet connection will slow to a crawl. Because of this, it is best practice to provide feedback to the user while the Ajax call is traveling back and forth from the server.

We've all seen those spinning pinwheels and loading messages in the browser while a request is happening in the background. These messages can go a long way in creating a better user experience. If users trigger an Ajax call and nothing happens because the request is lagging, they may think something is broken and leave the page. But a simple message of "loading..." can let them know something is going on, and they should stick around.

Listing 8.11 depicts the `ajaxCall()` function and how we might output a loading message (see the bolded text). This function is now also taking a third argument to define a region to place the loading message. We will also use the same region to output the actual content so the loading message is removed when the data is returned.

Listing 8.11   **Outputting a Loading Message**

```
/* define the Ajax call */

function ajaxCall(dataUrl, outputElement, callback) {

    /* use our function to get the correct Ajax object based on support */
    var request = getHTTPObject();

    outputElement.innterHTML = "Loading...";

    request.onreadystatechange = function() {

        // check to see if the Ajax call went through
        if ( request.readyState === 4 && request.status === 200 ) {

            // save the ajax response to a variable
            var contacts = JSON.parse(request.responseText);

            // make sure the callback is indeed a function before executing it
            if(typeof callback === "function"){

                callback(contacts);

            } // end check

        } // end ajax status check

    } // end onreadystatechange

    request.open("GET", dataUrl, true);
    request.send(null);


}
```

The Back Button

Page navigation through Ajax is a very popular trend, but one of the drawbacks is that because there is never a URL change, normal browser behaviors like bookmarking and using the Back button are inherently disabled. This produces a big usability problem.

Before the influx of HTML5 JavaScript APIs, fixing the Back button was a bit of an ordeal. Fortunately, we now have the **History API**, which allows you to, on-the-fly, update the URL of a document, which allows for accurate bookmarking along with normal Back button behaviors.

We will be getting in the History API a little later when we talk about HTML5 in Chapter 11, "HTML5 JavaScript APIs." For now it's important to note it as something you will need to code back into your Ajax applications.

Security

Sensitive information always needs to be encrypted before getting sent over the Internet. Usernames, passwords, social security numbers, bank accounts, credit card information—these are all types of data that are sent through the air unencrypted because of developer errors.

Sending unencrypted information through Ajax calls can lead to hacked accounts, identity theft, and general everyday headaches. If you're dealing with sensitive information, always remember to use an encryption layer before sending the data out to the world.

Putting It All Together

Throughout this chapter we have been adding to the core application we've been building during the course of this book and implementing the various Ajax methods into the main JavaScript file. Some things have changed, and some things were just added into the file for extra functionality.

Listing 8.12 shows the current state of the entire JavaScript file for the application. Notice that we are making two Ajax calls. The first call is to retrieve all the contacts, and the second call helps us perform the autocomplete feature. All the loops that were created to parse the old JSON object still exist, but they have been moved into the callback function of `ajaxCall()`. It may be easier to think of it as if the code blocks are the same as before, but are now wrapped in our `ajaxCall()` function; either way, very little of the core functionality has changed. You can see the changes in bold.

A couple other things to note that changed is that the `length` checker variable has now moved inside the Ajax call because we can't check the length of the JSON object until it is officially loaded. We are also now defining the output region as a variable to be passed into the `ajaxCall()` function.

Listing 8.12   **The Entire Contact Search Form JavaScript to This Point**

```
/* standard Ajax xhr function */

function getHTTPObject() {

    var xhr;

    if (window.XMLHttpRequest) { // check for support

        // if it's supported, use it because it's better
        xhr = new XMLHttpRequest();
```

```
    } else if (window.ActiveXObject) { // check for the IE 6 Ajax

        // save it to the xhr variable
        xhr = new ActiveXObject("Msxml2.XMLHTTP");

    }

    // spit out the correct one so we can use it
    return xhr;
}

/* define the Ajax call */

function ajaxCall(dataUrl, outputElement,callback) {

    /* use our function to get the correct Ajax object based on support */
    var request = getHTTPObject();

    outputElement.innerHTML = "Loading...";

    request.onreadystatechange = function() {

        // check to see if the Ajax call went through
        if ( request.readyState === 4 && request.status === 200 ) {

            // save the ajax response to a variable
            var contacts = JSON.parse(request.responseText);

            // make sure the callback is indeed a function before executing it
            if(typeof callback === "function"){

                callback(contacts);

            } // end check

        } // end ajax status check

    } // end onreadystatechange

    request.open("GET", dataUrl, true);
    request.send(null);

}

/* wrap everything in an anonymous function to contain the variables */
```

```
(function(){

    /* define the DOM elements and common variables you'll need */
    var searchForm = document.getElementById("search-form"),
        searchField = document.getElementById("q"),
        getAllButton = document.getElementById("get-all"),
        target = document.getElementById("output");

    /* define address book methods */
    var addr = {

        search : function(event){

            /* set the output element */
            var output = document.getElementById("output");

            /* start the Ajax call */
            ajaxCall('data/contacts.json', output, function (data) {

                // save the input value, contacts length and i to variables
                var searchValue = searchField.value,
                    addrBook = data.addressBook,
                    count = addrBook.length,
                    i;

                // stop the default behavior
                event.preventDefault();

                // clear the target area just in case there's something in it.
                target.innerHTML = "";

                // check the count, of course
                if(count > 0 && searchValue !== ""){

                    // loop through the contacts
                    for(i = 0; i < count; i = i + 1) {

                        // look through the name value to see if it contains the
➥searchterm string
                        var obj = addrBook[i],
                            isItFound = obj.name.indexOf(searchValue);

                        // anything other than -1 means we found a match
                        if(isItFound !== -1) {
                            target.innerHTML += '<p>' + obj.name + ',
➥<a href="mailto:' + obj.email + '">'+ obj.email +'</a><p>';
                        } // end if
```

```
                } // end for loop

            } // end count check

        }); // end ajax call

    },
    getAllContacts : function () {

        /* set the output element */
        var output = document.getElementById("output");

        /* start the Ajax call */
        ajaxCall('data/contacts.json', output, function (data) {

            var addrBook = data.addressBook,
                count = addrBook.length,
                i;

            // clear the target area just in case there's something in it.
            target.innerHTML = "";

            // check the count, of course
            if(count > 0) {

                // loop through the contacts
                for(i = 0; i < count; i = i + 1) {

                    // look through the name value to see if it contains the
➡searchterm string
                    var obj = addrBook[i];

                        target.innerHTML += '<p>' + obj.name + ', <a href="mailto:' +
➡obj.email + '">'+ obj.email +'</a><p>';

                } // end for loop
            } // end count check

        }); // end ajax call
    },
    setActiveSection : function() {

        // add a class of "active" to the wrapping div
        this.parentNode.setAttribute("class", "active");
```

```
        },
        removeActiveSection : function() {

            // remove the class from the wrapping div
            this.parentNode.removeAttribute("class");

        },
        addHoverClass : function() {

            // remove the class from the wrapping div
            searchForm.setAttribute("class", "hovering");

        },
        removeHoverClass : function(){

            // remove the class from the wrapping div
            searchForm.removeAttribute("class");

        }

    } // end addr object

    // activate auto complete on keyUp
    searchField.addEventListener("keyup", addr.search, false);

    // set active section on focus of the form field
    searchField.addEventListener("focus", addr.setActiveSection, false);

    // remove active section on blur of the form field
    searchField.addEventListener("blur", addr.removeActiveSection, false);

    // get all contacts when you click the button
    getAllButton.addEventListener("click", addr.getAllContacts, false);

    // add hover class on mouse over of the form field
    searchForm.addEventListener("mouseover", addr.addHoverClass, false);

     // remove hover class on mouse out of the form field
    searchForm.addEventListener("mouseout", addr.removeHoverClass, false);

    // activate search on form submit
    searchForm.addEventListener("submit", addr.search, false);

})(); // end anonymous function
```

Where Is Ajax Going?

Ajax, as it currently sits, is a surprisingly old technology, but we still use it in almost the same way we used it in the early days of its existence. With the speed the Web moves, sometimes we ask ourselves, what's next? Well, what's next for Ajax?

The question isn't so much what's next for Ajax, but rather, "What's next for client-side server communication?" That's really the goal of Ajax, to help us communicate with the server from the front-end and systematically refresh pieces of a Web application without reloading the entire document. As long as we're addressing the overall goal of a better user experience, the technology is almost irrelevant. Ajax will probably be around for decades more, whether there is a serious competitor or not. Some people will abandon Ajax for something like Web Sockets. Ajax was created to increase the responsiveness of the Web, making it more pleasurable to use. In the coming chapters we will talk about technologies that do just that—make the Web a more pleasing place to spend your time. Always, we should focus on an improved user experience.

Summary

In this chapter, you learned about Ajax. You first started off with a short history lesson about the origins of Ajax in its early days with Microsoft and then learned about how it came to be in its current form, along with the difference between synchronous and asynchronous server communication.

We broke down the individual pieces of the famous `XMLHttpRequest`, including `open` and `send` methods and the kinds of information that can be passed into each of them. We introduced a new JavaScript event called `readyState`, which is triggered by the Ajax call itself and returns five different state values you can check against before executing a block of code after a call has completed.

We talked about the different data formats that can be used when dealing with Ajax, namely: JSON, HTML and XML, and visited some positive and negative aspects of each, including some use-cases for each in the event you hit a time where you may want to use one over the other.

We also converted the Ajax call into a function that was applied to the autocomplete contact form application we've been building throughout the course of this book. We were able to reuse the function because it was written in a way where it was kept extensible by implementing a callback function.

We also talked about Ajax accessibility and why it is important to flag zones of your application by using ARIA so screen readers can identify certain areas of the page as being updated via Ajax. We also mentioned some common mistakes people make when using Ajax, such as failing to provide feedback to the user and how that incorporates with the guiding principles of progressive enhancement. (Are you sick of hearing about progressive enhancement yet?)

Last was a brief section on the future of client-side server communications, where user experience was addressed, and we talked about how some of the overall goals of Ajax can be met, whether it is with a technology like Ajax or something else entirely different.

Exercises

1. What are the five possible arguments in the `XMLHttpRequest open()` method, and which are optional?

2. What does Ajax stand for?

3. What JavaScript method is typically used to make repeat Ajax calls?

9

Code Organization

Don't skip this chapter—it's really important. If we were sitting next to each other or in a classroom setting, this is the point where I would ask if what we just went over made sense. All the previous chapters have given you the knowledge you need to do all the basics of JavaScript. Along the way we have addressed many of the action-oriented aspects of the language. You have a function or method, and an action is directly tied to it. `getElementById()` accesses the DOM; you know that now. You also know that using an `if/else` statement sets a custom condition to execute a block of code. You learned how to add, remove, and read items from an array either directly or by looping through them. You even know how to create functions and methods with JavaScript, how to store data externally, and how to access it with an Ajax call.

These aspects of JavaScript all depict the functions, or "things JavaScript can do." There is a lot more to the coding in this language than making something that "just works." Getting your code to work may be a primary goal, because what good is code that doesn't work? But besides getting it to work, you have to do a few more things:

- Get the code to work well (performance)
- Make the code easy to follow (readability)
- Make the code as reusable as possible

In this chapter we talk through the different aspects of code organization. It may not be the sexiest topic, but when our main focus is creating a good user experience, proper organization of your code can result in a better overall experience not only for the user visiting a site or application, but also for yourself and other team members who may need to work in the same codebase.

We address two main types of code organization in this chapter—areas I like to refer to as the script and style of JavaScript. We've been working a lot with the script aspect so far, which may make the phrase "the script of JavaScript" seem redundant. By this I mean the actual syntax of JavaScript, the functions, the objects, the methods, object-oriented models versus event-driven script models, and so on. All these aspects of JavaScript have specific uses, and we go over each of them, getting into the cases when you may want to use each and when something else may be a better choice. The key to solving any problem effectively is to use the right tool for the job. You will never be able to make a blanket statement to solve everything; otherwise, you might find yourself using a railroad spike to hang a photo on the wall, where a thumbtack would have been a better choice—or, for a more direct example, using a heavily nested JavaScript method instead of an anonymous function. These are all script patterns in JavaScript that will help your code make a lot more sense, not only for you, but for anyone else who gets in there.

The style aspect is a lot lighter than the script aspect of code organization. JavaScript style encompasses topics such as

- Comments
- Whitespace
- Line breaks
- Indentation
- Spacing

This is all part of JavaScript code design. With this, we get into aspects of team coding and generating a style guide/understanding. You learn how to use commenting to your advantage, and how it can help your overall coding effectiveness. In an ideal world you will be the only person working in your JavaScript file, but in reality there are a lot of reasons for someone else to be in a file you created. For this reason it is important to follow some formal style guide so the pain of looking through someone else's code can be kept to a minimum. We talk about some loose guidelines for coding standards and why it is just as important in some areas to not have coding standards. Making sure the standards you implement are seen as guidelines (and not laws to blindly follow) will help foster creativity and innovation within any development environment.

The code organization balancing act is something we have been talking about for the entire book. It's something that will need to be addressed individually (at some level) as a part of every project. Laying out some general rules, pitfalls, tips, and information will help you along the way.

General Coding Style Rules

There are some general over-arching style rules to the way you construct your code that you could safely apply to each project and treat as standard practice. These include things such as properly applying the concept of scope to your projects, creating a codebase that not only succeeds fast, but fails even faster (that sounds weird, I know but we'll get to it), all the while keeping your eye on the prize: creating a good user experience.

In a way, you have already been introduced to some general coding style best practice situations. So far throughout this book, we have been using something called **feature detection** to test for support of various features a browser may have; this is a specific coding style. Rather than testing for a device or browser that will constantly change over time, you test for the presence of a particular feature. It's always nice to have some general coding policies you can fall back on in a pinch. In this section, we talk about a few of them.

Scope

Scope is not a concept that is applicable only to JavaScript; it is widely used in all programming languages. JavaScript's application of scope may be a little different, but the overarching concept remains the same. Scope refers to the availability of resources within your JavaScript document. It will affect where you need to define your variables. We have been using anonymous functions a lot in the book to contain all the variables we're using. That is an example of what scope is. All the variables inside a function are contained within the scope of that function. That means you can't use a variable outside a function without returning the variable and then calling that function. It won't naturally come out.

Variable scope travels downhill. A variable defined inside a function can be used inside that function (you knew that), and then also travel into functions defined within that same function (that's kind of new). There is an example of this concept later on in this chapter, but the concept of variable scope traveling downhill (cascading if you will, to use a CSS term) is called **closure**. Mastering closure produces a lot of a-ha moments in the life of a JavaScript developer, so it's worth looking into in more depth. However, we will talk about that a little later in this chapter.

When dealing with variable definition and scope, we briefly mentioned **global scope**. Declaring something in the global scope makes it available to all functions, all the time. It's a very temping thing to do, and it can be helpful from time to time, but when you use the global scope too much, it's called **polluting the global scope**. What ends up happening is you use up all the good variable names and make it more difficult to create a maintainable application in the long run. Be sure to use the global scope aspect sparingly and responsibly. Listing 9.1 shows an example of how you might declare a variable in the global scope that is available to the entire document and all its containing functions. In this case, the partyStarter variable is declared and can travel downhill into either the pizzaParty() function or the declared anonymous function.

Listing 9.1 **Polluting the Global Scope**

```
/* the global variable */
var partyStarter = "Starlen";

/* a function to determine how many pieces of pizza everyone can have */

function pizzaParty(totalSlices, peopleCount) {

    "use strict";

    /* at this point the partyStarter variable is available because it's global */
```

```
    var fairness = totalSlices / peopleCount;

    // at this point fairness is set to a value
    return fairness;

}

/* wrap script in an anonymous function because we do that */

(function () {

    "use strict";

    /* at this point the partyStarter variable is available because it's global */

    var body = document.getElementsByTagName("body")[0];

    // call the function with arguments to output the returned value
    body.innerHTML = "<p>Dear " + partyStarter + ", Each person can have " +
➥pizzaParty(32, 10) + " pieces of pizza</p>";

    /* at this point "fairness is undefined" because it is
➥contained within the pizzaParty() function */

})(); // close anonymous function
```

Global variables, like anything in any programming language, have their place. It's more about using them responsibly and putting some thought into the content and naming of the variables. Setting global configurations of an application might be a good use for a global variable. Global configurations include: storing a base URL, directory information, an application name, or items that you know are going to be used over and over again that would be a waste of resources to continuously redefine. Everything has its place; it's all about finding that place and utilizing it without abusing it.

Listing 9.1.1 shows how you would clean up the global scope of this document by moving the partyStarter variable to a more logical place (bolded text in Listing 9.1.1) inside the anonymous function. This not only puts it in a better spot from a logic standpoint, but it contains the scope of the variable so it is no longer available to the pizzaParty() function. We weren't using it there anyway, so it's no matter.

Listing 9.1.1 **Cleaning the Global Scope**

```
/* a function to determine how many pieces of pizza everyone can have */

function pizzaParty(totalSlices, peopleCount) {

    "use strict";
```

```
    var fairness = totalSlices / peopleCount;

    // at this point fairness is set to a value
    return fairness;

}


/* wrap script in an anonymous function because we do that */

(function (){

    "use strict";

    /* moving the partyStarter variable out of the global scope */

    var body = document.getElementsByTagName("body")[0],
        partyStarter = "Starlen";

    // call the function with arguments to output the returned value
    body.innerHTML = "<p>Dear " + partyStarter + ", Each person can have " +
➥pizzaParty(32, 10) + " pieces of pizza</p>";

    /* at this point "fairness is undefined" because it is
➥contained within the pizzaParty() function */

})(); // close anonymous function
```

Failing Quickly

It sounds weird as a guiding principle to tell people that the code they write should fail quickly, but...your code should fail quickly. What does that mean exactly? We create if statements and conditionals to constantly check the state of something. The result of those conditionals is always either a pass or a fail (true or false). We use a lot of conditionals because without having those built-in checkpoints in our processes, many lines of unnecessary code would be executed, consuming a lot of valuable processor speed. Because of this, we use conditional statements to produce true/false scenarios that help run proper blocks of code.

The blocks that generate a false statement produce a failure and, depending on where we attach that conditional, the failure can either happen very quickly, or it can take much longer than necessary. Conditionals such as checking the length of an array before looping through it and checking for the presence of an HTML class on the <body> element are examples of conditional statements that fail very quickly. Because looping through information and parsing the DOM are both very resource-intensive functions, it is best to catch them as early as possible before moving onto something else. This is what I mean by creating code that fails quickly.

Listing 9.2 shows the code block from Listing 9.1.1 modified with a simple conditional statement that checks to make sure the amount of people set is greater than 0 and that the amount of pizza ordered is also greater than 0. You don't need to run the block of code outputting the calculation we made if no people are coming to the pizza party or if there hasn't been any pizza ordered. We can save a little bit of time by not executing the `pizzaParty()` function and just outputting an error message.

Listing 9.2   **Creating Code That Fails Quickly**

```
/* a function to determine how many pieces of pizza everyone can have */

function pizzaParty(totalSlices, peopleCount) {

    "use strict";

    var fairness = totalSlices / peopleCount;

    // at this point fairness is set to a value
    return fairness;

}

/* wrap script in an anonymous function because we do that */

(function () {

    "use strict";

    var body = document.getElementsByTagName("body")[0],
        partyStarter = "Starlen",
        peopleCount = 10, // the amount of people coming to the party
        pizzaCount = 4, // the amount of pizza partyStarter is ordering
        sliceCount = pizzaCount * 8; // the amount of slices available

    // make sure people are coming and pizza is being ordered

    if (peopleCount > 0 && pizzaCount > 0) {

        // call the function with arguments to output the returned value
        body.innerHTML += "<p>Dear " + partyStarter + ", Each person can have " +
➥pizzaParty(sliceCount, peopleCount) + " pieces of pizza</p>";

    } else {

        // create a fallback message
        body.innerHTML += "<p>You need to either invite people or order pizza</p>";
```

```
    } // end if statement

})(); // close anonymous function
```

User Experience

I know it must feel like I'm drilling this point into your head pretty hard, but that should show how important it is. Failing quickly, scope, looping performance, caching variables, using objects and methods—every one of these things can be traced back to our goal of creating a good user experience.

When you're going through your application making structural and style decisions about how to handle various pieces of your JavaScript, always keeping user experience in mind will guide your process. When we talk about user experience, we often focus on the end user of an application. But in reality, an aspect of user experience more commonly referred to as "maintainability" is equally important when developing an application. Maintainability is usability for people on your team or anyone who might be updating your code. It's not uncommon for maintainability to be sacrificed in favor of end-user usability. That's where the main focus should be, but as you go through the development process, you will have to constantly balance maintainability with performance and end-user usability.

If you hit a tough crossroad, it sometimes helps to ask, "What will be best for the end user?" and "How much will that affect our ability to maintain this code base moving forward?" If you can answer those two questions, you'll be well on your way to creating the best possible experience not only for your users, but for the other members on your own team.

Code Design

The concept of designing code is a touchy area with a lot of developers. Very often, especially with seasoned developers, people fall into a natural style of coding that they have used for years. For this reason, implementing a style guide for code can be a difficult task. Your styles should flow naturally with the overall process so they don't turn into something developers begrudgingly adhere to, fighting tooth and nail. Style rules are generally put into place when you're working on a team or sharing code publicly to minimize confusing points based on style alone. You're always going to hit spots while reading through code where there is a natural confusion, but you can make sure those points don't live at a stylistic level that encompasses elements like file naming, directory structure, indentation, and inline whitespace.

Front-end style guides are often taken too far, so it's important to not get so specific as to hamper creative freedom and implementing new practices. You hire people on a team because of their talent level, and to a certain extent you need to trust those people and their skills without holding them back with policy, red tape, and overly aggressive standardization.

Files and Directories

Dealing with JavaScript files and directory structures is pretty straightforward and follows much the same model as any type of front-end code like HTML or CSS. All JavaScript files should be contained within the same parent directory and all share the `.js` file extension. Using a `.js` file extension isn't actually required (I went on a stint of using a `.tim` extension for a short period of time—it was awesome), but it's one of those industry standards that exists because it makes perfect sense, and changing it would confuse people. File extensions should describe the coding contents of a file, `.html` contains HTML, `.css` contains CSS, `.json` contains JSON data, and `.js` contains JavaScript.

In an open source-based development world, you will most likely find yourself, in one form or another, using code that another developer wrote. There's absolutely nothing wrong with that; it's common to use a JavaScript library to fill in the developmental gaps that you don't want to deal with yourself. In the next chapter we get into JavaScript libraries and how they can help you code, but for now when dealing with JavaScript directory structures and external libraries, it is always a best practice to section them off into their own subdirectory of the parent JavaScript folder.

File naming conventions also come into play when dealing with external libraries. You may be using multiple plug-in files or add-on functionalities that are based off of the main library. In this case, it is best to preface the plug-in filename with the name of the actual library so you can quickly distinguish between library-base plug-ins and any other external code you may be using on a project.

Figure 9.1 shows a depiction of the file structure described earlier. As you can see, a "js" directory contains a subdirectory of "lib." This "lib" directory is where all the third-party code would go (code other people wrote). In this case the name of the application is "application" and the name of the external library is "library." The names of the actual directories would be up for debate on your team. Some prefer "script" or "javascript" rather than "js" but the overall principle still remains for sectioning off a directory specifically for JavaScript.

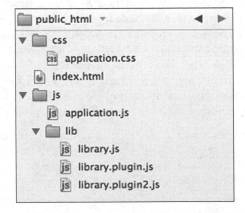

Figure 9.1   Suggested directory structure when dealing with JavaScript and libraries

> **Note**
>
> This structure model does not have to end at JavaScript. You could easily transfer it into your CSS directory if you were to use external CSS libraries as well.

In-document Script

Up to this point we have been putting JavaScript at the bottom of the document, so by now you should be familiar with how JavaScript blocks the loading of a page. By putting script at the bottom, you can create a faster loading page. This is nothing new, but it's important to remember because there may be times when you need to put a `<script>` reference at the top of the document to set up any object initializations.

JavaScript does not have to be grouped together. It's nice to have everything in one place, but in case the situation occurs where you need to add a JavaScript file reference to the top of the document, you shouldn't feel like it all has to be up there. Some can be at the top and the rest at the bottom where it belongs.

In the same note as the previous section, dealing with external libraries or multiple files not only affects your file structure, but it will also affect your in-document HTML. With more files, you will have more to link up at the bottom of your HTML document. Listing 9.3 shows what the bottom of your HTML document might look like if you were using an external library, a couple of plug-ins, and your own custom script. The order of the files is very important in this instance. Because the two plug-in files (and probably `application.js`) rely on `library.js` to function properly, you need to make sure that `library.js` is loaded before anything that depends on it. The files will load in the order they are listed; adding the library to the top of the list ensures that anything below it can access the dependencies.

Listing 9.3   **HTML When Dealing with External Libraries**

```
<!-- JavaScript -->
<script src="js/lib/library.js"></script>
<script src="js/lib/library.plugin.js"></script>
<script src="js/lib/library.plugin2.js"></script>
<script src="js/application.js"></script>

</body>
</html>
```

Because external library plug-ins are often very specific to a certain page of your site of the application, it is very temping to load that file only on the page where you need it. However, because of browser caching it is better to link up all your site's JavaScript all the time. When a user hits a page with the externally linked files, they will all be cached in the browser and most likely not redownloaded. For that reason, if you're linking multiple files (but try not to), it's best to link them all up and leave it alone.

In Chapter 2, "JavaScript in the Browser," when we mentioned browser performance we spoke of the HTTP request. A key aspect of creating a high-performance Web application is to cut down the HTTP requests as much as possible. In Listing 9.3 you probably noticed that we're starting to pile up the HTTP requests with the external library and plug-ins. This can be a problem. The solution is not to stop using external libraries; some of the libraries are really amazing (we'll get to that) because they cut down on your headaches of cross-browser compatibility a great deal. To cut down on HTTP requests, we do something called **concatenation** of the files. Concatenation needs to be run on the server, but what happens is that a server-side script will look through all your JavaScript files, pull out the contents, and dump them all into a single file. Because whitespace is almost irrelevant in JavaScript, the only thing that matters is that the files are combined in the correct order. It's best to have something running on the server that can do this for you, but you could certainly do it by hand as well. However, it's really hard to maintain, so I recommend automating the process if you can. Either way, the goal of using all the JavaScript you need while cutting down on the HTTP requests can be met.

Listing 9.3.1 shows what the bottom of the HTML document in Listing 9.3 would look like after the script has been concatenated, using only a single HTTP request to accomplish the goal.

Listing 9.3.1   **HTML with Concatenated Script**

```
<!-- JavaScript -->
<script src="js/application-combined.js"></script>

</body>
</html>
```

Variable Declarations

Good and consistent variable declarations and grouping can make working in someone else's code a very pleasant experience. In contrast, poor declaration patterns can make it an absolute nightmare.

When declaring variables, you can follow a few simple rules:

- Group all variables at the top of the containing function.
- Use clear and descriptive comments.
- Use a consistent grouping pattern.

Grouping patterns in variable declarations describe how they are arranged in your code. Because all your local variables begin with var and they will be grouped together, you can drop the var and separate them with commas. This is the pattern all the code samples so far in this book have followed. Listing 9.4 shows a variable definition block as a comma-separated list.

Listing 9.4   **A Variable Definition Block Example**

```
(function () {

    "use strict";

    var body = document.getElementsByTagName("body")[0], // target element
        partyStarter = "Starlen", // name of the person running the party
        peopleCount = 10, // the amount of people coming to the party
        pizzaCount = 4, // the amount of pizza partyStarter is ordering
        sliceCount = pizzaCount * 8; // the amount of slices available

    /* the rest of your function code */

}
```

Alternatively, variables can each be assigned a separate var declaration, depicted in Listing 9.4.1. The difference between the two methods is purely cosmetic. As long as the variables are grouped at the top of each function, the formatting is completely up to you. This is an area where a team meeting about a style guide would be a good idea; although the result of the code is the same, it's nice to use a similar format across a team. Each comment should also have its own individual comment.

Listing 9.4.1   **Multiline Variable Declarations**

```
(function () {

    "use strict";

    var body = document.getElementsByTagName("body")[0]; // target element
    var partyStarter = "Starlen"; // name of the person running the party
    var peopleCount = 10; // the amount of people coming to the party
    var pizzaCount = 4; // the amount of pizza partyStarter is ordering
    var sliceCount = pizzaCount * 8; // the amount of slices available

    /* the rest of your function code */

}
```

Variable and Function Naming

Variable and function names should follow the normal pattern for any type of front-end code. Names should be limited to using the standard 26-letter alphabet (a-z), numbers, and underscores (_). Avoid using unclear characters and symbols like: !@#$%^&*() when naming functions and variables.

Other than the contents of each name, you should consider some further constraints when naming. First and foremost, the name should make sense, and describe the actual content or action associated with a label. Second, the name should always start with a lowercase letter, never a number, and especially not an underscore.

Using an underscore in other programming languages typically represents a private value. Because this concept doesn't exist in JavaScript, prefacing a variable or function name with an underscore can be confusing to some; for this reason it is best to stick to lowercase alpha characters when starting out a variable or function name.

Listing 9.5 shows two different variable declarations. The first, `partyStarter`, is using a correct model by starting with a lowercase letter and following the camelCase syntax pattern. The second variable, `_partyAnimal!`, is an epic failure of variable declaration. Although it will work, starting with an underscore is confusing and inconsistent with other languages. If you're a programmer who has had to switch between languages in the same day, you know how frustrating it can become when coding styles collide. This variable is also using an exclamation point, which is bad practice in this area.

Listing 9.5 **Variable Naming Conventions**

```
(function () {

    "use strict";

    /* good variable name */
    var partyStarter = "Starlen";

    /* bad variable name */
    var _partyAnimal! = "The Ian";

})();
```

Comments

You can usually tell how good a coder someone is by the detail level of his or her comments. It's not the length so much, but the quality. Commenting your code is the first line of documentation. Sometimes it's for you and sometimes it is for others. But either way, using helpful and descriptive comments can cut down on ramp up time when jumping into a file (or jumping back into a file).

Make sure to be generous with your comments; they are often your chance to explain yourself and why you did a certain thing in you code. Was there a weird bug you needed to patch up? Are you setting up a declaration as a special application API hook? Maybe, but no one will know if you don't write it down.

When commenting your code, it is important to do your best to not state the obvious. You can safely assume that someone cracking open one of your JavaScript files knows the basics of the language (or they probably shouldn't be in there in the first place). If you're adding a class to a parent node, it isn't very helpful to leave a comment that says something like "add a class to parent"; anyone can tell that's what you're doing. A better comment would read something like "adding a class to the body element to act as a style flag for CSS and for JS to check the document state. The corresponding CSS lives in application.css." That would be a helpful comment to a developer coming into the code. Documentation can be a pain, but if you document well in your comments, you can dramatically cut down on the amount of external development documentation you need to create.

Listing 9.6 shows an example from the `pizzaParty()` function where the commenting leaves something to be desired.

Listing 9.6   **Example of Bad Commenting**

```
/* pizza party function */

function pizzaParty(totalSlices, peopleCount) {

    "use strict";

    // divide the total slices by the people <- no kidding?!
    var fairness = totalSlices / peopleCount;

    // return fairness value
    return fairness;

}
```

The comments in Listing 9.6 look like a computer wrote them. Not only are they amazingly unhelpful to someone viewing the document for the first time, but they're also super boring. Coding can always be a little more stressful than we would like, so don't be afraid to inject some humor into your comments. As far as brightening up someone's day when they're eyeballs deep in code, it doesn't get much better than reading a funny comment someone left. I've even caught myself laughing at comments I've written in the past. It's always a nice surprise and lightens the mood.

Listing 9.6.1 shows an example of commenting that might be a little more helpful.

Listing 9.6.1   **Example of Better Commenting**

```
/*
    determine how many slices of pizza each person can eat to get the maximum amount
 of fat in everyone's stomach.
    Taking 2 arguments to be a little more flexible / reusable
*/
```

```
function pizzaParty(totalSlices, peopleCount) {

    "use strict";

    // take the arguments and decide how many pieces per person is fair... life may
➥not be fair, but this function is!
    var fairness = totalSlices / peopleCount;

    // make the fairness value available
    return fairness;


}
```

Indentation

JavaScript doesn't have any rules about indentation and whitespace like a language such as Python may have. Because of this, it can be like the Wild West in some JavaScript files. Depending on the text editor you use, you can make life miserable for another person simply by pressing the Tab key a couple of times. Because no standards exist for the amount of space one "tab" is, it creates a lot of dissonance in the coding world. Unfortunately, there's not much we can do about how different programs use the Tab key. The solution is to use spaces instead.

Some programs will let you set the tab distance to a space value. If that's an option to you, it's certainly preferred to pressing the spacebar multiple times. A single indentation unit should equal four spaces. This is an industry standard (what a thing to have a standard around, eh?) and creates uniformity in your code. At times you need more than a single indentation unit, so they increment by four each time. Two indentations equal eight spaces; three equals twelve, and so on in that fashion until your eyeballs fall out of your head and your fingers cramp up.

We have been using this indentation pattern throughout the book. Figure 9.2 illustrates the anonymous function we have been using so far in this chapter and shows the level of indentation for some of the various lines of the code block.

When I first heard about the standardization of indentation in JavaScript, I thought it was way over the top and refused to pay attention to such a thing. But I ran into a few back-end developers who had requested that I move over from tabs to spaces because of the cross-editor formatting problems. I won't lie—if there wasn't a setting in my text editor to produce spaces rather than tabs, I probably would have fought the change tooth and nail. But it is a change for the best because you can make sure the code you write doesn't mess up the formatting of someone else's code, and vice versa. It's a small price to pay to avoid a coding headache.

Note

Using spaces instead of tabs will increase the overall size of your file, but don't worry about this excess whitespace; you can remove it with simple minification of the file before serving it up to the public.

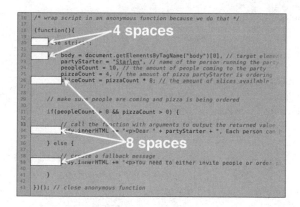

Figure 9.2   Indentation set to a four-space increment.

Whitespace

As mentioned in the previous section, JavaScript doesn't have a standard surrounding whitespace. So to a certain extent, it's up to personal preference. Whitespace should be used to increase the readability of your code. Using a lot of extra whitespace will increase the size of your JavaScript document. Normally, increasing the size of a document is a bad thing, but in this case (and also with comments), it can be a good thing, or more likely, a nonissue.

There are two types of files: development files and production files. Production files live on the server and get sent out to the public for consumption. Just like the concatenation method mentioned earlier, you can do something called "minification" on the server before a file goes live.

Minification is the process of removing all the whitespace from a document. Like concatenation, it is a server-side process. When a JavaScript file is minified, all the comments and whitespace are removed, and the file is shrunk down to a single line. A file is nearly impossible to work with after it has been minified, which is why you have development versions of your files as well. The development files will contain all the ample whitespace, formatting, and comments you need to effectively work.

Listing 9.7 shows a block of code (pizzaParty() function) with what I would call poor utilization of whitespace. Keep in mind that using whitespace for readability is a completely objective thing; what's good for one person may be horrible for another. This is another situation where you may want to come to an agreement with other team members on how to best handle whitespace.

Listing 9.7   **Code with Poor Whitespace**

```
/* determine  how many slices of pizza each person can eat */
function pizzaParty(totalSlices, peopleCount) {
    "use strict";
    // take the arguments and decide how many pieces per person is fair
    var fairness = totalSlices / peopleCount;
    // make the fairness value available
    return fairness;
}
```

Listing 9.7.1 shows a cleaned-up example of the same `pizzaParty()` function with better whitespace, creating more readable and maintainable code.

Listing 9.7.1   **Code with Better Whitespace**

```
/* determine  how many slices of pizza each person can eat */

function pizzaParty(totalSlices, peopleCount) {

    "use strict";

    // take the arguments and decide how many pieces per person is fair
    var fairness = totalSlices / peopleCount;

    // make the fairness value available
    return fairness;

}
```

When you combine file concatenation with minification, you can develop in a completely different environment that gets exposed to the public. You can keep your development code very modular, clean, and well documented, and in production you will get the smallest file with the best possible performance.

Statement Spacing

Creating a proper spacing scheme in your document can help increase the readability of your JavaScript. Along with using extra whitespace from line to line, adding a space between operators, variables, and values will create document consistency.

In this section we will look into the spacing patterns inside the conditional statement of our anonymous function from Listing 9.2. In Listing 9.8 you can see the highlighted sections of the conditional statement.

Listing 9.8   **Proper Statement Spacing**

```
if (peopleCount > 0 && pizzaCount > 0) {

    body.innerHTML += "<p>Dear " + partyStarter + ", Each person can have "
➥+pizzaParty(sliceCount, peopleCount) + " pieces of pizza</p>"; // semicolon at
➥the end of the statement

} else {

    body.innerHTML += "<p>You need to either invite people or order pizza</p>";//
➥semicolon at the end of the statement

} // end if statement
```

As a general rule, parentheses should have a space before and a space after. This principle can be applied to any conditional statement, functions, and any type of JavaScript loop. You'll notice in Listing 9.8 that the contents of the if statement are wrapped in parentheses and illustrate this pattern.

The else portion of the statement follows a similar pattern. Spaces should also be inserted to surround else and else if statements, as depicted in Listing 9.8.

Line Breaks

Lines in JavaScript can be broken at almost any point as long as the break doesn't come in the middle of a word. This can make breaking lines in your document feel a little weird and slightly ad hoc. Luckily, some conventions exist in the coding world that we can turn to for things like this.

There's a principle in Java (yes, that's Java, not JavaScript) that says that lines of code should not exceed 80 characters. Some Java-targeted text editors will even provide a vertical line on the screen to mark where your lines should break. With JavaScript, this is generally a good rule to follow, but more because around 60 to 80 characters is the point where text (any text) becomes harder to read and consume. No one expects you to insert a hard break at 80 characters in your JavaScript code, but it's something to be aware of.

Another option to consider for breaking a line of code is to do it at an operator. We have been breaking all our variables at an operator so far—the comma. The comma creates a natural coding breakpoint in JavaScript. Other operators like +, –, or = are also natural breakpoints. If you feel like your lines of code are getting too long, don't be afraid to go back and insert a few breaks where you see an operator. It can help improve readability a great deal.

Listing 9.9 shows the variable block we have been using, reinforcing the line breaks after each comma.

Listing 9.9   **A Variable List Broken at Commas**

```
var body = document.getElementsByTagName("body")[0],
    partyStarter = "Starlen",
    peopleCount = 10,
    pizzaCount = 4,
    sliceCount = pizzaCount * 8;
```

Math and Operators

The ability to do math is a core functionality of JavaScript, which goes hand in hand with the use of operators. Whether you're adding values, concatenating a string, setting a variable's value, or checking the condition of a certain state, using operators is something you will have to deal with on a day-to-day basis when coding JavaScript.

Of all the aspects in using spacing and whitespace in JavaScript, the usage of proper spacing when it comes to operators and math is an area where people tend to fall short. It's not uncommon for developers (even myself) to overlook spacing around an operator.

Each operator should have a space before and after. Listing 9.10 shows four types of JavaScript operators:

- === (exact match)
- += (append or increment and assign)
- + (concatenate strings or add numbers)
- !== (exactly not equal to)

Each operator in Listing 9.10 has a space both before and after.

Listing 9.10   **Spacing and Operators**

```
// finding an exact match for the partyStarter

if (partyStarter === "Starlen") {

    body.innerHTML += "<p>Yes, " + partyStarter + " is someone we all know!</p>";

}

// finding an exact mis-match for the partyStarter

if (partyStarter !== "Starlen") {

    body.innerHTML += "<p>No officer, I do not know anyone named " + partyStarter + ",
➥please take them away</p>";

}
```

Using math in JavaScript follows the same rules as math in the real world (except you use it more in JavaScript). Just like in the real world, you can perform math only on numbers. If you try to add two strings together, they will be concatenated rather than added; even if it looks like a number to you, it may not be a number to JavaScript. And just like in the real world, you can use addition, subtraction, division, multiplication, get percentages, and even group with parentheses. And it all follows the same procedural rule.

My sixth-grade teacher, Mr. Day (I feel like I can probably call him Richard now), taught me the math principle for the order of operations, PEMDAS or Please Excuse My Dear Aunt Sally (to the laymen). If you're not familiar, PEMDAS tells us which actions to do first in a math equation. It goes like this:

- Parentheses
- Exponents
- Multiply or Divide
- Add or Subtract

Listing 9.11 shows a `calculator()` function that takes three arguments and plugs them into an equation, which implements the order of operations principle.

Listing 9.11   **Using PEMDAS**

```
function calculator(a, b, c) {

    // do some math for us
    return (a + b) * c;

}

(function (){

    // save the result to a variable
    var result = calculator(1, 2, 3);

    alert(result); // returns 9

})();
```

Using eval()

The `eval()` method has the capability of evaluating or executing its argument. `eval()` is generally thought to be not a safe function for casual use (or to ever use). A couple things to remember right off the bat with this method are

- `eval()` is terrible aka "evil"
- Don't use `eval()`

That's pretty much all you need to know about using eval(), and many people leave it at that and take it as a blanket statement. But what kind of author would I be if I left it at that?

There are a few reasons to not use this method, but really, why would I even bother bringing it up if it's so bad? It's a method that's out there, and it's actually extremely easy to use and pretty helpful. Unfortunately, the small upside of using eval() is dwarfed by the enormous downside.

Because of eval()'s core functionality of evaluating and executing any string that is passed into it as an argument, this makes the method extremely insecure and very likely one of the largest security holes in the entire language. By passing strings into the method, you are basically saying, "Do whatever you'd like here." Because of that, consuming third-party scripts can leave you extremely vulnerable to injection hacks.

Security is the most obvious problem with using eval(), but using it can also make debugging your script more difficult because it will not report proper error codes and line numbers. You're much better off using some of the eval() alternatives when a situation comes up.

You've already come across a situation where you could have used eval(), but we chose one of the alternative methods instead. In Chapter 8, "Communicating with the Server Through Ajax," when we were pulling the JSON data file and saving it to a variable by using the JSON.parse() method, you could have used eval(). However, this is exactly what we don't want to do because consuming a data feed like that and evaluating the contents can be very dangerous. In our case, it wasn't dangerous because we had full control over the data in a static file on disk, where the likelihood of an attack is pretty low. However, if it were an external script or being outputted from a database, the likelihood of an injection hack increases quite a bit. That's why we use JSON.parse() instead of eval(). It's a good habit to get into, especially because consuming remote JSON data is an extremely common practice.

In Listing 9.12 you can see what the Ajax call from Chapter 8 would have looked like if we had chosen to use eval() rather than JSON.parse(). It is a small change on the surface, but an enormous change under the hood.

Listing 9.12   **Ajax Call from Chapter 8 Using eval()**

```
request.onreadystatechange = function() {

    // check to see if the Ajax call went through
    if ( request.readyState === 4 && request.status === 200 ) {

        // save the ajax response to a variable
        var contacts = eval("(" + request.responseText + ")");

        // make sure the callback is indeed a function before executing it
        if(typeof callback === "function"){

            callback(contacts);
```

```
        } // end check

    } // end ajax status check

} // end onreadystatechange
```

As you can see in Listing 9.12, eval() is taking a single argument, which is the JSON data returned from the Ajax call.

Listing 9.12.1 shows the same Ajax call from Chapter 8 with JSON.parse() returned to its original position, replacing eval(). This is a much safer way to pull in and access the JSON data because it is no longer susceptible to injection attacks. Seriously, don't use eval().

Listing 9.12.1   **Ajax Call from Chapter 8 Using an eval() Alternative, JSON.parse()**

```
request.onreadystatechange = function() {

    // check to see if the Ajax call went through
    if ( request.readyState === 4 && request.status === 200 ) {

        // save the ajax response to a variable
        var contacts = JSON.parse(request.responseText);

        // make sure the callback is indeed a function before executing it
        if(typeof callback === "function"){

            callback(contacts);

        } // end check

    } // end ajax status check

} // end onreadystatechange
```

Taking Style Guides Too Far

All the code design and style techniques we've been going over should be taken as guidelines to help you along the way in developing a style guide that works best with your own process. Principles such as spacing, whitespace, and commenting are all in place to help your development, whether you're working on a team or by yourself.

When you're setting your style guide for JavaScript, be sure to not tighten it in the wrong places. If you're taking it to the point of defining specific methods that should be used in certain situations, you're probably going way too far. Style guides are just that, guides, they're not rules for you to blindly follow, and they should not be built to the point where they negatively impact creativity. Creativity and innovation is what has powered the Web since its early days. If you see to it that your style guides are more helpful than hurtful, you will be sure to foster an environment where some amazing things can happen. Automate the stuff people don't want to do, and you'll leave them open to create a strong base and innovative future.

Code Structure

By now you know that code blocks get wrapped into functions. We have explored beyond that of a normal function and onto types like anonymous functions and nesting functions inside objects to create the elusive JavaScript method. The function alone can take many different versions, and deciding which one to use can greatly affect your application and how it performs.

In this section we are going to take a look the `pizzaParty()` function and how it would look if we were to transform it into all the different function types. We'll also talk about when it might be a good time to use one over the other.

Functions

The normal function call is something we have not only been using in this chapter, but throughout the entirety of the book to this point.

The `pizzaParty()` function we have been using is a standard function. It begins with the `function` keyword, followed by the function name, argument list, then the function content itself. This function also returns a value from the calculation that is being made.

All the following functions will have the same functionality as this example, but we will explore the different ways to achieve the same outcome and discuss how they are different from the others. Listing 9.13 shows the `pizzaParty()` function as it has been throughout the chapter, for reviewing purposes.

Listing 9.13   **The Normal `pizzaParty` Function**

```
/* determine how many slices of pizza each person can eat */

function pizzaParty(totalSlices, peopleCount) {

    "use strict";

    // take the arguments and decide how many pieces per person is fair
    var fairness = totalSlices / peopleCount;

    // make the fairness value available
    return fairness;

}
```

Usage

This style of function is good to use in a relatively small JavaScript application where you want to be able to reuse the `pizzaParty()` calculation more than once. Because it takes more processing time to visit the function and call it than to call it inline, you wouldn't want to pull this functionality out into a function unless you were going to use it multiple times.

Anonymous Functions

Nothing in the anonymous function can be reused. The variables can be, but only within the scope of that same function (remember scope?).

Listing 9.14 shows the `pizzaParty()` function if it were to be written as a single anonymous function instead of an anonymous function and standard function. This function is self-executing and will run on its own from top to bottom.

The differences in Listing 9.14 are that `fairness` is now set to be a normal variable in the definition block, where the calculation is happening, and instead of calling the `pizzaParty()` function and outputting the returned value, we are now outputting the `fairness` variable. Overall, not much has changed, but it is a little less flexible now (which is okay sometimes).

Listing 9.14   **If `pizzaParty` Were One Large Anonymous Function**

```
(function () {

    "use strict";

    var body = document.getElementsByTagName("body")[0],
        partyStarter = "Starlen",
        peopleCount = 10,
        pizzaCount = 4,
        sliceCount = pizzaCount * 8,
        fairness = sliceCount / peopleCount;

    if (peopleCount > 0 && pizzaCount > 0) {

        body.innerHTML += "<p>Dear " + partyStarter + ", Each person can have " +
➡fairness + " pieces of pizza</p>";

    } else {

        body.innerHTML += "<p>You need to either invite people or order pizza</p>";

    } // end if statement

})();
```

Usage

Because we aren't calling the original `pizzaParty()` function more than once, it is faster to use it as part of the anonymous function, forgoing the time it takes to travel up to the function. It is a slight performance enhancement, but this is an instance where throwing a blanket policy over extracting all functions may not be the best way to attack this individual issue.

An anonymous function is probably the best for this situation, but if we ever wanted to use that calculation again, it would either need to be rewritten or pulled out into another function.

Functions as Variables

Functions can also be declared as variables. There is no function difference between this function and the original `pizzaParty()` function. They both produce the same outcome and are even called the same way `pizzaParty(argument1, argument2)`.

This is a stylistic choice and leans more toward the function as an object/method style of development. Listing 9.15 shows this style of function declaration.

Listing 9.15   **Example of a Function as a Variable**

```
var pizzaParty = function (totalSlices, peopleCount) {

    "use strict";

    // take the arguments and decide how many pieces per person is fair
    var fairness = totalSlices / peopleCount;

    // make the fairness value available
    return fairness;

}; // semicolon at the end, because it's still a variable

/*
    to call: pizzaParty(sliceCount, peopleCount)
*/
```

Usage

The usage for this function syntax is the same as the normal function call syntax, if you have a block of code that you need to execute more than once. However, because it is so stylistically different, it is pretty rare to see the two occupying the same document.

Functions as Methods

Our autocomplete contacts search form employs this structural pattern for the functions (methods) within the application. This function also produces the same outcome as the others, but with a much different path to execution.

When using a function as a method, the syntax and nesting is the most notable. Our pizzaParty() function has now been split into a party object and a pizza method. This opens up opportunities to add more party-related methods into the pizza object, further grouping and sectioning off this functionality in our application.

Listing 9.16 shows what the pizzaParty() function would look like if we converted it into an object containing a method.

Listing 9.16 **pizzaParty** Function as a Method

```
var party = {

    pizza : function(totalSlices, peopleCount) {

        "use strict";

        // take the arguments and decide how many pieces per person is fair
        var fairness = totalSlices / peopleCount;

        // make the fairness value available
        return fairness;

    } // end method

}; // end pizza object

/*
    to call: party.pizza(sliceCount, peopleCount)
*/
```

> **Note**
>
> The function call for using a method is slightly different because you not only have to enter the object, but also travel down to the function (method) itself.

Usage

Using objects and methods works very well with larger applications with multiple categories of functionality. Objects are used to group similar methods together to help foster better organization within your code.

The Pizza Party application doesn't have enough functionality to merit this function nesting, but if we had plans to expand it later into adding something like a beverage method, this pattern of objects and methods would work very well with that. In Listing 9.16.1 you can see what the party object would look like if we were to expand it by adding a beverage method.

Listing 9.16.1   **pizzaParty Function as a Method**

```
var party = {

    pizza : function(totalSlices, peopleCount) {

        "use strict";

        // take the arguments and decide how many pieces per person is fair
        var fairness = totalSlices / peopleCount;

        // make the fairness value available
        return fairness;

    },
    beverage : function(fluidounces, peopleCount) {

        // create the same thing, but for drinks

    }

};
```

As you can see in Listing 9.16.1, just like we did in the autocomplete contacts search form application, adding a second method to an object is a process similar to creating a comma-separated list of variables.

JavaScript Development Patterns

In addition to choosing which function syntax to use, a decision must be made about development patterns in JavaScript. To talk about development patterns, we will need a new application.

This application will simulate audio controls. It will have a very basic HTML structure and some CSS for presentation. From there we will talk about two very common JavaScript development models that can be applied to this example to achieve the same outcome. The two development patterns we'll be going over are

- Functions and Closures pattern
- Event-driven pattern

In Listing 9.17, you see the basic HTML structure for this audio-controls application. Most of it is pretty standard, but note that there is an external CSS file that we will be creating content for to help visualize the actions that we will write into the button functionality. The document also contains a div with two buttons identified as play and stop, respectively. And, of course, our external JavaScript file is linked up at the bottom of the document.

Listing 9.17   **Example HTML for JavaScript Patterns**

```
<!doctype html>
<html lang="en">
<head>
    <title>Chapter 9</title>

    <!--meta cluster-->c
    <meta charset="utf-8">

    <!--css-->
    <link rel="stylesheet" href="css/audio-controls.css">

</head>
<body>

<div id="controls">
    <button id="play" type="button">Play</button>
    <button id="stop" type="button">Stop</button>
</div>

<!--js-->
<script src="js/audio-controls.js"></script>

</body>
</html>
```

The contents of the CSS file are very basic. We'll be adding 20px of breathing room around the
containing element. There are two CSS objects: one for when the player is set to "playing" and
another for when the player is set to "stopped." We are using shades of gray so it is easier to see
what is going on in the browser. Listing 9.17.1 shows the contents of audio-controls.css.

Listing 9.17.1   **Contents of audio-controls.css**

```
#controls { padding:20px; }

.playing { background:#eee; }
.stopped { background:#ccc; }
```

Functions and Closures Pattern

The first development pattern we will be going over is called "Functions and Closures." I briefly
mentioned closures early on in this chapter as a model by which variables can travel downhill
inside a containing function. This pattern of utilizing closure allows you to encapsulate everything inside a single object and create a form of public API that can be used throughout the
application while keeping all the other functions and variables local to the original object.

In Listing 9.17.2 you can find a `controls` object defined that takes a single argument, the `controls` containing element. Inside this object, everything should look familiar. Right off the bat you can see three variables being defined: one for the argument, one for the Play button, and another for the Stop button.

Below the variable definitions are normal event listeners, both of which are tied to the `click` event and executing their respective functions.

After the listeners are set up, you will find the actual `play()` and `stop()` functions being declared. This is where the concept of closure comes into play. Both functions are using the argument variable `audioControls`, which was defined outside each function but inside the parent `controls` object. This is an example of a variable traveling downhill into other functions from the parent.

As a whole, this function does everything we need, but you still have to return the data to be able to pull the actions out of the function. That is why at the end of the controls object you see the functions `play` and `stop` being returned. They are returned without the parentheses because using parentheses causes a function to execute immediately, and we certainly don't want that. This is how you set up an API that is available to the application while keeping its contents private.

Listing 9.17.2   **Example of Functions and Closure in JavaScript**

```
/* function and closure development pattern */

var controls = function (el) {

    var audioControls = el,
        playButton = document.getElementById("play")
        stopButton = document.getElementById("stop");

    // set up event listeners like normal
    playButton.addEventListener("click", play, false);
    stopButton.addEventListener("click", stop, false);

    function play() {

        // accessing parent function variable - this is closure
        audioControls.setAttribute("class", "playing");

    }

    function stop() {

        // accessing parent function variable
        audioControls.setAttribute("class", "stopped");
```

```
    }

    // set up a natural API to return
    return play, stop;

};

(function () {

    var element = document.getElementById("controls"),
        action = controls(element);

    // Use the API
    action.play;
    action.stop;

})();
```

Play and stop functions are as easy as calling the controls object, passing it the proper argument, and accessing the API we set up. After implementing this code, you should be able to open the HTML document in a browser and switch between clicking the Play and Stop buttons. The action should be toggling a class on the container element, and the CSS should be changing the background color.

Event-Driven Pattern

The second development pattern we will go over is called "event-driven." This pattern is a little more straightforward because you set up functions and then call them with event listeners. It is especially good if you don't care about setting up a public API for your application. Event-driven JavaScript uses a little less code when compared to other patterns, and many enjoy this method because it is thought to be short and to the point.

In Listing 9.17.3, you can see the same functionality contained in Listing 9.17.2, but coded in an event-driven pattern. In this pattern you will notice a lot of the same elements. We have two functions: play() and stop(), the two button variables and their respective event listeners set up. The main difference with this pattern is that instead of the public API, you have the two functions now publicly available.

Listing 9.17.3   **Example of Event-Driven JavaScript**

```
/* Event-driven JavaScript */

function play() {

    // apply a class to the parent node of whatever was clicked
    this.parentNode.setAttribute("class", "playing");
```

```
}

function stop() {

    // apply a class to the parent node of whatever was clicked
    this.parentNode.setAttribute("class", "stopped");

}

(function(){

    // save the audio controls to variables
    var playButton = document.getElementById("play"),
        stopButton = document.getElementById("stop");

    // set up the play event listener
    playButton.addEventListener("click", play, false);

    // set up the stop event listener
    stopButton.addEventListener("click", stop, false);

})();
```

The event-driven JavaScript pattern may feel a little more comfortable to you because it's the model we have been using through the course of this book. But both methods have their place; if one feels more comfortable to you versus the other, you should certainly feel free to explore that option. They're both extremely popular patterns and perform very well in the browser.

Summary

In this chapter, we took a large bite out of the various options and standards you have to consider when constructing your JavaScript file. We talked more about how to deal with the constant balancing act between performance and maintainability by following some industry standards surrounding such topics as whitespace, using robust comments, proper indentation, and clean spacing in conditionals, functions, and around operators. All these are elements of a style guide that can help you code more effectively.

From there we went over the different options you have when choosing a function structure and when to use options like anonymous functions over something more robust like an object/method model.

Last, we talked about a couple of popular JavaScript development patterns—a function and closure model and an event-driven model, each of which have valid uses in client-side development. We also talked about the differences between the two patterns.

Exercises

1. What are the four things you want to accomplish when building your JavaScript?

2. Why shouldn't you start a function or variable name with an underscore?

3. When is it best to use an anonymous function?

10

Making JavaScript Easier with Libraries

In this chapter, I make your life easier. Bold statement, I know, but that's exactly what we're here for. So far in the course of writing all these chapters, I have been doing my absolute best to present the JavaScript language in a unique and true-to-life way with the idea that it will ease the pain of learning something that may have been presented in other mediums as overly complicated. However, when some people learn JavaScript, it is a very natural flow with their build process, but for others, learning a development language like JavaScript can be very hard. I realize that. We do our best to create an understanding and organic flow to the learning experience to aid in the creation of what we call "ah-ha moments," where everything you've been learning suddenly makes sense, like magic.

Because JavaScript and the Web as a whole is one giant work in progress, there are a lot unknowns, gaps in functionality, and developing standards that we need to work either with or around. Depending on where your love affair with JavaScript currently is, this can either be a delight or a nightmare.

This chapter is an exploration and introduction to JavaScript libraries. Previous to this chapter you have seen some very brief references to libraries and how we use them. This chapter elaborates on the concept of libraries in general and how they are used in JavaScript. We go over a lot of different aspects that encompass the concept of using someone else's code; we talk about the good, the bad, and some alternatives. We also explore some library methods and how they map and relate to their native JavaScript counterparts.

Working with a JavaScript library will make your life easier, and there are entire books dedicated to touring through each one (not each one, but the popular ones, for sure). At some point in your JavaScript career, you will most likely use a library of some kind; in fact, there is a good chance that you've heard of some of the libraries we will be going over. It's very easy to get lost and overreliant on them, but if you keep in mind that it's still just JavaScript, you will be miles ahead and have the ability to switch between various libraries with a minimal learning curve. As you go through this chapter, keep in mind one important concept that a surprising number of people forget about libraries: **it's all still JavaScript**.

JavaScript Library Basics

A JavaScript library is a collection of functions and methods presented in a reusable format. Libraries can be a set of personal assets and functions that you build for an individual project or, more commonly, a set of assets and functions. They are carried from project to project to help reduce development time by saving and reapplying the common coding patterns over and over.

You may not have noticed it, but we have been building a sort of custom JavaScript library throughout this book. I'll admit that it is an extremely small library, but anytime you write a flexible function or method, you have the ability to reuse it beyond the scope of the current project. The `ajaxCall()` function from Chapter 8, "Communicating with the Server Through Ajax," is a great example of the kind of asset you would find built into a library because it was built in a very flexible manner and is easily reused with any local JSON data file. In fact, that's how many of the original JavaScript libraries started. There was a single person collecting frequently used functions who then gave them out for the world to use.

As I said, libraries can be personal collections of code that you save and transport from project to project, but most of the time the libraries you interact with will be collections of JavaScript methods that *other* people wrote. Whether they're libraries, toolkits, or frameworks, they are all basically a collection of JavaScript some other person (or a team of people) wrote for you and others to consume.

As with anything, there are always ups and downs to using a library. There are a lot of them in the wild and it can be an overwhelming experience trying to choose the correct one for the job on a particular project.

There are two very different ends of the spectrum when it comes to opinions about using libraries in JavaScript. Many are heavily in favor of using them, and many others lean in the other direction. It will be completely up to you as to which side of the fence you want to be on; hopefully, this chapter will help you come to a conclusion. The debate about whether to use a library will go on for decades and probably won't come to an end. However, it really doesn't matter because we're all out to accomplish the same goal on a project, and whatever set of tools you choose to accomplish that goal will be the right ones for the job, whether it's a JavaScript library, a back-end framework, or 100% custom code.

In this section you're going to learn some of the basic concepts behind the learning process when working with a new library, the purpose of creating a library, what goes into a library, and how libraries can save you time in the long run. If JavaScript is causing you any sort of headache at this point (it's common, don't worry), you can think of libraries as your well-known headache medicine that our lawyers won't let me explicitly call out by name. Most of the time it will stop your head from throbbing, although sometimes it doesn't, and be sure you don't take too much or you can find yourself in some serious trouble.

The Library Learning Process

There is a learning process that everyone goes through when exploring libraries in general. Most stick to this thought process so tightly that it is almost comical to observe a fellow developer or designer travel through it. The steps will inevitably take you from loving libraries to hating them, eventually settling somewhere in the middle. You may even become one of those really smart people who answer every question by saying, "It depends," when asked your opinion about using libraries.

When you're new to JavaScript, you experience a lot of frustrations due to inconsistent browser support, knowledge gaps, and struggling to find your coding groove with code organization. In a nutshell, there's a growing laundry list of things that you don't want to deal with, whether you fully understand them or not. It's a completely natural reaction to want to automate the boring stuff so you can focus on the more interesting pieces. For some people, focusing on interaction design is high on their list, so they may use libraries to handle the more hardcore aspects of JavaScript, like server communication (Ajax). Others who may enjoy the developer side of JavaScript can use libraries that allow for easy and immediate user-interface patterns so they don't have to worry about the design side of things.

When you discover which aspects of the language you like and which ones you don't, you will probably start filling the gaps of things you don't like with libraries and let someone else do the heavy lifting you don't want to do. This is the first step of getting into a library. In step 1 you love libraries because they do what you don't want to do, and there's nothing to worry about. You will even start discovering aspects of the library that can enhance the parts of the job that you really like. Libraries make things easier; it's really their only job and they're very good at it.

As you get deeper into developing your JavaScript based on a library system, you will probably get to step 2 in the learning process where you begin to tighten up your general JavaScript skills in areas where you were previously very weak, and you begin discovering that there is a lot of code in the library that you don't need anymore. Maybe you're using only a few of the predefined methods at this point. In step 2 you start to hate libraries and feel like you can succeed without relying on them. At this point you will begin distancing yourself from libraries and start building applications with only native JavaScript. As you step through your new non-library-based JavaScript applications, you rediscover a lot of the frustrations you had to deal with when you first started. You may even start building your own library before realizing that someone already took the time to assemble all the common functions people use. Then, like magic, there you are at step 3 using libraries again.

Even through you're back to using a library, step 3 in the learning process is very different from step 1 because of all the knowledge you have gained along the way. This is the point where you've now come to the conclusion that libraries can be both good and bad; it all depends on how you use them (there's that "it depends" statement). Libraries can be used very elegantly and can be integrated into your normal code, or they can be used in ways that overpower an application. It all depends on how you use a library whether it's a good or a bad thing. We get into the good and bad later on in this chapter.

Syntax

Learning a library is similar to learning a new language (spoken language, not coding language). Suppose that your primary language is English. You may not know all the words in the English language, but you know the ones you use and maybe a bunch that you learned while studying for the SATs. Learning a JavaScript library would be like trying to learn Spanish after already knowing English. It's all about learning new syntax and discovering a new way to communicate the same thing.

The correct way to learn a library, much like learning a second language, is to have a solid grasp of your first language (JavaScript/English) before moving forward. Otherwise you end up saying statements like *Mi perro walked to la biblioteca*, and never understanding why that's a pretty weird statement as a whole. The two languages have the same communication goals, but they accomplish them differently. And learning a library is very similar.

All the functionality of a library is already native to JavaScript. Things like accessing the DOM or executing an Ajax call can all be done, but a library does it in a different way; mastering a library is all about learning the special way a library solves a particular problem. Most libraries use syntaxes that are generally very different from others, so taking the time to discover which features are best suited for you and how to most efficiently apply them to a project is time well spent.

Focusing on the Goal

As mentioned earlier, libraries allow you to focus on the interesting stuff while (to some extent) automating the parts that are overly complex or that you don't want to deal with. Either way, it will speed up your development process a great deal and focus on the project goals.

Unless your project is to write an extensible JavaScript library, chances are that when you sat down with the client or initial development team, the goals for the project did not include things like the following:

- Build a powerful JavaScript method to handle multiple levels of cross-browser compatible Ajax functionality.
- Create a DOM node selection system that uses a more readable syntax.
- Make simple animation models that can be reused.

Nine times out of ten, your project goals will look something more like this:

- Increase conversions.
- Create an engaging user experience.
- Make it perform well in a browser.

The steps you take to achieve those goals will vary from project to project, but one of the most compelling reasons to use a library—and where the power really is—relies on the fact that libraries allow you to focus on reaching those project goals much more efficiently. At that point it doesn't matter if the library is something that you personally wrote and is being carried from project to project or if it is something that a third-party wrote for open source use. It doesn't matter, because the goal of the library in that use-case is to remove complications from the process and guide your focus back to areas of a project that are much more high impact.

This is a great use of libraries, getting out of the way and letting you more effectively accomplish the goals for the project, which will help create a better outcome in the same amount of time.

Creating Shortcuts

Creating shortcuts to code is, at its core, what libraries do. It is important to remember this because some of the shortcuts, although extremely helpful, can actually hurt in the long run. There's no question that libraries make coding easier. If they made it more difficult, I can guarantee that not only would no one use them, but this book would be a chapter shorter. Easier is not always better, but it *is* easier, and that's why learning JavaScript before learning a JavaScript library is so important. I realize that seems like a "no kidding" kind of statement, but you would be surprised at the amount of people who learn a particular library before getting into the native language.

Knowing JavaScript and how a library creates its shortcuts to "easier" functions and methods will help you selectively use a library without flooding your application with unnecessary coding shortcuts.

This brings up the interesting debate over why you would even use a library that creates unnecessary shortcuts in the code. As I mentioned, all libraries have their ups and downs. You're not always going to utilize all the methods available to you in a given library. The benefit lies in that you can choose what you want to use on a project from the library, use the same library on another project, and choose a completely different set of features to utilize. It's a way to keep your coding sanity.

I still remember the day I was using a popular JavaScript library and realized that every method I was using was just a shortcut to another method that is native to JavaScript. The difference was that someone with a vastly better understanding of JavaScript architecture wrote it. After I realized that, I began writing much more efficient code, sprinkling in the library shortcuts where they were applicable, but more important, I started to realize where I didn't need the help of a library and where the code I was writing could be more efficient than that written in the library.

I cannot stress this fact enough—when you're coding with whichever library you choose, be sure to keep telling yourself that it's all still JavaScript. Even if it looks a little different from what you are used to, you can still use the code you feel will be the best for an individual situation. Just because you're using a library doesn't mean it is the best solution for 100% of the code you write. Later on in this chapter we will go over some specific library examples and how they map back to what you've already learned in previous chapters. We will also discuss when library code is less or more efficient/extensible than what you may be writing for yourself.

Fixing Browser Issues

What is the worst part of any front-end developer's job? If you ask 100 front-end coders (HTML, CSS, JavaScript people) 99 of them will tell you that what they hate the most is testing and fixing code that breaks across different browsers and platforms. Unless you're that one person who gets fired up about something else, this is where you will really love working with a JavaScript library.

A few years ago, there was a development in the CSS world that was called the "CSS Reset." The man himself, Eric Meyer, came out with the idea of fixing all the browser inconsistencies by resetting margin, padding, sizing, positioning, and border values to a baseline starting point in an attempt to cut down on the cross-browser problems, testing headaches, and hacks we all dealt with on a day-to-day basis. It worked amazingly well. We all loved the CSS reset, other than a few folks (but you'll get that with everything). It saved everyone a lot of time and frustration. We still had to cross-browser test, but using a reset made the experience much more bearable. JavaScript libraries do something similar.

Libraries *will* solve your cross-browser JavaScript problems. There were a few specific examples in previous chapters where we had to do support checks before moving forward with our code. The checks in question were general support checking, like the XMLHttpRequest and addEventListener, but were targeted to browsers. Although the methodology of checking for support rather than checking for a specific browser still applies to this model, we're really checking because they don't work in older versions of Internet Explorer; so when you do your browser testing, everything will work. What libraries do is create method shortcuts to things like a support check for the XMLHttpRequest and methods like addEventListener and return the correctly supported method—all behind the scenes. You rarely have to engage in JavaScript browser testing when using a library because they are all (generally) extremely well tested before being released to the public through various rounds of quality assurance.

No one likes browser testing, so this is another great use for a library. Knowing JavaScript and learning a library in great detail will help you indentify the spots in JavaScript where you know there will be browser issues and use the cross-browser-tested methods written in the library in appropriate situations. It will also allow you to identify places in the library where there are no cross-browser issues in the native JavaScript version of a method, so you can avoid any unnecessary overhead.

As browsers get more advanced and modern JavaScript methods become globally supported while old browsers slowly die off, the need for some of these library functionalities will fade away. That day may be on the horizon, but the horizon is still pretty far away. If the only function of a library was to save you from dealing with cross-browser support and building JavaScript fallbacks into your code for better support, I would still say they're worth using. Fortunately, they do a lot more than that.

Popular Libraries

As you go about the JavaScript development life, you will probably be choosing a go-to library (if you haven't gotten one already). There are currently an overwhelming amount of libraries to choose from and truth be told, most people choose by popularity. Picking the most popular library probably isn't the greatest way to go about things, but there is certainly something to be said as to why a particular library is the most popular. It may actually be the best overall; it may have the best documentation, a really strong community, or it may have just been the first to market.

When you're choosing a library, you should take into account everything that you commonly do on a project. Because you're probably not going to switch libraries on every project (that would be silly), you should do your best to make an informed decision based on the set of criteria you define for yourself. And there is nothing wrong with picking a few, using them on different projects, and picking the one that feels the most right for the way you like to code. When it comes down to it, you can read all the documentation, articles, books, and reviews you want about something, but until you use it in a real-life situation it is very hard to tell how something will work with your personal preferences and style.

However, you have to start somewhere. There are so many libraries out there and so many factors to take into account that it is hard to filter out which are at the top of their games, which are on the rise, and which are quickly falling into obscurity.

With any open source project (libraries included), documentation and community is often a critical component. Picking the most popular option will usually yield the best results if that is your only criteria. Some JavaScript helpers categorize themselves as libraries, some are referred to as toolkits, and others stick to the term framework pretty tightly.

Some subtle differences exist between the three terms, but they all accomplish the same goal of making JavaScript easier to use. Libraries and toolkits are the most common, because they are seen as a giant ball of (well-organized) functions and methods for you to reuse. Libraries generally come in the form of a single file you attach to your HTML document. Some toolkits come in the form of a few separate files that are conditionally included into the document. Frameworks are the only term that doesn't quite fit the bill when held up to libraries and toolkits. Frameworks are much more than simple libraries; they can *contain* libraries (like one that we will go over) but they speak to an overall structural change in the way you code JavaScript, offering many more tools. The outcome of a framework is usually that you will be using a very distinct coding style, whereas a library would be freer to be used however you would like, with little structural constraint imposed on the coder. Let's start off by looking into a popular framework, YUI.

YUI

YUI is a free and open source JavaScript and CSS framework whose goal is to create rich interactive Web applications. It is a fully featured and lightweight framework built with modularity in mind. It was built, and is supported by, the front-end engineers at Yahoo!. If you're looking for a well-documented framework or library, you can safely stop your search at YUI. The documentation of YUI is among the best in the industry. It also has a strong user community surrounding it. It also doesn't hurt to be backed by one of the most popular companies on the Web.

YUI differs from other libraries in that it is modular in nature, which allows it to contain the same amount of features as every other library but perform much better because you load only the parts you need. This allows it to be very scalable for large Web applications.

Some of the features in YUI include utilities for

- Event binding
- Traveling through the DOM
- Cache
- Data Storage
- Ajax

YUI has too many features to effectively list here, but you can find an extensive list of all the features, widgets, and tools at yuilibrary.com, along with all documentation and community forum activity. Something to note about the widget list in YUI is that there is an active widget targeting an autocomplete functionality for a search form. This is a perfect example of where using a library would have saved us some time. If we had used something like YUI to build out the autocomplete search form, all that functionality, including the Ajax, would have been built for us already. Of course, nothing would have been learned, but those are the types of common JavaScript actions that you will find in libraries and frameworks. They are built for the sole purpose of saving you time in your development process.

YUI as a whole is called a framework because it contains the YUI JavaScript Library, the YUI CSS Library, and other tools such as the YUI Online Code Compressor, which will safely minify your code for you. All these tools inside the framework can be used independently, but they fit very well together and are intended to be used as a single unit (aka, framework). The YUI CSS Library contains styles, which map directly to classes that are added to the DOM when you use the various widgets available in the framework (like autocomplete). Pairing up the CSS and JavaScript like that helps keep clean styling of elements by default to prevent the perception that there may be a problem if a widget looks a little off when loaded without the accompanying CSS file.

All the information, data, and documentation on the YUI Framework is located on yuilibrary. com (deceptive URL, I know, it's a framework). Many beginners find YUI to be a little overwhelming with its modular nature. It works very well when building large-scale Web applications. Yahoo! Mail was written using YUI; the library's modular nature makes it very easy to scale while keeping performance at the forefront. However, if you need something a little more lighthearted for a smaller application or site, it's probably worth taking a look at the elephant in the room: **jQuery**.

jQuery

At the time of this writing, jQuery is, by a large margin, the most popular JavaScript library available being used on more than 50% of all the top websites. It was written by John Resig and released in 2006. It is currently being actively maintained by a small team of developers. jQuery, like YUI and most other JavaScript libraries, is open source and free to the public.

jQuery is a library in the true sense of the word. It's a collection of predefined functions and methods loaded into your documents through an external script for you to access and use as you see fit. jQuery is a very large library and as I mentioned previously in this chapter, you're probably not going to use the entire thing (nor should you). What jQuery does best is make things easy. That probably feels redundant because the goal of any library is to make things easy, but jQuery does an especially good job of that.

Due to its ease of use, jQuery has lowered the barrier of entry for a designer to start coding with JavaScript. The jQuery team has done a great job in lifting the veil off of JavaScript and making the language accessible to anyone who needs to code with it. For better or for worse, it isn't uncommon for a designer to list jQuery as a skill set and omit JavaScript. jQuery is so immensely popular that many people fail to see it as actual JavaScript. But again, don't forget **it's still just JavaScript**.

The jQuery library contains almost everything you would need to build everything from a small marketing site to a robust Web application, and the browser support for features in the library goes all the way back to Internet Explorer 6. There are countless books, articles and blog posts written about every aspect of jQuery, including full API documentation on jquery.com. Because it is the most popular library available right now, the community and support surrounding jQuery is unmatched by any other.

The jQuery library can be downloaded from jquery.com. You can get a production version of the library, which has been minified and compressed (no whitespace), or a development version, which is larger but maintains all the correct whitespace and comments. The development version of jQuery can be a great learning resource; it is well commented and built by some of the best JavaScript minds in the industry. If you're going to learn, you might as well learn from the best, right? For our purposes, we won't be tearing apart any jQuery core functionality, so the production version is probably the best. Figure 10.1 shows you where to download the library from jquery.com.

Figure 10.1   Downloading a production version of jQuery from jquery.com

Clicking Download jQuery will link you directly to the raw JavaScript file. To download it, you can either copy the code directly from the browser and paste it into a `jquery.js` file, or you can save it from the browser. This is an odd point of confusion for a first-time downloader because the Download button doesn't actually download anything. After you have the file downloaded, we'll add it into a similar file structure like the one we've been using to this point. Figure 10.2 shows a basic file structure with an `index.html` file and a `js` directory with two JavaScript files: `jquery.js` and `script.js`. `jquery.js` is the library, and `script.js` is any custom JavaScript we want to write; this is the same process as before, the only difference this time is that we also have jQuery in the directory structure.

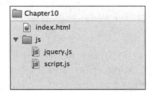

Figure 10.2   A snapshot of the current directory structure

After downloading jQuery, the next step is to attach it to the document. We can't use a library that we're not including in the HTML document. Just like how we have been including `script.js` into our HTML documents, we need to include `jquery.js`. Listing 10.1 opens up the index.html file in Figure 10.2, showing a skeleton HTML file with both JavaScript files linked up.

Listing 10.1   **Skeleton HTML Document Linking Both JavaScript Files**

```
<!doctype html>
<html lang="en">
<head>
        <title>Chapter 10</title>
        <meta charset="utf-8">
</head>
<body>

<!--js-->
<script src="js/jquery.js"></script>
<script src="js/script.js"></script>

</body>
</html>
```

It is important to remember that the order of the files in this context matters quite a bit. Because jQuery contains method we want to use, and the document renders from top to bottom, you need to be sure that the library is fully loaded before any script we custom write is utilized in any of jQuery's methods.

In the next section we dive into the actual code of jQuery. We talk about the new syntax you encounter and what exactly is going on with it. We step through many of the topics covered in previous chapters of this book, along with some code samples, so you can see the physical difference between the way native JavaScript looks and how JavaScript powered by jQuery looks.

jQuery Basics

The popularity of anything is usually related to its barrier to entry. This concept is particularly true in the case of jQuery. It's one of those things like playing bass guitar; it's easy to play but tough to master. jQuery echoes this sentiment in many ways, from its revolutionary selector engine, to the natural implementation of Ajax, to its plethora of predefined methods and functions collected with thoughtful care focused around the goal of helping you do more while writing less.

This style of development has opened jQuery up to an audience of designers who would have otherwise feared an entry deep into JavaScript. In this section, you are introduced to the basics of jQuery by circling back to elements of JavaScript you've already learned throughout the course of this book. By mapping the methods in jQuery to methods in native JavaScript, you see exactly what pieces of the library to use and which methods you may want to do without.

To effectively depict the basics of jQuery, we'll need an HTML document to root around in. Listing 10.2 shows a basic HTML structure of a container div and three other divs classed with module. There is also some basic CSS embedded into the <head> of the document to create a standard three-column layout.

Listing 10.2   **Sample HTML to Show jQuery's Functionality**

```
<!doctype html>
<html lang="en">
<head>
        <title>Chapter 10</title>
        <meta charset="utf-8">

    <style>
        #container {
            overflow: hidden;
        }

        .module {
            width:33%;
            float: left;
```

```
            background: #eee;
        }
    </style>

</head>
<body>

<button type="button">Don't click the button</button>

<div id="container">

    <div class="module">
        <p>Hello module one!</p>
    </div><!--/.module-->

    <div class="module">
        <p>Hello module two!</p>
    </div><!--/.module-->

    <div class="module">
        <p>Hello module three!</p>
    </div><!--/.module-->

</div><!--/#container-->

<!--js-->
<script src="js/jquery.js"></script>
<script src="js/script.js"></script>

</body>
</html>
```

At the bottom of the document, in bold in Listing 10.2, you can see that we are linking up to the jQuery source (`jquery.js`) that we downloaded from jquery.com, followed by `script.js`, which is where we will put our custom jQuery-based code.

document.ready

At the heart of the jQuery library, and its claims to fame, is the `ready()` method. The `ready()` method is bound to the `document` and takes a single argument, which is the entirety of the JavaScript you're attaching to the HTML document. It is a listener-type method, which will hold off execution of any script contained within it until the entire DOM is loaded.

Previous to this chapter, we went over the `load` event to execute script when the entire DOM is loaded. The `load` event will hold off on execution until every asset, including images, has been successfully received. Waiting until images are received can take longer than you might prefer to wait, and this is where jQuery's `ready()` method differs from the native `load` event. The `ready()` method will not wait for all images to be received before executing code. Instead, it waits only until the DOM is constructed, which provides a smoother experience.

This behavior simulates including a script reference at the bottom of the document, which we have been doing for the entire course of this book. It's not technically needed in our case, but the `ready()` method is a central topic in jQuery, so for the purposes of this section, we will be wrapping all executed code with it.

Listing 10.2.1 shows jQuery's `ready()` method and how you would attach it to the document.

Listing 10.2.1   jQuery's `document.ready` Method

```
$(document).ready(function () {

    // jquery goes here

}); // close document.ready
```

You probably noticed in Listing 10.2.1 that we're not using a normal method of attaching a method to the `document` the way we would do with something like `document.getElementById()`. There's a dollar sign ($) and parentheses surrounding the `document` declaration. This is your first introduction to a jQuery selector. By wrapping `document` with `$()`, we are saying, "Hey, I want to use a jQuery method on this element." This is the pattern you will consistently be using in jQuery. You will be very familiar with the selector engine as you dive deeper and deeper into the library.

Selectors

A large barrier of entry for the design community with JavaScript was the nonintuitive way you have to attach methods to elements in the DOM. jQuery solved this with the *Sizzle* selector engine, which allows you to use CSS syntax to select elements in the DOM. *Sizzle* was added shortly after the initial release of jQuery and exploded in the Web design world when designers finally understood how to create simple cross-browser compatible commands in JavaScript without soliciting help from a developer.

As mentioned previously, the jQuery selector syntax centers around the dollar sign ($). The dollar sign is used to signify jQuery code and activate the selector engine. Wrapping `$()` around any CSS selector will select that element (or group of elements).

Listing 10.2.2 shows three ways to get an element by its ID value. The first two should look familiar, because we have covered them earlier in this book; they are native to JavaScript. The third item is how you would accomplish the same thing using jQuery. jQuery has shortcuts to almost everything, and this is the first stop: jQuery's way to select an element by ID.

Listing 10.2.2   **Selecting an Element by ID**

```
// native JavaScript version
var container = document.getElementById("container");

// native JavaScript - newer version
var container = document.querySelector("#container");

// jQuery version
var container = $("#container");
```

Because these methods are shortcuts to the native methods in JavaScript, they will give you the performance boost of using native JavaScript. This is a concept you need to be conscious of when using a library. Libraries are best when used to minimize the work you would have to do in creating cross-browser code that is flexible and extensible. Listing 10.2.3 is an example of where you would want to use a library. Because the functionality of getting an element by its class name is not well supported in native JavaScript, using jQuery for it assures that you won't have to write complicated code to make this feature work the way you want it to.

Listing 10.2.3   **Selecting an Element by Class Name**

```
// native JavaScript version
var module = document.getElementsByClassName("module");

// native JavaScript - newer version
var module = document.querySelector(".module");

// native JavaScript - newer version, return array
var module = document.querySelectorAll(".module");

// jQuery version
var module = $(".module");
```

Although it may not seem like it, jQuery goes through a series of checks when using something like the example in Listing 10.2.3. You see only the nice clean version of the selector $(".module"), but behind the scenes the library is running through feature detection checks against the browser you're using to see which native method it should use for the highest efficiency possible.

It first checks querySelectorAll, then getElementsByClassName, and then if all else fails, it will use a custom-written function to return the element or elements requested by class name. These are the same steps you would have taken if you were to write this code yourself, so using a library in this way saves you valuable development and browser testing time.

Traveling Through the DOM

Using the HTML example from Listing 10.2, we will begin to travel around the DOM, like we did in Chapter 4, "Accessing the DOM," but this time we'll use the jQuery library shortcuts.

All the functionality of moving up, down, and side to side in the document object model you have already done has also been rebuilt within jQuery. You may remember that when using native JavaScript, you can run into problems with whitespace in your code, causing false returns as you travel around the document. This isn't a problem in jQuery, which is another benefit of using a library (it takes care of many common problems).

In Listing 10.2.4, you will find four methods of traveling around the DOM:

- parent()— Get the immediate parent node.
- parents()— Look through all parent nodes until you find a selector match (can travel multiple levels).
- find()— Travel down the DOM until you find a match (can travel multiple levels).
- siblings()— Get sibling elements that match the selector.

You may notice the addClass() method, as well; this will (you guessed it) add a class to the selected element. This is in place so you will be able to tell that the elements are indeed being selected if you were to view the **generated** source code. addClass() takes a single parameter, which is the class to be appended to the element.

Listing 10.2.4   **Traveling Through the DOM with jQuery**

```
// travels up one level
$(".module").parent().addClass('module-parent');

// travels up multiple levels
$("p").parents("#container").addClass('p-parents');

// travels down
$("#container").find(".module").addClass('container-find');

// travels sideways
$(".module").siblings(".module").addClass('module-siblings');
```

Just as in native JavaScript, jQuery contains shortcut methods for more fine-grained travel through the DOM. There are shortcuts to jump to the first item in an array of DOM nodes, to the last item, and ways to move either one node up or down with the next() and prev() methods.

Listing 10.2.5 shows how to use these shortcut methods to jump into and travel around the DOM. In this example we are again using the addClass() method to show in the generated source code where the elements are being targeted. These are very common methods to use in jQuery, but it is important to remember that they are just more readable shortcuts to native JavaScript methods.

Listing 10.2.5   **First, Last, Next, and Previous DOM Nodes**

```
// get first module
$(".module").first().addClass('first-module');

// get next module
$(".module").first().next().addClass('second-module');

// get last module
$(".module").last().addClass('last-module');

// get previous module
$(".module").last().prev().addClass('second-to-last-module');
```

Adding Style Information

Generally speaking, adding style information to the DOM through JavaScript is not a good idea. If you can accomplish the same task by adding a class to an element and using CSS from there, you should—it not only performs better but also keeps all styling information in the presentation layer where it belongs.

There will be times, however, when you need to apply dynamic styling to an element with JavaScript—for instance, a positioning value that needs to react to a moving cursor (a drag-and-drop interface). jQuery makes adding style information to a DOM node very easy with the css() method. This method takes a single argument, which is an object containing all the CSS you want to apply to an element.

In Listing 10.2.6 you can see that we are adding a height of 300px and a font color of red to all the div elements with a class of module. Just about any CSS property can be added to a DOM node with this method. The syntax is important to note for when we go over JavaScript animation (awesome, right?).

Listing 10.2.6   **Adding Style Information with jQuery**

```
// set the height of all nodes that have a class of module to 300px
$('.module').css({
    'height': '300px',
    'color': 'red'
});
```

Binding Events

Binding an event in jQuery isn't much different from binding an element with native JavaScript. There are methods in jQuery that map to each type of event in JavaScript, including `click`, `mouseover`, `mouseout`, `submit`, `change`, `blur`, `focus`, `keyup`, `keydown`, and any other event you can think of. There are also shortcut events to common actions like `hover()` and `toggle()`, which are very convenient. Rather than using both `mouseover` and `mouseout`, two separate events, you can bind to `hover()` and create the same effect. This is an example of a library saving you some time. Like jQuery's motto: Write less, do more.

Each event in jQuery can be passed a callback function, which contains the action you want to accomplish, just like a normal event binding. With jQuery's syntax, you do not need to be concerned about the browser support of an event listener versus an event handler; it will take care of that for you.

In Listing 10.2.7 you will find the jQuery you need to attach a `click` event to the button from Listing 10.2. This action should result in an alert window that reads "you got me!" All event bindings in jQuery use this syntax, so you can substitute `click` with any event you choose, like `focus` or `blur`.

Listing 10.2.7   **Binding a `click` Event with jQuery**

```
// bind a click event to the only button element in the document
$('button').click( function () {

    // anonymous function that shows an alert
    alert('you got me!');

}); // close click anonymous callback function
```

Animation

The capability to combine events and the `css()` method syntax to create JavaScript animations is one of the most popular features in jQuery. For this, the library exposes an `animate()` method that contains CSS properties you want to animate to.

The `animate()` method takes three arguments. The first is the CSS properties to animate, like you used with the `css()` method. The second argument is the duration of the animation in milliseconds. The third (optional) argument is a callback function you want to execute when the animation is finished.

In Listing 10.2.8 you can see that we are still binding a click event to the `button` element, but instead of showing a JavaScript `alert()` we are animating the height of each `.module` from wherever it is (it's at `300px`) to `0px`. This animation should take `500` milliseconds. After the animation is complete, the third argument will activate and the button text will change to "now what, smart guy?" This is how you animate in jQuery. The animations can get pretty complex, but this is always at its core. When you animate the DOM node, you are dynamically updating CSS properties.

Listing 10.2.8   **Simple jQuery Animation**

```
// bind a click event to the only button on the page
$('button').click(function () {

    // animate all the heights of each module to 0
    $('.module').animate({
        'height': '0px'
    }, 500, function () {

        // after the animation is complete, change the button text
        $('button').text('now what, smart guy?');

    }); // close animate anonymous callback function

}); // close click anonymous callback function
```

jQuery Nonbasics

All the basic stuff in jQuery is great. The selector engine and DOM shortcuts combined with ease of animation in the library makes it a powerful script right out of the gate. Other than animation, the basic stuff is just that, basic. You already knew how to accomplish all those tasks in native JavaScript, so the benefit of learning the jQuery versions of them is more for your convenience if you choose to move ahead with the library.

The big savings of jQuery (or any library for that matter) are what I call the nonbasics. They're not quite "advanced" topics, but they are far beyond the basics of the library and are where the real benefits of loading that oversized JavaScript library into your application begin to pay off.

There are three major areas in jQuery where the library really steps up to the plate: Ajax, loops, and a concept called **chaining functions**. To properly address these issues, we will be taking a step back into the JavaScript file we have been working with for the autocomplete search form. We will be replacing the custom Ajax function we made with a jQuery version and combining that with the jQuery loop syntax to create the same effect of autocomplete searching, but by using a library.

Using Ajax in jQuery

Remember all those `loops` and `if` statements we had to write when creating the Ajax call from the autocomplete search form? You may be upset when you find out how easy it is to make Ajax requests with jQuery. Ajax is one of those things that many people consider the saving grace of a library because of all the cross-browser problems and checking that needs to happen behind the scenes to create a successful-Ajax call.

The Ajax call we wrote in previous chapters was pretty specific to our purposes. We needed an Ajax call, which returns a JSON object that will be parsed. Although that is an extremely common case, the ajax() object in jQuery offers up an extremely flexible API where you can easily set configurations for your call, whether it's a GET or POST, using JSON, HTML, XML or script. It also offers straightforward options for accepting callbacks in the case of a successful call or a failed call.

In Listing 10.3, you can see the basic setup structure for an Ajax call, which uses the jQuery method. This specific call will retrieve the contacts.json file, return it, and output the contents in the JavaScript console. You could also parse this data directly with a basic for loop.

Listing 10.3   **Basic Ajax Call with jQuery**

```
$(document).ready(function () {

    $.ajax({
        type: 'GET', // set request type GET or POST
        url: 'data/contacts.json', // data URL
        dataType: 'json', // type: xml, json, script, or html
        success: function(data) {

            // if the call is a success do this
            console.log(data.addressBook);

        },
        error: function () {

            // if the call fails do this
            alert('an ajax error occurred');

        }
    }); // end Ajax call

}); // close document.ready
```

getJSON

The ajax() method by itself is very flexible, but because our application is using JSON, we can utilize an Ajax method built into the jQuery library that was specifically created to properly parse JSON data. This method is called getJSON() and it is a shortcut to the normal ajax() method.

getJSON() takes two arguments. The first is a URL to the JSON data, and the second is the function you want to execute upon a successful data return. In Listing 10.3.1 you can see that we are passing the data URL into the getJSON() method and using an anonymous callback function to save the data to a variable and check the length of its contents. This probably looks familiar because it's what we do right before every single loop we have gone over up to this point in the book.

Listing 10.3.1   **Ajax Call with jQuery Targeting Toward JSON Data**

```
$(document).ready(function () {

    // start Ajax call
    $.getJSON('data/contacts.json', function (data) {

        var addrBook = data.addressBook,
            count = addrBook.length;

        // clear the target area just in case there's something in it.
        $('#output').empty();

        // check the count, of course
        if (count > 0) {

            console.log(addrBook);

        } // end count check

    }); // end ajax call

}); // close document.ready
```

> **Note**
>
> jQuery contains shortcuts to other jQuery methods, which are eventually mapped to native JavaScript methods. getJSON() is an example of this. It is important to remember that passing from one shortcut to another has performance implications. Wherever possible, you should use the shortest path possible.

Looping Through Data in jQuery

Now that we have set up our Ajax request with the getJSON() method, the next step is to loop through and output the data that is returned with the jQuery each() method.

This method is among the most popular because it's very human-readable and makes sense. The each() method says, "for each of these things, do something," which is the same thing a normal for() loop says, but in jQuery you don't have to worry about that mashup of weird variables being passed as arguments into the native for() loop. It's very straightforward and easy to use, which is why people like it.

This method takes two arguments. The first is the data you are looping through (the JSON object in this case), and the second is the function you want to execute on each item. The callback function also requires two arguments, similar to that of a normal for() loop.

Listing 10.3.2 takes our Ajax call to the next step by creating the output and looping through the JSON object that was returned. This is the same process we have been using, but with jQuery syntax instead.

Listing 10.3.2   **JSON Data Ajax Call with a Loop Through the Response**

```
$(document).ready( function () {

    // start Ajax call
    $.getJSON('data/contacts.json', function (data) {

        var addrBook = data.addressBook,
            count = addrBook.length;

        // clear the target area just in case there's something in it.
        $('#output').empty();

        // check the count, of course
        if (count > 0) {

            // loop through the contacts
            $.each(addrBook, function (i, obj) {

                $('#output').append('<p>' + obj.name + ', <a href="mailto:' +
    ➥obj.email + '">'+ obj.email +'</a><p>');

            }); // end each

        } // end count check

    }); // end ajax call

}); // close document.ready
```

It is worth noting at this point that the each() method in jQuery is among the worst performing methods in the library. It's a function (the loop), which calls a callback function (the output) on top of being a shortcut back to the original native JavaScript loop. This is very far for a process to travel, especially when you could use a normal native loop instead.

This is one of the performance bottlenecks that can happen when using a library. It is important to be aware of situations like this so you can identify where it is appropriate to use the library methods and when you might be better off using native JavaScript. Because there aren't any support issues with normal loops in JavaScript, there is little reason to use the jQuery each() method.

Chaining Functions

Function chaining in jQuery is, again, one of the more attractive features in the library. It allows you to add an endless amount of methods to a single DOM node without repeating the declaration over and over. To an extent you have already been exposed to this concept in Listings 10.2.4 and 10.2.5. Using the parents() method in conjunction with addClass() is called **chaining functions**. There are very few restrictions for chaining methods. Just about anything can be chained.

The ajax() method exposes a few extra API methods to check the status of an Ajax call. They are error(), success(), and complete(). In Listing 10.3.1 there was no error checking in the getJSON() method. Luckily, these extra Ajax status methods can be chained to the end of the getJSON() method to help us execute functions that check status and conditionally fire off logic.

Listing 10.3.3 shows how you would go about chaining these methods to the getJSON() method and alert the status of your Ajax call.

Listing 10.3.3 **Chaining Functions with Ajax Methods**

```
$(document).ready(function () {

    // start Ajax call
    $.getJSON('data/contacts.json', function (data) {

        var addrBook = data.addressBook,
            count = addrBook.length;

        // clear the target area just in case there's something in it.
        $('#output').empty();

        // check the count, of course
        if (count > 0) {

            // loop through the contacts
            $.each(addrBook, function (i, obj) {

                $('#output').append('<p>' + obj.name + ', <a href="mailto:' +
➥obj.email + '">'+ obj.email +'</a><p>').hide().fadeIn();
```

```
        }); // end each

    } // end count check

}).error(function () {

    // if there was an error during the ajax call
    alert('there was an ajax error');

}).complete(function () {

    // if the ajax call completed (whether it was successful or not)
    alert('your ajax call was completed');

}).success(function(){

    // if the ajax call was a success
    alert('your ajax call was a success');

}); // end ajax call

}); // close document.ready
```

Using chaining not only can save you valuable whitespace in your code but also keep your logic in the correct execution order by forcing you to think about when each method is to be executed.

Extending Libraries Through Plug-ins

A plug-in is a built-in way to extend the functionality of a library. As mentioned earlier, no library will meet 100% of your needs; you will inevitably have to extend what it does for your own personal use. Often you will find yourself using the same library functionality numerous times. When this occurs in the normal flow of native JavaScript development, you would probably pull that functionality out into an object or function that you can reuse whenever the situation arises again.

When you create that function, you also want to make it as easy as possible for others to use it. There are certain things in a library that are in place so you can extend the functionality while still using the library. These are called **plug-ins**. Often these plug-ins are released to the open source community, which is why it's so important that they are closely tied to the library you are writing them for.

In this section we will be starting with a normal function and converting it into a jQuery function to see the actual difference between the two methods of reusing code.

Building a Plug-in

Many times the first step to creating a plug-in is writing it as a normal JavaScript function and later discovering that it might be helpful to others or yourself as a plug-in. Converting a function into a jQuery plug-in is pretty straightforward, but let's start off with the plug-in itself.

Suppose you find yourself in a situation where you are creating a lot of HTML data tables that need to have a zebra striping effect, where every other table row needs to have a background color of light gray.

Listing 10.4 shows a function called `zebraStripe()` that takes two arguments, one is the wrapping element (probably a table) and the other is the element you want to add the striping effect to (probably the table row). The function then takes the arguments, finds only the odd rows, and sets the background color to #ccc (light gray).

Listing 10.4   **Zebra Striping Function**

```
// define your zebra striping function
function zebraStripe(wrapper, elToStripe){

    $(wrapper).find(elToStripe + ':odd').css({
        'background': '#ccc'
    });

}


// wait for the document to be loaded
$(document).ready( function () {

    var output = $('table),
        tr = output.find('tr');

    // call the function with 2 required arguments
    zerbraStripe(output, tr);

}); // close document.ready
```

Calling the function in Listing 10.4 is like calling any function in JavaScript and passing it the two required arguments. This function will work perfectly fine with jQuery, but the syntax is not quite there yet. When calling the function, we are not using the normal jQuery selector syntax to attach it to a DOM node. This is where we want to convert the normal JavaScript function into a jQuery plug-in.

There is a distinct template for creating a plug-in for jQuery, which includes the plug-in name, default options, options that the user can overwrite, a loop, and the actual striping code from the `zebraStripe()` function. Listing 10.4.1 shows the `zebraStripe()` function converted to a jQuery plug-in.

Listing 10.4.1   **Zebra Striping jQuery Plug-in**

```
// enclose the plug-in so no variables leak out
(function($){

    // define and name the plug-in
    $.fn.zebraStripe = function(options) {

        // define default options
        var defaults = {
            elToStripe: "tr"
        };

        // let options be customized by the user
        var options = $.extend(defaults, options);

        // loop through each element you're attaching the plug-in to
        return this.each(function() {

            // use the attached element and option value
            $(this).find(options.elToStripe + ':odd').css({
                'background': '#ccc'
            });
        }); // end loop
    };

})(jQuery);


$(document).ready( function () {

    // attached zebra strip plug-in to the #output div
    $('#output').zebraStripe({
        elToStripe: "tr" // if you want to change the option (we didn't)
    });

}); // close document.ready
```

You can see that the difference between the normal function and the jQuery plug-in is how they are called. The plug-in is utilizing the jQuery selector engine, which feels more natural when working with the library. The second argument in the first function is now an option inside the function. This pattern probably looks familiar from the JSON object and also the jQuery `css()`, `animate()`, and `ajax()` methods.

Writing your jQuery code in the form of a plug-in won't always be the answer, but because you will most likely be using plug-ins that others have built, it is nice to know how they are put together, which may give you the skills to contribute back to the vast community associated with whichever library you choose to work with.

The Good of Libraries

As we have said throughout this chapter, all libraries have their good sides and bad sides, even jQuery. It's not so much about poking holes in individual libraries, such as discussing whether YUI is better than jQuery, or whether they're better or worse than other libraries. If you choose to use a library over writing your own custom code from scratch, it's important to know exactly what you're getting into. Before choosing a library, you first have to weigh the good and bad of using a library at all. In this section we're going to try to stay positive and go over some of the better aspects of using a library.

There's a large upside with using a JavaScript library, the biggest advantage is what we have already gone over, where they fix the cross-browser issues inherent to JavaScript that no one wants to have to deal with. Libraries can be extremely helpful in streamlining and helping you keep focus on a project in more efficient areas. In this section we will look over some of the better aspects of choosing to code with a JavaScript library at your side.

Popularity and Community

Some libraries are good because they're popular, some are popular because they're good (more likely), and some are both. I think we can agree that choosing a library only because it's popular is a terrible idea. The library (or any codebase you work with) should be the best tool for the job regardless of how popular it is. Popularity may be a factor in your decision-making process because it usually comes with a strong community and good documentation and support, but it shouldn't be the only factor in your decision.

Having a strong support community around an open source project like a JavaScript library can make your development experience almost pleasurable. Communities for open source projects can create anything from libraries of plug-in functionality to meet up groups, to discussion forums, free online tutorials, and even entire books. There are entire books dedicated to helping you learn JavaScript libraries, so there is certainly something to be said about surrounding yourself with a strong community.

The more popular libraries will also be more widely distributed among websites and applications, increasing the probability that users may already have the library you're using within their browser cache, eliminating the need for them to redownload it from your site. Not having to download the library over and over will help improve the overall performance of an application.

Content Delivery Network

A content delivery network (CDN) is a large, distributed collection of servers that deliver content based on a user's geographical location. You might be asking how exactly this relates to using a JavaScript library. It does and it doesn't. Using CDN to serve up content to users based on where they are is considered to be a best practice in Web development. If content is sent to a user from a geographically closer location, it stands to reason that the content will reach the user faster. This *is* in fact the case and how this relates to using a library is that many (popular) libraries can be centrally hosted through a third-party CDN.

Google is one of the companies that generously collected a large amount of the more popular JavaScript libraries and now centrally host them on its own custom content delivery network, which you can directly link to from your HTML document.

The list of JavaScript libraries hosted by Google includes the following:

- jQuery
- jQuery UI
- Dojo
- MooTools
- Prototype
- Ext Core

If you don't have a CDN of your own to work with, using a central service like this to host your library can significantly improve the performance of your site or application by not only utilizing the geographic loading capabilities of a CDN, but also freeing up an HTTP request from your domain, allowing more assets to be loaded in more quickly.

Listing 10.5 shows a sample HTML snippet depicting how you would link to jQuery hosted on the Google CDN.

Listing 10.5   **Linking to the Google Hosted jQuery**

```
<!-- load jQuery from the Google CDN -->
<script src="http://ajax.googleapis.com/ajax/libs/jquery/1/jquery.min.js"></script>
<script src="js/script.js"></script>

</body>
</html>
```

Just like before, linking to the remote library happens at the bottom of your HTML document.

Efficient Code

It is a general assumption that if someone took the time to assemble and release a public JavaScript library, the individual or team putting it together is very good at writing efficient JavaScript. Using a library that someone else put together will usually make sure that the code and predefined method you are using (using, not writing) were written with efficiency and performance in mind. A lot of performance bottlenecks can exist in JavaScript, and having all of that worked out behind the scenes for you by a team of people who write JavaScript for a living can help your project start off on the right foot.

In using a library, you can generally expect that things like looping, parsing the DOM, and executing flexible Ajax calls will be done in the most efficient way possible. Because library code is open source and free to the public, it is always under heavy scrutiny. It may sometimes be frustrating to the authors, but it usually results in a long list of bugs and feature requests submitted by the public. There is a lot of value in having such a huge audience of Quality Assurance testers constantly poking holes in the codebase. This will either result in the library being dropped (survival of the fittest) or the creation of a really great, strong, and efficient JavaScript library that you can use with confidence.

The best part of this is that if you find a performance hole in a library, you can tackle it in a few different ways:

- Submit a bug report to the author.
- Do nothing and wait for a library version update.
- Ignore that part of the library and use native JavaScript for that part instead.

This circles back to one of the original points of working with libraries—that it's still just JavaScript and you shouldn't feel obligated to use something in a library that you think could be done better.

The Bad of Libraries

Libraries can cause just as much frustration as they shield you from if you let them. Just like everything in life, JavaScript libraries are not 100% good. There are probably just as many reasons to *not* use them as there are *to* use them. In this section we're going to get negative with hopes of appealing to the pessimist in you about libraries. It's important to not only know the good about libraries, but also the bad before you start on your journey.

When libraries are used in a responsible manner, they can do amazing things, but unfortunately, because the barrier to entry for JavaScript has been lowered so much by some libraries, they mask the actual language and can prevent developers and designers from writing efficient front-end code. I say "front-end code" instead of "JavaScript" because while using libraries, many people fall into the trap I've been mentioning: using JavaScript in various places where CSS may be a better option. This issue is often amplified when using a library. There are also a few other downsides to library usage.

Overhead

Libraries are large. You won't be using every feature contained within the library, but in most cases the entire library needs to be included and downloaded if you want to use *any* features in it. This can create a lot of unnecessary overhead in your site or application forcing a user to download, especially when you are trying to performance tune a user experience.

Unfortunately there isn't a whole lot you can do about the overhead caused by using a library. You need to weigh the cost of the extra file size you're having a user download versus the level of interaction you're relying on the library to provide. Most of the time, using the library will win, but you would be surprised to find out how many times a JavaScript library is loaded into a document, and it either isn't being used at all or it is being used in a way that is easily replaced with native JavaScript.

Performance

We've already kind of talked about the performance implications of using a library. There are a couple different levels to be aware of. There is the performance hit you take simply by downloading all the extra code and also the performance problems internal to the library itself within the methods and functions that are made available to you.

I mentioned in the section of this chapter about looping through data with jQuery that it is among the worst performers in the entire library because of the chain reaction it causes as it executes all the required functions in its path back to the original JavaScript method. That is a very common pattern in library usage. It is important to remember that everything in the library is just a reference to a method that is native to JavaScript; therefore, they will never be able to perform better in a browser than if you were to use native scripting. There will always be a link back to the original method, and that distance will always take time to travel.

Keeping that in mind, you will be able to make intelligent decisions about when to use a library method and when it is best to use something native and preserve some performance.

Overreliance and Shelf Life

Overreliance on a library can be a pretty serious problem for a developer or designer. Many times people learn libraries before learning the core language. This goes far beyond the scope of JavaScript; it is a problem in any programming language where there is a jump to learning a framework or library before learning the underlying language. With JavaScript, you see the scenario previously mentioned where a library is loaded into a document to perform an incredibly simple task that could be achieved with far less code. Because of this overreliance on the library, there isn't a way to performance tune an application because there's only so much you can do while staying within the library itself. Because library code is already optimized, you can do very little without breaking out of the library and back into native JavaScript.

Another problem with libraries is their shelf life. Sure, some are very popular and stay around for years, but remember, this is the Web we're talking about. It's a medium that changes almost daily and gets flooded with new technologies to try out. All libraries and frameworks will eventually die off. If you are heavily using a library without ever learning JavaScript, and one day you notice that your favorite library has a shiny new competitor, it's only a matter of time before that library you learned drops in popularity and fades into the background. It happens with everything. Learning the core language of JavaScript will help you be a better, more flexible, front-end coder. It will allow you to use libraries when you want, switch to new ones when others die, and most important, not use them at all. In an industry that moves as fast as the Web does, it's important for you to be flexible in what you can learn.

Using Microlibraries

Each time a major library, toolkit, or framework releases a new version rich with features, there is always an inevitable side-effect of the library growing to a larger file size. This leads to developers and designers constantly questioning whether the load time and overall weight of a library is worth the benefit of using a full-featured library. With the constant need to keep a watchful eye on performance, you can't blame someone for searching for a smaller but more targeted solution to his or her front-end development problems.

In real-life development scenarios, you will probably need only a handful of features from whatever library you choose. Maybe you like using jQuery's selector engine or the way it handles complex features like animation, or you want to take advantage of the advanced Ajax support for various data formats. Whatever it is, there will be a lot of helpful shortcuts in the library, but it would be naive to think that any library will solve all your problems. There will certainly be requirements that are not met and cannot be solved with a prebuilt plug-in that you will have to custom build for each project. That's the nature of the beast. At times you will ask yourself if loading in a large library is the right tool for the job. If you can accomplish your goals with less code, by all means, you should do that.

If you come to point where you're questioning your good old standby library because of its size relative to how much you're utilizing it on a project, you may want to look into using a micro-library. Using a microlibrary will help you directly assemble the pieces you need to complete a project, making sure that there is no code to be wasted. This modular format is very attractive to a lot of developers and designers because there is little waste, and performance can be finely tuned.

With all that in mind, let's take a look at some of the ups and downs (good and bad) in using microlibraries.

The Good

If you were to take a library like jQuery and pull it apart into all its different functions, it would form a bunch of microlibraries. There would be one for DOM parsing, one for Ajax functionality, one for animations, and so on in that fashion until the entire library was broken up into pieces. It's similar to dinner being a project, and if you went grocery shopping every day, you would get only what you need to make dinner and nothing more. It makes that one project very targeted and efficient.

Many microlibraries are highly focused on solving a specific problem. Because of this, little code is wasted and not used. This is the complete opposite of using a catchall library where there will be a lot of code you don't use. Less waste means less code processing, which means better performance and a cleaner experience for your users.

Many think that using a module architecture in JavaScript is the wave of the future because of the way it cuts down the amount of code you need to solve a problem. This very well may be the case if the individual libraries integrate well with other microlibraries.

Another positive aspect of using microlibraries is that they are easier to learn. With something like jQuery, there can be multiple ways to solve even the simplest of problems; the endless number of methods and functions to learn can leave your head spinning and never knowing if a single solution is the best. Because the microlibraries are so focused, they can help you tackle very specific problems in very efficient ways.

The Bad

As with all things in life, there are bad elements and good elements, and microlibraries are no different. Although the microlibraries are usually significantly smaller than their library counterparts, that doesn't necessarily mean the code is more efficient. This is where many people trip up when choosing a path to explore. Microlibraries can be very temping when comparing a 3K-sized file to a 30K-sized file, but it is always important to think about efficiency when dealing with performance and waste. Just because they're smaller doesn't necessarily mean they perform better.

There are a few downsides to using these smaller, more focused libraries. Basically all the reasons for using a major library like jQuery or YUI are the reasons to not use a microlibrary. Documentation is a major problem with microlibraries. Not that it doesn't exist, but you will most likely use 3 to 6 microlibraries on a project, each of which has its own set of documentation and a repository that you will need to be familiar with if you ever run into a snag while writing your code. Having to jump back and forth between documentation sources can really put a damper on your development process.

When building a project using multiple microlibraries, you will need to make sure they all work well together. Some will, and some won't. This is what happens when you piece together things from all over the Web. It applies to anything from CSS to JavaScript to whichever back-end language you choose. Whenever you need to integrate multiple sources into a single source, you will most certainly experience situations that don't go quite as planned. This is one area where using a full-featured library would ease the pain of integrating many features because they all live in the same library and have been thoroughly tested, so they work well in the same environment.

Building with this modular mindset can be a great model to follow with your development process. However, major libraries and frameworks are available that practice the same methodology of using only the code you need. YUI, as briefly mentioned earlier in this chapter, is a great example of an established JavaScript framework, with a team of developers and support and documentation behind it that offers a modular framework that can help you optimize performance. Many of the major libraries are moving over to this modular model, and they are worth exploring before diving into a custom collection of microlibraries that may not offer the proper amount of sustainability and support your project requires.

Summary

In this chapter, we went through everything you need to know about JavaScript libraries, from the mental process you will inevitably go through as you learn more and more about JavaScript all the way to specific syntax examples from jQuery.

Learning when to use a library can be more important than actually using a library. We talked about the purpose of JavaScript libraries and how they help fix frustrations you may encounter as a front-end coder. Libraries help tackle the most common problems in the JavaScript language, such as cross-browser headaches, and complicated functions, such as the animation of DOM nodes and creating rich user experiences with minimal effort.

We also talked about two popular libraries: YUI and jQuery. From there we dove into the jQuery library with its innovative (CSS-based) selector engine. You learned how to add and animate style information, bind events, and travel around the DOM before moving on to some of the less-basic topics in the library, such as Ajax and looping through data.

We again used the autocomplete search form application to illustrate how to apply Ajax methods to the codebase. We then moved on to extending libraries through plug-in development and used a zebra striping function as an example.

We also talked about some of the reasons to consider when making a decision on whether to use a library, balancing them with the reasons you may want to consider in the other direction of shying away from library usage, along with the option to use a combination of microlibraries as a replacement for full-featured libraries.

Exercises

1. What is a JavaScript library?
2. What is a plug-in?
3. What is a content delivery network?

HTML5 JavaScript APIs

This chapter begins our exploration into HTML5 and its accompanying JavaScript APIs. It's not uncommon to hear the term "HTML5" and immediately jump to the typical structure-based mind-set that has been associated with HTML thus far. Certainly no one would blame you for immediately thinking like that, especially now that you have knowledge of progressive enhancement, but a lot of features that shipped with HTML5 are not solely targeted at building an HTML document. A whole slew of JavaScript APIs were built with the intention of tying into the new elements, and even some that live independently from the DOM.

The official W3C specification for HTML5 has gone through so many revisions that it's hard to keep up with which features are in the spec and which have been removed. When a feature gets removed from the specification, it doesn't mean it is no longer a feature; it can be quite the opposite. Although items get removed and dropped, many features get removed because they're too large to be contained inside the same specification as other HTML5 elements. One such example is the Geolocation API we talk about later in this chapter.

Is Geolocation in the current HTML5 specification? No. Was it? Yes. It wasn't removed because we didn't want the feature; it was removed because it needed its own dedicated specification. This has happened quite a bit with other features, as well. Although what is officially HTML5 can change from day to day, the cool features available probably don't. In truth, it's more important to focus on the individual features, such as Geolocation or the History API or audio and video implementation because, although the specification is nice to have as an official document, what we really care about is which browsers have implemented the features and if they're handling them in a consistent manner.

As this chapter progresses, we go over the two most glaring sections of HTML5: the mark-up and the JavaScript APIs. We introduce some of the new structural elements available in the language and some very common accessibility enhancements that have been added into the specification in the form of ARIA roles. It's going to be a wild ride through the world of HTML5, so have a seat, buckle in, and let's get started.

What Is HTML5?

HTML5 is the concept of semantic markup bundled with JavaScript APIs. The term "HTML5" has, over the past few years, ballooned into somewhat of a monster catch-all term that people use when talking about the bucket of new features that have been added to our Web development toolkit. However, very few things added into HTML5 would be considered "new" to the Web community. Yes, the elements are new and the JavaScript APIs hadn't been seen before. But the core concepts haven't changed much. I'll explain.

Arguably, one of the greatest things about HTML5 was the user-centered approach to the design of the fifth version of the language. Wait, user-centered design of code? It sounds weird, but that's exactly what happened. Just about everything in HTML5 already existed in one form or another before the language was formalized. Did we validate form fields? Yes. Could we get someone's geographic location? Yes. Could we play audio and video in the browser? We sure could. What about calendar-style date pickers? Yes, even those existed before HTML5. Most of the main features were around already; we were just creating them as nonstandard objects, whether it's validation on the server or a date picker built with JavaScript.

What happened was that the powers-to-be (the W3C) looked at all the struggles and hacking that was going on in the community and decided to formalize them into the language. Because of the way this model was implemented, just about everything in HTML5 is usable right now. For example, you can implement HTML5 form validation and create a fallback sequence of JavaScript validation, and then server-side validation. Using this model assures that every user will get the best possible experience, even if it's not the exact feature-rich one that you initially intended. If a browser doesn't support a given feature, it will gracefully degrade to a secondary experience. This method can be applied to all the HTML5 features that previously existed in other forms before their formalization.

Not *all* the features existed beforehand, however, and some are even still being added. We go over a few of the JavaScript APIs in this chapter. A few fall into the "we could already do that" category, and others won't. Either way it will be a fun journey discovering the features you can play with as you move forward with JavaScript. Let's get started by getting to know some of the new elements before moving onto the JavaScript APIs.

The Markup (aka HTML)

At first glance, with HTML5, the new elements immediately jump out and command attention. The W3C listened to the community and planned for the future when architecting the abundance of new elements. We have everything from basic structural elements like <header> and <footer> to others like <video> and <audio> that tap into what seems to be a very powerful API that allows us the freedom to create more user-friendly applications while further distancing ourselves from reliance on Flash for saving data and intense animation.

Because the main focus of this book is JavaScript, we won't be spending a lot of time talking about the HTML5 elements, but the topic of HTML5 in general does open the door to discuss the JavaScript APIs that were shipped out with the fifth version of this language. Some of the elements came with JavaScript hooks available in them, which we get into later in this chapter. But for now, let's go over some of the basics of HTML5 in the new elements you're probably already running into.

Creating Better Semantics

The goal of creating more meaningful content wrappers was a central goal of the W3C when the HTML5 specification was being put together. Creating more meaningful layouts means that more standards can be created around them. When compared to meaningless layout elements like the <div> (no offense), you can really see the benefit in replacing it with an <article>, or even a <section>; both have more semantic meaning than a normal <div>.

When you take a look at the new elements, it looks like they're just replacing our common <div> IDs; and in a way, it's true. But they can be used more than once on a single page where they behave more like classes and normal HTML elements that you can use over and over to retain a semantic structure. Whether it's a normal website, a blog post, or a full-featured application, you have the ability to embed more meaning into a document.

Elements like <header> and <footer> are not meant to represent only the top and bottom of the current document. They also represent the <header> and <footer> of each document section, much the way we use <thead> and <tfoot> in data tables.

The benefits of using these structural elements is mainly due to the fact that they are extremely well defined and provide a great way to semantically structure your document. However, these elements do need to be used with some careful thought because they can very easily be overused. Figure 11.1 shows how you might use the new HTML5 elements to lay out a page.

Building More Accessible Content

Some time before the HTML5 specification was released there was an accessibility specification called WAI-ARIA; for short, we call it ARIA now. We went over some of the ARIA attributes in the Ajax chapter, having to do with creating accessible Ajax content. There is much more to using ARIA than the Ajax purposes; you could also flag normal areas of a document to give meaning beyond the semantic elements.

Let's take a look into the <header> element, for example. A <header> is obviously more descriptive than a <div>, but because it can be used multiple times in a single document (an element you can use only once isn't of much use), the meaning could in theory change, depending on the context. At the very top of a document, the <header> may serve as an area reserved for branding information or a banner, whereas another <header> that is inside an <article> or <section> element could very well be acting as a header for that individual section of the document, not the entire document. The same situation could be applied to any element, but you will more likely see it a lot with the <header> and <footer> elements. These elements by themselves are meaningful, but with ARIA attributes, you can add even more meaning.

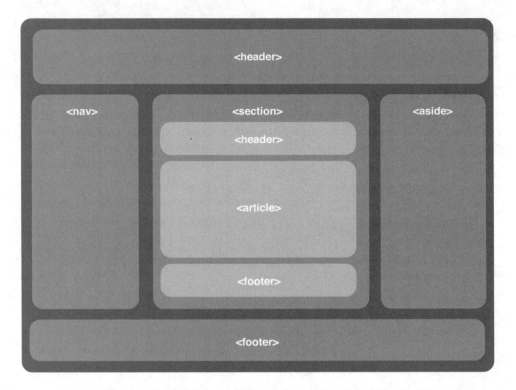

Figure 11.1   Illustration of a page using the new elements

ARIA opens up the role attribute to be applied to elements. A popular type of ARIA role is called the *landmark* role. These roles are meant to represent navigational landmarks in the document. The landmark ARIA roles you will often see include the following:

- application
- banner
- complementary
- contentinfo
- form
- main
- navigation
- search

There are four total categories for ARIA roles. The other three are abstract roles (command, input, range, and so on), widget roles (alertdialog, menu, menuitem, progressbar, and so on), and document structure roles (article, definition, heading, math, and so on). All exist to aid in the accessibility of your HTML document. By describing areas like this you can provide an easier form of navigation to users visiting your site by way of an assistive technology (a screen reader).

Listing 11.1 shows an HTML document marked up with the new HTML5 elements utilizing ARIA landmark roles.

Listing 11.1   **Adding Descriptive Roles to the New HTML5 Elements**

```
<!doctype html>
<html lang="en">
<head>
        <title>Chapter 11</title>
        <meta charset="utf-8">

</head>
<body>

<header role="banner">
   <hgroup>
        <h1>Site title</h1>
        <h2>Site slogan</h2>
   </hgroup>

</header>

<nav role="navigation">
   <ul>
        <li><a href="/">Home</a></li>
        <li><a href="/blog">Blog</a></li>
        <li><a href="/portfolio">Portfolio</a></li>
        <li><a href="/contact">Contact</a></li>
   </ul>
</nav>

<section>
    <article role="main"></article>
    <aside role="complementary"></aside>
</section>

<footer role="contentinfo"></footer>

</body>
</html>
```

The JavaScript APIs

HTML5 isn't just HTML—there are a lot of JavaScript pieces as well. The specification released a lot of JavaScript hooks into the language and a handful of new features, such as the data storage methods we explored earlier, `localStorage()` and `sessionStorage()`, which are both JavaScript APIs in the HTML5 specification.

As we step through some of the JavaScript APIs built into HTML5, there will be some themes you've probably heard of before, like location-based services, media embedding, and server communication. As I mentioned earlier, they're familiar because they predate HTML5. Some of the APIs we'll be exploring are the formalizations of theses concepts.

The navigator Object

The `navigator` object is a root-level object in JavaScript that reports back information about whichever browser a user is visiting with. It's been around for a long time, so the `navigator` object by itself isn't anything revolutionary, but it does return some helpful information:

- Browser name
- Brower version
- Platform
- If cookies are turned on or off
- If Java is enabled
- User agent string

Previous to HTML5, that's the only information the `navigator` object would report back; in the post-HTML5 world, let's take a look at all the data we have now. Listing 11.2 shows a JavaScript console log that is being passed the `navigator` object.

Listing 11.2 **Sending the `navigator` Object to the JavaScript Console for Analysis**

```
console.log(navigator);
```

If you run the code from Listing 11.2 in a browser and open the debug, you will be able to see all the information currently being returned in the `navigator` object. As you will see, it's a lot more than it used to be. Figure 11.2 shows the console log from Firefox 11.

Exploring the `navigator` object is kind of a pro tip for discovering new browser features, because this is where a lot of the new items get added as browser information. As you can see, the Geolocation API lives inside this object, but as you search down the list you see some that you may not recognize, such as `mozBattery` and `mozVibrate`. These are some of the newest features added to the browser, and we will get to explore them in a little more detail when we go over the Device API later in the chapter.

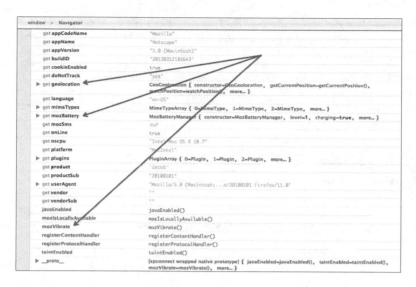

Figure 11.2   Graphic of the `navigator` object console log

Geolocation

For years now, we have had the capability of grabbing a user's IP address, running it through some process on the server, and outputting the user's general location. The concept of Geolocation in itself is not new to the Web; you see ads for local businesses all the time online. The process of parsing an IP address can be accurate enough to locate a user for purposes of serving up ad information, but if you want more specific data, like exact latitude and longitude to alert them of businesses within walking distance, you need something with a more fine-grained output model. This is where Geolocation comes into play.

As you saw in the previous section, Geolocation is part of the `navigator` object in JavaScript. To see all the properties and methods available, you could do another console log but also include the secondary object like: `console.log(navigator.geolocation)`.

One of the most helpful methods available within the Geolocation API is the `getCurrentPosition()` method. This method returns all the information you need to locate a user. The information returned includes

- Latitude and longitude
- Position accuracy, reported in meters
- Altitude
- Altitude accuracy, reported in meters
- Heading
- Speed

Some of the objects won't return most of the time, such as altitude, speed, and heading, unless the target is actually moving or off the ground, but it's nice to know that they're there if you need them.

The most common usage for this API is to get a snapshot of the latitude and longitude of a user. Listing 11.3 shows how to return relevant positioning data from the Geolocation API into the browser. This script will run attached to any HTML document because we are outputting the data into the <body>.

Listing 11.3   **Geolocation Example to Return All the Data Available**

```
// an anonymous function to contain the variables
(function () {

    // define a function to output all the data returned from navigator.geolocation
    function getPositionData(position) {

        var body = document.getElementsByTagName("body")[0];

        body.innerHTML += "<p>Latitude: " + position.coords.latitude + "</p>";
        body.innerHTML += "<p>Longitude: " + position.coords.longitude + "</p>";
        body.innerHTML += "<p>Position accuracy (in meters): " +
➥position.coords.accuracy + "</p>";
        body.innerHTML += "<p>Altitude: " + position.coords.altitude + "</p>";
        body.innerHTML += "<p>Heading: " + position.coords.heading + "</p>";
        body.innerHTML += "<p>Speed: " + position.coords.speed + "</p>";

    } // end success function

    if(navigator.geolocation) {

        // using getCurrentPosition to return positioning data
        navigator.geolocation.getCurrentPosition(getPositionData);

    } else {

        // apologize to the user for teasing them
        alert("sorry, this browser doesn't support the Geolocation API");

    } // end support check

})(); // End anonymous function
```

Geosecurity

A major concern with gathering geodata from a user is security. There are a lot of times a user may not want to let a site report latitude and longitude. Because of this, all supported browsers have implemented a permissions system to deal with geolocation. Most of them come in the form of a pop-up message asking for permission to get the user's current location. After you have permission, you can continue with the data. There is no way to do so without permission from the user.

Gathering location-based information from a user can be a very powerful and interesting thing when used properly, but super annoying when used poorly or in an unethical manner. If you keep the user's needs in mind, you will be sure to use the data in a responsible and useful way.

Audio and Video

Again, embedding audio and video into an HTML document isn't a new concept, but until HTML5 standardized the way to do such a thing, we were reliant on third-party plug-ins like Flash and QuickTime for embedding media. The standardization of this area means that anyone is able to access the content from anywhere and from any device without the previous limitations and security holes that go along with a technology like Flash.

The <audio> and <video> are more than just new elements in the HTML5 specification. They also have JavaScript API hooks included to tie into features such as creating custom audio and video controls. The elements both come with default controls built into the interface and designed by the browser makers. Listing 11.4 shows what a normal HTML5 audio player would look like as HTML. Note the controls attribute; this is how you use the default generated media controls available in the browser.

Listing 11.4   **Normal Audio Element with Standard Attributes**

```
<audio id="player" controls preload="auto" autobuffer>
    <source src="audio/demo.mp3">
    <source src="audio/demo.ogg">
</audio>
```

Notice the two <source> elements inside the <audio> element in Listing 11.4. This shows how you can create fallback support inside the element itself. We have been familiar with browser support of various elements and methods throughout the book, so there is that aspect of rendering this new element, but there is a secondary support consideration when dealing with media files in the browser. The browser has to support both the element and the audio/video file format to play properly.

Stacking multiple <source> elements lets the browser travel down the list and play whichever format it supports. If it supports multiple formats listed, it will take the first one it hits.

If you don't like using the default controls, for whatever reason, the audio and video APIs contain hooks so you can remotely, with JavaScript, create actions like: play, pause, volume up, and volume down. There is no stop option, only pause. To remove the default controls, you just need to remove the controls attribute, but remember to create new controls.

Listing 11.4.1 shows an HTML document with an `<audio>` element with default controls turned off and a set of three buttons, which we will tie the play, pause, and volume actions to.

Listing 11.4.1   **Complete HTML Structure for Creating Custom Audio Controls**

```html
<!doctype html>
<html lang="en">
<head>

    <title>Chapter 11 - Audio and Video</title>
    <meta charset="utf-8">

</head>
<body>

    <audio id="player" preload="auto" autobuffer>
        <source src="audio/demo.mp3">
        <source src="audio/demo.ogg">
    </audio>

    <div id="controls">
        <button type="button" id="play">play/pause</button>
        <button type="button" id="vol-up">volume up</button>
        <button type="button" id="vol-down">volume down</button>
    </div>

<!--js-->
<script src="js/html5.js"></script>

</body>
</html>
```

You already know how to bind a click event to a button, so this is more about getting to know the API. The player will return objects related to its current state that you could check against when dealing with the play/pause button. The methods available are pretty straightforward in `play()` and `pause()` to initiate the actions. There are also similar options to access and manipulate the volume object inside the player.

Listing 11.4.2 shows the JavaScript needed to attach the play, pause, and volume actions to their respective buttons in the HTML of Listing 11.4.1.

Listing 11.4.2   **Creating Custom Controls for Audio or Video Elements**

```javascript
// anonymous function to contain the variables
(function () {

    var player = document.getElementById("player");
```

```javascript
// play or pause the audio file
function playPause() {

    // if the audio is paused, play it
    if (player.paused) {
        player.play();

    // if the audio is playing, pause it
    } else {
        player.pause();
    }
}

// turn down the volume by .1 each time
function volumeDecrease () {

    // check to see if the volume is already all the way down
    if(player.volume > .1) {
        player.volume -= .1;

    } else {
        alert("minimum volume level");
    }
}

// turn up the volume by .1 each time
function volumeIncrease () {

    // check to see if the volume is already all the way up
    if(player.volume <= .9) {
        player.volume += .1;

    } else {
        alert("max volume level, see an ear doctor");
    }
}

// set up your listeners
document.getElementById("play").addEventListener('click', playPause, false);
document.getElementById("vol-up").addEventListener('click', volumeIncrease,
➡false);
document.getElementById("vol-down").addEventListener('click', volumeDecrease,
➡false);

})();
```

The script from Listing 11.4.2 can be a lot to consume, but what we're saying for the play button is: If the song is playing, pause it; and if it's paused, play it. We can do this by checking the available object in the API. The same goes for the volume buttons. Because volume is reported as a value from 0 to 1, you can increment (or decrement) by .1 for each click until you reach the min or max volume levels.

History API

The History API allows you to manipulate the browser's address bar and history contents. This is one of the features in the HTML5 JavaScript APIs that didn't previously exist. There was a clear need for it with the influx of Ajax, so it was created. It is generally used to preserve meaningful URLs while loading in Ajax content. One of the downsides of using Ajax as a main navigation feature in a Web application is that the URLs don't change unless you force them to change. This can make for an uncomfortable user experience where sharing URLs and bookmarking is part of the natural process of interacting in the browser. The history APIs solve this by allowing meaningful (and real) URLs to be pushed into the address bar and maintained in the browser history (both forward and back).

To help illustrate the History API, we will be using the HTML document from Listing 11.5. You will also need to create the referenced documents: cat.html, dog.html, and bird.html. These files are not complete documents, just HTML snippets (a paragraph) that we will pull in with an Ajax call as we step through the example.

Listing 11.5   **HTML Documents to Show the History API**

```
<!doctype html>
<html lang="en">
<head>

    <title>Chapter 11 - History API</title>
    <meta charset="utf-8">

</head>
<body>

    <p>
        <a href="cat.html">Cats</a> |
        <a href="dog.html">Dogs</a> |
        <a href="bird.html">Birds</a>
    </p>

    <div id="output"></div><!--/#output-->
```

```
<!--js-->
<script src="js/html5.js"></script>

</body>
</html>
```

pushState()

The history API opens up a related method called pushState(). The pushState() method extended the history object and takes three arguments. This is the method used to change the address bar URL. The three arguments are data, the page title, and the new URL. Data and page title are information passed to the history object, but you will see the URL change in the address bar.

Something important to note about the pushState() URL argument is that it will push anything you put into it; because there is no browser refresh, the URL does not have to be valid. It is recommended that it be valid, but it's not required.

Listing 11.5.1 shows a basic loop through all the links in our document and a click event being attached to each. This is the first time we have used a loop to apply event listeners to a DOM node, but it is a perfectly valid way to automate the event binding within a document.

Inside the event listener we are storing the href attribute (the URL to be pushed) and the link text (title to be sent) to variables. These variables are then passed into the history.pushState() method. At that point you should see the URL in the address bar change to whatever was in the link that was clicked.

Listing 11.5.1   Example of Implementing the History API

```
// anonymous function to contain the variables
(function(){

    var links = document.getElementsByTagName('a'),
        linkCount = links.length,
        output = document.getElementById("output"),
        i;

    if(linkCount > 0) {

        // loop through all the links on the page
        for (i = 0; i < linkCount; i = i + 1) {

            var obj = links[i];

            // attached a click event to each link
            obj.addEventListener('click', function(e) {
```

```
        e.preventDefault();

        // store the href and text of the link you clicked
        var href = this.getAttribute("href"),
            title = this.innerHTML;

        // push the new URL in to the address bar
        history.pushState(href, title, href);

    }, false);

  } // end loop

} // end counter check

})();
```

> **Note**
>
> The `pushState()` method is not a free-for-all method when pushing URLs into the address bar. There is a domain-based restriction when changing a URL. This guards against cross-site scripting and external URL injection into the browser's history.

Now that we have disabled the clicking of these links and activated the `pushState()` method to change the URL in the address bar, we should probably find a way to load in the contents of the URL that is being pushed. Believe it or not, you already know how to do that. It's a simple Ajax call that is to be executed when a link is clicked.

One slight difference exists in this type of Ajax call versus the Ajax call from previous chapters. In this call we will be requesting HTML content, and in the other we were requesting JSON content. Therefore, we need to make one small change to the `ajaxCall()` function we created. Because HTML doesn't require any extra parsing, you can remove the `JSON.parse()` method that was surrounding the `responseText;`.

Listing 11.5.2 shows the `ajaxCall()` function with `JSON.parse()` removed for your reference. The `getHTTPObject()` function we created will remain the same.

Listing 11.5.2   Slightly Modified Ajax Function from Earlier

```
/* define the Ajax call */

function ajaxCall(dataUrl, outputElement, callback) {

    /* use our function to get the correct Ajax object based on support */
    var request = getHTTPObject();
```

```
        outputElement.innerHTML = "Loading";

    request.onreadystatechange = function() {

        // check to see if the Ajax call went through
        if ( request.readyState === 4 && request.status === 200 ) {

            // save the ajax response to a variable
            var data = request.responseText;

            // make sure the callback is indeed a function before executing it
            if(typeof callback === "function"){

                callback(data);

            } // end check

        } // end ajax status check

    } // end onreadystatechange

    request.open("GET", dataUrl, true);
    request.send(null);

}
```

Using the slightly modified `ajaxCall()` function from Listing 11.5.2, it is easy to add in an asynchronous page loading functionality to the `click` event that has already been created by inserting it right after the `pushState()` method.

Listing 11.5.3 shows the `ajaxCall()` function taking its three normal arguments, just like before: the URL, the output target area, and a callback function. The callback function will output the HTML snippet into the document. When this is combined with the URL change we already made, it creates something that looks like an instant page load with a bookmarkable URL.

Listing 11.5.3   **History API with Ajax**

```
// anonymous function to contain the variables
(function(){

    var links = document.getElementsByTagName('a'),
        linkCount = links.length,
        output = document.getElementById("output"),
        i;

    if(linkCount > 0) {
```

```
        // loop through all the links on the page
        for (i = 0; i < linkCount; i = i + 1) {

            var obj = links[i];

            // attached a click event to each link
            obj.addEventListener('click', function(e) {

                e.preventDefault();

                // store the href and text of the link you clicked
                var href = this.getAttribute("href"),
                    title = this.innerHTML;

                // push the new URL in to the address bar
                history.pushState(href, title, href);

                // make the ajax call to get the HTML snippet in the page
                ajaxCall(href, output, function (data) {
                    output.innerHTML = data;
                });

            }, false);

        } // end loop

    } // end counter check

})();
```

popstate

If you try this example in a browser, you will notice one glaring problem with it: the back and forward buttons don't work as expected. Sure, you can hit them and the URL steps back or forward to what it was, but the content isn't changing. That works because we have been pushing data into the history object with `pushState()`.

Obviously, the back button not working is going to create a weird user experience, so it does need to be fixed. Luckily, the history API gives us a new event called `popstate`. `popstate` listens for the back and forward buttons to be activated. When this happens you can access the data previously stored in the history object (the URL you want) and create another Ajax call to load in the appropriate content.

Listing 11.5.4 shows how you would set up a listener on the `popstate` event, access the data, and execute another Ajax call (you're probably an old pro at Ajax calls by now).

Listing 11.5.4   **Activating the Back Button with the History API**

```
// listen for the popstate event (forward and back buttons)
window.addEventListener("popstate", function(e) {

    // access the history state (the URL that was saved)
    var storedHistoryData = e.state;

    // make the ajax call to get the HTML snippet in the page
    ajaxCall(storedHistoryData, output, function (data) {
        output.innerHTML = data;
    });

}); // end listener event
```

When combining pushState() and popstate with Ajax, you can simulate the normal browsing experience without a single page reload, creating a more seamless user experience.

Web Workers

Web workers are HTML5's attempt at creating a better user experience in an area that to this point has been one of the most brutally hacked spaces on the Web: server communication. That's right: Ajax. Workers are not around to replace Ajax; they exist to supplement the server communication model that is currently in place.

JavaScript is blocking in nature and you know that; it's why we put JavaScript references at the bottom of the DOM and why we execute a single request at a time. Related to how JavaScript blocks communication is that it also runs on a single thread in the browser. Consider a thread like a road, and there is only one road at any given time. When JavaScript is traveling down that road, nothing else can happen. Any other Ajax request going on will be blocked until the original call is sent and returns successfully. The single threading problem in JavaScript has always been around, but only recently has it become a larger issue. As we rely on JavaScript and Ajax to create richer and more responsive Web applications, the requests begin to collide and block responsiveness, creating a clunky user experience.

Web workers help alleviate that problem by opening up a secondary thread in which you can pass data back and forth through. Web workers live in a separate JavaScript file, which is referenced from the main JavaScript file. Because of security concerns, workers do not have access to the DOM; their sole purpose is to fetch and return data to the main file. Organizing your script execution and data retrieval into a worker can improve your overall user experience. Web workers open up a new methods and a new event to use that provide ways to pass information to a worker, catch it, and send back the processed data to the main file. The new additions include

- postMessage (data)
- message event

postMessage()

The `postMessage()` method is, to use a baseball term, the pitcher. `postMessage()` takes a single argument, which represents the data or information you want to send to the other file. Because data can travel from the main file to the worker and also from the worker back to the main file `postMessage()`, it is used on both sides. Using `postMssage()` will pass whatever information is available into the receiving file and trigger the `onmessage` event.

message event

The `message` event is triggered after the `postMessage()` method is called. The receiving file will wait for the `message` event to trigger an action. Listening for the message event is the same process as waiting for any other event, like a click to be triggered. The only difference is that instead of a user triggering the event, you will be triggering it programmatically when you are ready to send and process data.

This event combined with the `postMessage()` method will allow you to offload some of the server communication or processing work to the Web worker while your main file continues on with its normal communication model. To depict how a Web worker can run in parallel with another script that is constantly executing, we set up the HTML in Listing 11.6. There is a button to start the worker that we will bind an event to, a couple `div` elements for catching the output, and another button to terminate the worker.

Listing 11.6   **HTML Document to Display Web Worker Functionality**

```
<!doctype html>
<html lang="en">
<head>

    <title>Chapter 11 - Web Workers</title>
    <meta charset="utf-8">

</head>
<body>

<button type="button" id="start">start worker</button>
<button type="button" id="stop">stop worker</button>

<div id="timer"></div><!--/#timer-->
<div id="output"></div><!--/#output-->

<!--js-->
<script src="js/html5.js"></script>

</body>
</html>
```

The first step to using a Web worker is to create a new instance of the worker you want to use. The instance contains a path to the worker file. It should be another JavaScript file, probably in the same directory as your main file.

Listing 11.6.1 shows the JavaScript needed to create an instance of a Web worker that we will use later on. The workers will be contained within the /js directory and live in a worker.js file, but you should feel free to rename it to anything that makes sense. There is not standardization around naming conventions for worker files.

Listing 11.6.1   **Initializing a Worker**

```
// create a new instance of the worker
var worker = new Worker("js/worker.js");
```

To illustrate worker functionality, we will be returning to the same contact JSON data that we have been using throughout this book, but for brevity we will be embedding it into the main JavaScript file. With this format the data that will be passed into the worker will be the entire contacts object. If we were to leave the contact information in an external JSON file, the data passed to the worker would simply be the data URL where the worker would target an Ajax call.

As a refresher, Listing 11.6.2 shows a dump of the addressBook information saved to a contacts variable that will be passed into the worker.

Listing 11.6.2   **Contact Information Data the Worker Will Be Parsing**

```
var contacts = {
    "addressBook" : [
        {
            "name": "hillisha",
            "email": "hill@example.com",
        },
        {
            "name": "paul",
            "email": "cleveland@example.com",
        },
        {
            "name": "vishaal",
            "email": "vish@example.com",
        },
        {
            "name": "mike",
            "email": "grady@example.com",
        },
        {
            "name": "jamie",
```

```
            "email": "dusted@example.com",
        }
    ]
};
```

To accurately show a worker in action, we will be setting up a scenario where there is a process constantly running in the main file while passing information to the worker that will be processed and returned to the browser. In the main file we will be setting up a simple counter function that increments (counts up) every half second. To do this we are using the `setInterval()` timing method that we used in the Ajax chapter to make calls over and over.

After creating the counter functionality, we will set up three event listeners. The first is a normal `click` event that will start the worker. To start the worker, we are calling the `postMessage()` method on the `worker` instance we created at the beginning of the document. We're also passing in the contacts data to be sent to the worker for processing.

The second listener utilizes the message event to wait for a reply from the worker. When the event is triggered, the data will be returned and outputted to the DOM.

The third listener will terminate the worker and add a `disabled` attribute to the start button. After terminating the worker, `postMessage()` won't work, which is why we are disabling the button.

Listing 11.6.3 shows the contents of html5.js, the script file containing the worker initialization.

Listing 11.6.3   Main JavaScript Contents in html5.js

```javascript
// anonymous function to contain the variables
(function () {

    // create a new instance of the worker
    var worker = new Worker("js/worker.js");

    var btnStart = document.getElementById("start"),
        btnStop = document.getElementById("stop"),
        timerOuput = document.getElementById("timer"),
        workerOutput = document.getElementById("output"),
        num = 0;

    // create a script that is constantly running to block the normal flow
    setInterval(function () {
        num = num + 1;
        timerOuput.innerHTML = num;
    }, 500);
```

```
// add click event to the start button to activate the worker
btnStart.addEventListener("click", function() {

    worker.postMessage(contacts); // send contacts data to the worker

}, false);

// set up message listener
worker.addEventListener("message", function(e) {

    workerOutput.innerHTML += e.data;

}, false);

// add a click event to the stop button to terminate the worker
btnStop.addEventListener("click", function() {

    worker.terminate();
    btnStart.setAttribute("disabled", "disabled");

    alert("worker has been terminated");

}, false);


})();
```

The second step to setting up your worker is to create a worker file to process information that is getting sent through the postMessage() method being called in the main JavaScript file. At the top of the main file, you can see that we are referencing a worker file called worker.js. This is where all your worker scripting will live, on the secondary thread.

Setting up the worker is similar to the way you set up the main file, only in reverse. In the main file you first called postMessage(), then waited for the message event to be triggered from the worker response. In the worker file it's the opposite. You first set up an event listener to wait for the message event to be triggered carrying the information from the main script file, then process the information, and call postMessage() to send it back. All of this happens in parallel to what is going on in the main JavaScript file, on the main thread.

In our case, the worker file is receiving the entire contacts object that can be parsed through and returned to the main JavaScript thread/file. Normally this would require a loop, but in this instance a loop would execute far too quickly to be able to see anything going on. To slow down the process, we will again be using the setInterval() timing method with the execution time set to half a second. In other words, for every half second, the function will send an item from the data set to the main JavaScript file. Listing 11.6.4 shows the contents of the worker.js file.

Listing 11.6.4   **Worker Script in worker.js**

```javascript
// anonymous function to contain the variables
(function(){

    // set up an event listener to catch the message
    addEventListener("message", function(e) {

        var data = e.data.addressBook,
            dataCount = data.length,
            counter = 0;

        // send the data every half second until it reaches the end
        setInterval(function(){
            if(counter < dataCount){
                postMessage("<p>" + data[counter++].name + "</p>");
            }
        }, 500);

    }, false);

})();
```

If you open this example in a browser, you should see the original timer counting up from the main JavaScript file and the results of the worker's postMessage() data processing appear every half second. This is an example of two script processes executing at the same time in JavaScript.

Figure 11.3 shows an illustration of how postMessage() and the message event work together in the context of a Web worker.

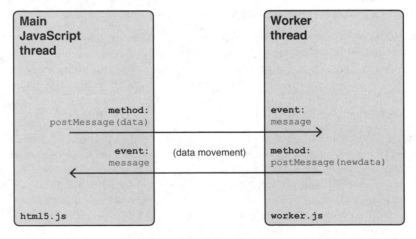

Figure 11.3   An illustration of worker and main thread communications

Device API

With the Device API we can further narrow the gap between building a native device application and developing purely on the Web. It is one of those things out on the bleeding edge of the Web. At the time of this writing, very few browsers and devices support this specification, but it's by far one of the coolest things on the horizon of JavaScript. We finally have a pathway to gaining advanced access to the device a user is visiting with.

Up to this point in Web design and development, the limitations of getting advanced access to device capabilities have been one of the very few barriers to creating our "one Web" goal and building all applications on a single code base of HTML, CSS, and JavaScript. This limitation has been attributed, mostly, to the negative security-base stigma JavaScript has carried with it for years. Even though we are still very weary of JavaScript's known problems, we have been able to move the Web forward in a responsible manner. One of the first major steps in that direction is the Device API.

Parts of the API have been added into JavaScript and other parts in HTML. The Device API opens up a new world of opportunities with connections to device information, such as the battery life and current available bandwidth, coupled with the ability to shock the world and actually vibrate a user's phone from a browser, which will help create a Web that is more targeted to the needs of a user and provide the best possible user experience customized for each person.

In this section we will be taking a peek at the Device API and three of its major components: the Battery Status API, the Vibration API, and the Network Information API. Each API we will be going over has an official draft specification with the W3C and will be the future of client-side interaction in the browser.

The Battery Status API

The initial specification for the Battery Status API came out in 2010 as part of the System Information API specification, but within a year it broke off into its own working draft so it could be more readily available and implemented independently. It was thought to have enough merit to stand on its own, and since then the specification has grown in a robust document and has gained support in Firefox 10+.

This API provides a way for you to retrieve the battery life and status of a device from the browser, which will allow you to design an efficient Web application that can respond to the amount of power left in the device to provide the best experience possible. It can be used to defer or scale back excess processing when the device is not charging. For example, if you are trying to create the real-time data illusion we went over in the Ajax chapter by using `setInterval()`, you could adjust the amount of Ajax calls to the server, conditionally based upon the amount of battery life.

You may have noticed from Figure 11.2 that inside the `navigator` object was something labeled `mozBattery`. This is the object, in Firefox, for the Battery Status API. It provides all the information you need to find out about a device's battery life. The API will return four types of information:

- Battery level (number from 0 to 1)
- Battery charging status (true or false)
- Battery charging time (how long until the battery is fully charged)
- Battery discharge time (how long until the battery is dead)

Each piece of information can be accessed through the `navigator` object, like `navigator.battery.level`. In addition to the new objects, this API also opens up four new JavaScript events to constantly monitor the battery status:

- `chargingchange` (when the level increases)
- `chargingtimechange` (when charge time changes)
- `dischargingtimechange` (when discharge time changes)
- `levelchange` (whenever the battery level changes)

Attaching an event listener to these events will help you customize processing if a user stays on your site for an extended period of time. Listing 11.7 shows an example of how to implement the Battery Status API with the official W3C syntax. This example can be used with any HTML document, because it will append output information into the `body`. It should show you the current battery information for your device.

Listing 11.7   **Using the Battery API**

```
// anonymous function to contain the variables
(function(){

    var battery = navigator.battery,
        body = document.getElementsByTagName("body")[0];

    function updateBatteryStatus() {

        body.innerHTML += "<p>Battery level: " + battery.level * 100 + "%</p>";
        body.innerHTML += "<p>Battery is charging: " + battery.charging + "</p>";
        body.innerHTML += "<p>Battery charging time: " + battery.chargingTime +
➥"</p>";
        body.innerHTML += "<p>Battery discharging time: " + battery.dischargingTime +
➥"</p>";

    }

    // detect if the battery status API is supported
    if(battery) {

        battery.addEventListener("chargingchange", updateBatteryStatus);
        battery.addEventListener("levelchange", updateBatteryStatus);
```

```
        updateBatteryStatus();

    }

})();
```

Because it is an experimental object, you may have to use the vendor prefix to get the example in Listing 11.7 to work properly. In Firefox the battery object is `navigator.mozBattery`, and in Chrome/Safari it is `navigator.webkitBattery`. Vendor extensions for experimental properties in JavaScript work the same as they do in CSS, but with a slightly different syntax. So if you use a JavaScript object prefaced with `webkit` or `moz`, you know you're living at the edge of the Web.

The Vibration API

The Vibration API is another one of those bleeding-edge JavaScript APIs that isn't implemented very well quite yet, but it does exactly what you think it does. It provides you programmatic access to the vibration mechanism of a device. Of course, it will work only if the host device has a vibration mechanism in the first place. You probably won't be able to vibrate someone's Apple IIe, even if you can find a way to get it to run the latest version of Chrome.

The official W3C specification for this API doesn't appear to enforce vibration limitations out of the box, so chances are this is going to be one of the more fun APIs to play around with after support starts to take off. I imagine it will result in a lot of dropped phones as well if we start randomly vibrating websites. You certainly need to be careful with something like this, even though it is meant to be used to provide tactile feedback in gaming and not as a generic notification system.

Just like the Battery Status API, the Vibration API is part of the `navigator` object in JavaScript, and it is accessed much the same way. It takes a single argument, which can be a numerical value representing the length of the vibration (in milliseconds) or an array of numbers representing a vibration interval. Listing 11.8 shows the two syntax possibilities for calling the `vibrate` object.

Listing 11.8   **Basics of the Vibration API**

```
// vibrate for 1 second
navigator.vibrate(1000);

// vibrate for 1 second with an array
navigator.vibrate([1000]);
```

Listing 11.8 shows the two formats of the Vibration API. The array option exists to set up interval vibrations. For example, if you were to enter three numbers into the array, the first and third represent the length of two vibrations, and the second value is the amount of time the API should be paused before executing the second vibration.

Listing 11.8.1 shows a JavaScript snippet you could use to utilize this API. We are setting up a click event on a button that will vibrate the device two times with a half second pause in the middle. We are also using a form of feature detection to check to see if the user's browser has support for the API before trying to execute the code block.

Listing 11.8.1   **Using the Vibration API**

```
// anonymous function to contain the variables
(function(){

    // attach a click event to a button with an ID of "vibrate"
    document.getElementById("vibrate").addEventListener("click", function(){

        if(navigator.vibrate) {

            // vibrate for 1 second wait half a second, then vibrate 2 seconds
            navigator.vibrate([1000, 500, 2000]);

        } else {

            // apologize to the user for teasing them
            alert("sorry, this browser doesn't support the vibrate API");

        } // end support check

    }, false);

})();
```

The Battery Status and Vibration APIs are two of the best examples of the type of fine-grained access you will have to the device. Having both of these APIs in your toolkit will help you create truly unique experiences for your users.

The Network Information API

The Network Information API is the last item in the Device API that we're going to check out. It's one of those APIs that the user really has no idea about. I always say that Web development is like cinematography in a movie; when it's great you never really notice it. This API is a testament to that statement. It has the potential to be the most powerful API released to date, so let's get to it.

The Network Information API provides access to information about the underlying connection of a device. What does that mean? It means you can run light connection and bandwidth tests on a device before loading in assets. Similar to what we spoke about with the Battery Status API, you can modify the user's experience based on available resources.

One of the biggest problems right now with building a one Web experience is asset management. Building a design that works in all browsers and all screen resolutions is a difficult task that is made even harder with the problems that arise with the constrained bandwidths of a cellular network. The Network Information API allows us to throttle back assets such as high-resolution images if the available bandwidth doesn't lend well to large graphics. We can load images that are more appropriate for the data exchange rate, again ensuring a smooth user experience. It's all about user experience, but I'm sure you know that by now.

Accessing connection information is the same as anything else in the `navigator` object. You first travel in the `connection` object, then `type` like: `navigator.connection.type`. The API returns a numerical value, which maps to a connection speed.

To illustrate this principle, let's see if we can solve the asset management problem with this API and a few lines of JavaScript. Listing 11.9 shows an HTML document containing a reference to an image. By default we're loading a small image into the DOM and utilizing an HTML5 custom data attribute to provide the source for a large image that will be loaded in if the extra bandwidth is available.

Listing 11.9   **HTML Document to Show Off the Network Information API**

```
<!doctype html>
<html class="no-js" lang="en">
<head>

    <title>Chapter 11 - Network Connection</title>
    <meta charset="utf-8">

</head>
<body>

<img src="images/small.jpg" data-large="images/large.jpg">

<script src="js/html5.js"></script>

</body>
</html>
```

In Listing 11.9.1, you will find the JavaScript that goes with the HTML in Listing 11.9.

In this example we are running a normal for loop over each image on the page, checking to see if the connection speed is either unknown, Ethernet, or WIFI (0, 1, 2 `type` codes), and if true, we are grabbing the large image source and loading it into the DOM.

Listing 11.9.1   **Checking the Network Connection to Load Larger Images**

```
// anonymous function to contain the variables
(function (){

    // Check bandwidth level is supported
    var connection,
        connectionSpeed,
        images = document.querySelectorAll("img[data-large]"),
        imageCount = images.length,
        i;

    // create a custom object if navigator.connection isn't available
    connection = navigator.connection || { 'type': '0' };

    if(imageCount > 0 && connection.type === '0' || connection.type === '1' ||
➥connection.type === '2') {

        for (i = 0; i < imageCount; i = i + 1) {

            var obj = images[i],
                largeImg = obj.getAttribute('data-large');

            obj.setAttribute('src', largeImg);

        }

    }

})();
```

All the device APIs we've been talking about are pretty far out there as far as support. But being ahead of the game is half the battle. All we need is one device to pick up support before these APIs start to take off. There are already rumors swirling about for support of these features in the very near future (if they're not here already).

Luckily, with a healthy mix of condition statements and feature detection we can start coding for these features today, then sit back and watch as they gain more momentum in the community. Let's take a closer look into how we can use some of these features right now.

Using This Today with Feature Detection

This chapter has been chock full of cutting-edge development techniques. Some of them have very good support, some "work where you expect them to work," and others don't have much support right now. When you get to that point in building on the front-end where you're using these cutting-edge techniques, specific browser support information stops being useful. You're fully aware that what you're using isn't going to work in all browsers.

Knowing that a feature isn't going to work in all browsers or devices allows you to set up something called **feature detection**. We have been mentioning (and using) this method throughout the book. It's always important, but especially important when using some of the newer additions to both HTML and JavaScript.

Feature detection is a front-end methodology where you check for the presence of an object before executing a block of code depending on it. When you boil it down to its core, feature detection accomplishes two things:

- Creates fallback features when something isn't supported
- Prevents blocks of unsupported code from being executed

If an object isn't supported, it will return as undefined, so you can set up your conditional statement based on that assumption.

Listing 11.10 depicts the familiar example of feature detection we used when detecting for geolocation support earlier in this chapter.

Listing 11.10   **An Example of Feature Detection in Geolocation**

```
if(navigator.geolocation) {
    // you have geolocation
} else {
    // the navigator.geolocation object came back as undefined, you don't have the
➥features
}
```

This model of feature detection can be applied to anything in JavaScript, and many things in HTML. If you're like me and always want to use the latest and greatest APIs available, this will be the way you do that. Because we are always striving to create a rich experience for all our users, detecting for feature support is a necessary exercise to achieve consistency and relevancy across multiple Web environments.

Summary

In this chapter, we lifted up the hood of some of the HTML5 JavaScript APIs that have begun to explode on the Web development community the past couple years. We started by going over the general purpose of the HTML5 specification, how it was very focused on the developers, and how the language was already being used. We discussed how the new structural elements in HTML5 create a cleaner semantic markup structure and open up a new world of accessibility options with the influx of the WAI ARIA specification.

From there, we jumped into a few of the JavaScript APIs, like geolocation, media embedding, accessing browser history, and forcing URL changes, and an improved server communication model with Web workers.

We then moved a little further out on the ledge and got in to the bleeding edge of the Web with the Device API. We talked about the different ways you can gain fine-grained access to hardware capabilities like battery life, a vibration mechanism, and even network information to conditionally load assets based on the available bandwidth at any given time.

We closed this chapter by talking about a central theme of the book: feature detection. We went over reasons that you should use this style of development and referenced previous examples where we had been applying it throughout the book.

Exercises

1. What are the four types of ARIA roles?

2. What information can be returned from the Battery Status API?

3. What connection types are returned from the Network Information API?

Moving Forward with JavaScript

In this chapter, we take a look into some areas of JavaScript that may help you move on to the next level in your coding journey. Many times when a book is finished you're left with that empty feeling, thinking "now what?" With the content presented in this chapter, I hope to lead you in a direction so you can decide for yourself what the best path moving forward is. This includes a brief review of the content we've gone over throughout the course of this book as a way to refresh your memory of how far you've come. Unless you've sat down to read this book in a single sitting (which would be amazingly impressive), I'm sure there are some gaps in the topics we went over. Even though many of the examples retain much of the information, there are always pieces that slip through the cracks. Hopefully, in our short review we can fill in those cracks.

The JavaScript you have learned to this point has been pretty generalized, with the goal of creating a solid knowledge-base that you will need to have to continue learning and building in the language. However, every person who sits down to learn JavaScript comes in with a different background and mind-set. Some of us are designers, some of us are developers, and others don't quite know yet.

If you are a designer, you will be using JavaScript in a very different way compared to how a developer would use it. This is in part because of how diverse JavaScript can be as a language. Although the basic knowledge of DOM manipulation, data storage, looping, and server communication will always be necessary to a developer or a designer, moving toward your goals can be a very different experience.

We keep the overall user experience in mind, but a designer might focus on user interface, animations, and special design-level issues where a developer might focus on data transfers and building the DOM in an efficient way. This chapter addresses both paths and shows how you might continue your path from here.

After the review, this chapter is broken up in the two distinct parts:

- JavaScript for Designers
- JavaScript for Developers

Plenty of people overlap the two areas, and if you're still trying to figure out which road to travel, I hope this division will give you some insight into what you might have to look forward to in each area. As you're reading, if one area feels more "awesome" than the other, you may have your answer for how you can progress to the next level of learning JavaScript.

A Brief Review of Key Topics

Looking back on what you've learned so far is an important step in moving forward. When you sit down to learn a topic as massive as JavaScript, it's natural to forget some things and have to review. Luckily, this is a book, and you can always flip back to check out a code sample to jog your memory. Reviewing at this point is especially important because we're talking about moving forward with the language, and you can't effectively do that without taking a step back and going over what you already know. This is a good practice with anything you're learning. If you can create natural checkpoints in the process, you will be able to evaluate your progress and make sure you're still on the path you want to be on.

We went over a lot of core JavaScript topics through the course of this book, and you took in a lot of information that will help you in the future. Some major concepts like progressive enhancement and accessibility will serve as reminders and point you in the right direction as you move from project to project. These methodologies will guide your development strategies at a high level and help you plan out the style in which you design and build for the Web. Although we spoke about them in the context of JavaScript, the concepts in progressive enhancement and creating accessible content stretch far beyond in limitations of a behavioral language like JavaScript. These topics will also bleed into your HTML, CSS, and even back-end technologies like PHP, Python, or Ruby (or maybe even back-end JavaScript, ::hint hint::).

There are also topics more specific to the execution of JavaScript development, such as manipulating the DOM, storing data, and dealing with server communication. These are the topics that build your JavaScript skill set. You use these to do the actual coding on a project. They include all the interaction design, Ajax calls, loops, and event models. The style you choose to pursue in this area will focus on performance, responsiveness, and creating an application or site that can scale to both traffic and a forever-changing list of devices. Being responsible in your JavaScript usage isn't always the sexiest of topics, but in the end if you're keeping user experience in mind, choosing the right tool for the job is all that matters. Knowing the capabilities of JavaScript as well as its limitations can be the difference between a good career in JavaScript and a great career in JavaScript.

Progressive Enhancement

I realize that by now the concept of progressive enhancement has been drilled into your head quite a bit, and that's because it is so vitally important in the development and design processes. Progressive enhancement is a layered approach to Web design that focuses on the accessibility of content at all times. It recognizes that the consumption of content is the main goal of any visitor to the Web, and therefore it should always be available to the user regardless of the medium by which it is delivered (phone, desktop, tablet, paper airplane, and so on).

Progressive enhancement also leads into areas such as accessibility and graceful degradation, both topics that were central methodologies throughout the content of this book and that will guide you as you continue designing and developing for the Web.

When the topic of accessibility is approached, it is generally from the angle of a disabled user accessing a site from some kind of assistive technology. We spoke about two major areas of accessibility in the form of WAI-ARIA. Both are within HTML, flagging zones of a document to more accurately describe the contents, and also from a server communication model in making Ajax and the asynchronous updating of a document (without a page refresh) visible to a screen reader by announcing when an area is updated.

Accessibility goes beyond screen readers and disabled users, of course. It speaks to the main goals of progressive enhancement, creating a system where content is always available to the user, whether it is being accessed through a fully featured desktop medium, a screen reader, a mobile device, a tablet, or another device that for some reason is browsing with JavaScript turned off.

Users browsing with JavaScript turned off are a concern that shrinks with every passing day, but until the option is removed from the browser altogether, it is something we will all have to be aware of.

These are the main principles of progressive enhancement, denying no one access to what they need. Step one is learning and implementing these guides. Step two, which we will get into a little later in the chapter, is breaking them. Of course there is a difference between ignoring rules altogether and breaking them. The rules of progressive enhancement should never be ignored, but breaking them in responsible ways when it's the right tool for the job can create some interesting scenarios in your path to creating a great user experience.

DOM Manipulation

Manipulating and traveling around the DOM are main concepts in JavaScript development. There are very few examples of interface design where you don't have to manipulate the DOM in one way or another. Whether you're outputting data after an Ajax call or adding and removing classes to a DOM node based on a user interaction, you'll be doing DOM manipulation in one form or another. It is a skill that both designers and developers need to possess to effectively code with JavaScript.

We went over a lot of different ways to enter the DOM. There are JavaScript methods like `parentNode`, `firstChild`, and `lastChild` that take advantage of the parent-child DOM relationship when you're traveling around a document. Others, like `nextSibling` and `previousSibling`, allow you to travel horizontally within an HTML document. You learned that there is always a way to get to a DOM node; if it exists, you can get to it with JavaScript. This includes the more direct methods of DOM entry, such as `getElementById`, `getElementsByTagName`, and the newer, less supported `querySelector` and `querySelectorAll`. By now you are, hopefully, pretty comfortable with how to target a specific DOM node; throughout this book, you have been using each of the various methods when entering a document. We have talked about the various levels of support for all the DOM methods, and even explored the world of JavaScript libraries and how the methods map back to their related methods in native JavaScript.

When manipulating the DOM for interface design, it is important to keep performance in mind because it is our first line of defense when molding a user experience. Using an event-driven JavaScript model means that many things that happen in an interface are triggered by soliciting user feedback, in the form of events. When users click, swipe, pinch, rotate, or interact with a page in any way, they expect some feedback immediately. That feedback could be modal window closing, a tab exposing itself, or even the appearance of a loading graphic until data is received. Because this feedback needs to be created as fast as possible, it can be invaluable to the overall user experience to be able to recognize points in an interaction where you can accomplish the same task with CSS that you were trying to create with JavaScript, because at this point CSS rendering in a browser happens significantly faster than that of JavaScript. The action of adding/removing a `class` can allow you to offload some processing to nonblocking CSS instead of custom building features in JavaScript that already exist within another language that is readily available and possibly served from cache.

Listing 12.1 shows you an example of how you could use JavaScript to manipulate the DOM by adding a class to an area and simulate a smooth hide/show interaction. You should get used to adding and removing classes to DOM nodes, because it represents a main (a very powerful) feature in JavaScript. As browser support for advanced CSS features grows, you will find yourself using this model more and more so you can focus JavaScript resources on creating more real-time data and interaction models.

Listing 12.1   **Example of Using CSS with JavaScript**

```
/* the CSS */
.hide-and-move-up {
    opacity: 0;
    position: absolute;
    margin-top: -100%;
    transition: all linear .5s; /* add vendor extensions */
}



/* the JavaScript */
var modalWindow = document.getElementById("modal-window"),
    closeButton = document.getElementById("close");

/* when the close button is clicked apply the class */
closeButton.addEventListener("click", function(e){

    modalWindow.setAttribute("class", "hide-and-move-up");

}, false);
```

You may look at the example code in Listing 12.1 and note the use of a transition effect to create some form of an animation, and wonder if that breaks the wall of progressive enhancement by embedding behavior into your CSS. Adding behavior into CSS can be a hot topic, because many believe it should be solely contained within the JavaScript behavior layer. The secret to the whole thing is that to some degree, there has always been behavior in CSS with the :hover pseudo-class. With the influx of transitions and keyframe animations into CSS, you can make the presentation of you project pop a little more while offloading some of the process burden that has been shouldered by JavaScript.

Data Storage

Storing data is another JavaScript core concept that we spent a lot of time utilizing. As you stepped through the examples in this book, the data storage methods became more and more stable. We started off by using simple variables to store information like strings, numbers, and Boolean values; this was also applied to storing references to DOM nodes. From there, the storage models moved into a more robust system by adding in different types of arrays (lists of data), like associative arrays and multidimensional arrays. Using data storage in these ways showed you that you don't have to rely on flat data models in JavaScript just because there is no real concept of a database. Using a combination of variables and arrays can create a very robust and flexible data source for an application.

After we toured through arrays and variables for storing data, we looked into saving information in objects—JSON objects, to be more specific. This led into us moving data storage to an external JSON file and stepped right into an Ajax interaction model to consume external data (pretty smooth, right?). These are all ways you can store information in various formats for direct use within your application.

Listing 12.2 shows all the different forms of data storage that we have gone over to this point.

Listing 12.2 **Application Data Storage**

```
// storing data in variables

var name = "Tim",
    city = "Boston",
    age = "107";


// storing data in arrays

var dude = [];

dude["name"] = "Tim";
dude["city"] = "Boston"
dude["age"] = "107"
```

```
// storing data in a JSON object

{
"dude" : [
    {
        "name": "Tim",
        "city": "Boston",
        "age": "107"
    }
]}
```

Using data in this direct way with variables and object storage is the most common data interaction you will be using, but on the other side of the coin lives another form of storage. Browser data storage is how you leave your mark on a user, and we went over two ways to accomplish this: localStorage and sessionStorage.

With these methods of storing information in the browser, you can take some of the data objects you have been transferring on the server and save it locally to the browser in either a persistent way (it stays there) or a session-based way (deletes when the browser closes). Listing 12.3 gives you a refresher on how you might save and retrieve the "dude" JSON object to/from the browser's storage methods.

Listing 12.3   Browser Data Storage

```
// storing data in the browser

localStorage.setItem("dudeInfo", JSON.stringify(dude));
sessionStorage.setItem("dudeInfoSession", JSON.stringify(dude));

// getting saved data

localStorage.getItem("dudeInfo");
sessionStorage.getItem("dudeInfoSession");
```

Getting the data from the browser is just as important as being able to set it. Mastering data storage in JavaScript will help you far beyond this language because the JSON format crops up in all programming languages as the preferred method of data storage in many cases, especially when dealing with client-server communications.

You will also frequently see JSON-formatted data when working with third-party APIs, so being able to take that data, consuming and working with it in a similar way to what you do with locally stored data, will help streamline your development process. This is a great example of not developing with blinders on. If there is a choice to be made in data formats (XML versus JSON) you might want to examine the application as a whole and indentify which format is more common for the situation in which you are using it.

Server Communication

Ajax is the elephant in the room when you talk about JavaScript server communications. We were able to use Ajax in a logical way when we were building the autocompete search form application, but often Ajax is not used in a logical way. It is one of the most overused methods in JavaScript, by far, mostly due to its "coolness factor" and marketing popularity. For this reason you will see a lot of Web applications that are hacked together with too much JavaScript and are hampered with crippling performance issues because of poor planning and lazy development.

Many developers who are dealing with Ajax will ignore the rules and build a model of progressive enhancement by adding the behavior layer way too early in the process. For whatever reason this happens, it creates more problems than it solves by relying on a cross-browser sensitive language like JavaScript for your application's core functionality and not providing a way for the experience to degrade gracefully in the browser. This is what I was referring to earlier by saying that there is a difference in ignoring progressive enhancement rules and breaking them.

We took server communication one step further when we got into Web workers and the HTML5 JavaScript APIs. By talking about creating a better user experience by freeing yourself from the single-thread, blocking nature of JavaScript, we opened up another door in client-side server communication. Using Web workers is not that dissimilar from using CSS together with JavaScript. They're extremely different technologies that do very different things, but they accomplish their goals by offloading some of the processing put onto a main JavaScript file.

JavaScript certainly has its shortcomings, but using these technologies together in a responsible and well-thought-out way can ensure that you are using them all in the most logical way, to create the best possible user experience.

JavaScript for Designers

JavaScript is such a diverse language that you can have two people with expert-level knowledge who do completely different things. There are interface designers who work heavily with JavaScript but never get into the heavy data manipulation side of the language. There are also JavaScript developers who never get into the interface side of things.

Up to this point in the book, all the JavaScript knowledge you have attained has addressed the needs of both the design and development communities. But as you move forward, you will probably find yourself leaning toward one particular side or the other, especially as time progresses and the techniques get exponentially more complex. Chances are that if you are already a Web designer, you might settle on using JavaScript as an interface design tool, and if you're already a developer, you might use it as a developmental language. Either way, the focus is always on user experience—from two very different angles but always meeting in the middle.

This section is targeted toward a level of JavaScript you might find yourself getting into if you are designing an interface. We'll call it JavaScript for Designers for now, but I'm sure you'll find that the path to designing is dusted with development.

Advanced Interface Design

For many years, interface design has been pigeonholed into a pretty standard environment in the form of a desktop (or laptop). To a large extent, this is still the case. You will still be designing interfaces that are interacted with through a keyboard and mouse, but they will also have to be flexible enough to work within other contexts, such as a touch interface.

With interface design it is important to focus on the features of a given environment. For instance, screen size is a feature. With screen size you can use CSS media queries to modify the design of an application to best fit the environment, because the design lives in the presentation layer, which is why we deal with it in CSS. Using the JavaScript method of adding and removing classes also allows you to easily modify how a class behaves based on screen size. This is a bonus side effect of building your interface in a way that interlaces CSS and JavaScript wherever possible. You will get the performance benefits of CSS combined with the event-driven model that is built into JavaScript.

Touch capabilities is another device feature. This feature will affect your JavaScript directly because it is a behavior and is dealt with in the behavior layer. When building a touch interface, there are a lot of features you may want to be inherited from the nontouch interface to the touch version. Because it is important to create a consistent user experience across multiple devices so your users don't get confused, you can either build a function library to be used for both touch and nontouch (mouse events) alike, or you can map touch events to mouse events. A lot of events in a touch interface simply will not map directly to a mouse event, like a pinch-zoom. But a lot of events, like `mousedown` and `touchstart`, can be directly related to each other in a logical way.

Listing 12.4 shows how you would set up two event listeners attached to the document, one event for `mousemove` and another for `touchmove`. This model works if you want to do two separate things for the similar actions, or if you plan to use them independently.

Listing 12.4 **Using Mouse and Click Events**

```
// set up mousemove event
document.addEventListener("mousemove", function(e){

    alert('got it!');

}, false);

// set up touchmove event
document.addEventListener("touchmove", function(e){

    alert('got it!');

}, false);
```

If the mousemove event is going to do the same action as a touchmove (like a drag action), you can save yourself some code writing by directly mapping the mousemove event to the touchmove event and binding your events to the mousemove event instead of both. This sounds a little complex, but it really means that you will write an event listener for the mousemove event, and whenever a touchmove event is triggered, you will force the mousemove event to also trigger so that its accompanying function will also execute. You can map any event to any other event in this way to ensure that you aren't writing (or maintaining) any extra code.

Listing 12.4.1 shows exactly how you might map touch events to mouse events, allowing you to execute the same function without handling separate events. There is a lot going on in the example, so let's take a look at it and go step by step.

Listing 12.4.1   **Mapping Touch to Click**

```
// declare a function to map touch events to mouse events
function mapTouches(e) {

    e.preventDefault();

    var first = e.touches[0], // get the first touch
        type = "",
        simulatedEvent = document.createEvent("MouseEvent"); // initialize a phantom
➥mouse event

        switch(e.type) {

                // if the event is touchstart map it to mousedown
                case "touchstart":

                        type = "mousedown";
                        break;

                // if the event is touchmove map it to mousemove
                case "touchmove":

                        type = "mousemove";
                        break;

                // if the event is touchend map it to mouseup
                case "touchend":

                        type = "mouseup";
                        break;
```

```
        default:
            return;

    }

    // set all the values of the phantom event
    simulatedEvent.initMouseEvent(type, true, true, window, 1, first.screenX,
➥first.screenY, first.clientX, first.clientY, false, false, false, false, 0,
➥null);

    // trigger the event on the item in context
    first.target.dispatchEvent(simulatedEvent);


}
```

When a user touches a screen, an array of the touch coordinated for each finger is available to the browser in the touch object. You can see that in Listing 12.4; we are accessing the touch object and grabbing the first item in the array: touch[0]. After that, you can access the event type by returning the type object of the event (e.type). This is what you will be testing against, reflected in the switch statement. As you can see, we are running a switch that checks for the event type, and if one returns true, we are then resetting the event type object to whatever mouse event we choose to map it to. From there, we continue to initialize and set up the phantom event that is now mapped from a touch event to a mouse event.

Creating and Executing Phantom Events

In Listing 12.4.1 you may have noticed two methods that we haven't used before: createEvent() and initMouseEvent(). These are the two methods that are used to trigger the events that have been mapped in the switch statement. There are three major steps in making a phantom event:

- Create an instance of an event type.
- Initialize the actual event and give it properties.
- Trigger the event.

The createEvent() Method

createEvent() is the method used to create an event of any type. It takes a single argument, which is the event type. Normally you would think the event type is something like click, blur, focus, keyup, or something like that, but because we are creating the event programmatically, you need to take it one step back from there. The options for event types that can be created from the createEvent() method are

- UIEvents
- MouseEvents

- MutationEvents

- HTMLEvents

We won't be getting into the other event types at this point, but for our purposes we only need to know that we're using MouseEvents to create the event.

After the MouseEvent is created, the next step is to initialize the event with the initMouseEvent method. In a normal event, this step is also taken care of for you. At this point you have to name the event and give it all the appropriate properties that a regular event has. It's like creating a custom event that happens to have the same name as a normal event. The initMouseEvent method takes 15 required arguments. The first argument is the most important, the name of the event. We set the name of each event in the switch statement by returning the type object, so that is what gets passed through the method. Listing 12.4.2 shows the information and steps in creating this event by using the createEvent and initMouseEvent methods.

Listing 12.4.2 **createEvent() and initMouseEvent()**

```
// initialize a phantom mouse event
var simulatedEvent = document.createEvent("MouseEvents");

// set all the values of the phantom event
simulatedEvent.initMouseEvent(type, true, true, window, 1, first.screenX,
➥first.screenY, first.clientX, first.clientY, false, false, false, false, 0,
➥null);
```

The dispatchEvent() Method

Now that the event is fully created and mapped to the touch event we want, the last step is to trigger the event. In our case the events like touchstart, touchmove, and touchend are triggering their mouse counterparts: mousedown, mousemove, and mouseup (or click). Because these events are now tied together, whenever the user on a touch device executes one of the events listed, it will automatically trigger the mouse event, executing the event listener attached to it (we haven't set up the listener yet, don't worry).

As I mentioned, now that the events are all mapped correctly, the next step is to trigger the event. This is done with the dispatchEvent. This method is attached to the object in context; in our case, that is the first touch by the user and the target on the finger (first.target).

In Listing 12.4.3 you can see the dispatchEvent method being passed the simulatedEvent object. This is the last step in creating and mapping the events together, but we still have to set up the event listeners that will execute the function.

Listing 12.4.3 **dispatchEvent()**

```
// trigger the event on the item in context
first.target.dispatchEvent(simulatedEvent);
```

Now that the entire mapping has been built into the mapTouches function, you get to take a look at something that seems a little more familiar in event listeners. The mapTouches function still needs to be fired off when each of the touch events occurs. For this we set up a series of listeners for each of the events listed in the function: touchstart, touchmove, and touchend, each of which executes the mapTouches function individually.

Listing 12.4.4 shows how to set up the event listeners with each touch event so the events are mapped together. Below that you will see a normal mousemove event, which opens a JavaScript alert.

Listing 12.4.4 **Listening for Touch Events**

```
// anonymous function to contain scope
(function(){

    // set up the event mapping listeners
    document.addEventListener("touchstart", mapTouches, false);
    document.addEventListener("touchmove", mapTouches, false);
    document.addEventListener("touchend", mapTouches, false);

    // test out the mappings with a mousemove event
    document.addEventListener("mousemove", function(e){

        alert('got it!');

    }, false);

})(); // End anonymous function
```

Now that the events are properly mapped and the listeners are set up, you should be able to execute the code in Listings 12.4–12.4.4 in a touch-capable browser, swipe your finger across the page, and see the alert window pop up. This means your events are properly mapping. If you were to disable the mapping and try again, it wouldn't work.

CSS Transforms in JavaScript

Any style that can be added with CSS can also be added with JavaScript, but as I mentioned a few times before, that's generally not a good idea because CSS is so much faster than JavaScript. If you can use CSS to apply styles, you should. There are times when you will want to use JavaScript to apply dynamic styles to a DOM node. By dynamic styles, I don't mean styles that are added after the document has been rendered, but rather styles that need to respond to user-interaction patterns. A pinch-zoom on an object, a drag and drop, or the rotation of an object in the browser by the user are all examples of when you would have to write styles dynamically to respond to how users are moving their finger, fingers, or mouse.

Because we're applying CSS transforms with JavaScript, we are going to focus on an example of creating a pinch-zoom effect on an object. To effectively test a pinch-zoom, you need either a touch-capable device or a simulator.

In the chapter about HTML5 JavaScript APIs, I mentioned that some of the experimental properties in JavaScript are treated the same as they are in CSS, by adding vendor extensions. The extensions have a similar syntax (-moz- vs. Moz, -webkit- vs. Webkit, and so on) and when dealing with transforms in JavaScript, they need to be utilized the same way. Unlike the way in CSS that we pile up all the vendor extensions, in JavaScript we have functions, objects, and variables at our disposal, and we can use them to detect the proper vendor extension that needs to be applied.

Listing 12.5 shows a function called getTransformExtension that lists all the possible extensions in a properties array, then loops through them checking each for a match in the element that is passed through as the sole argument. When a match is found, the correct property will be returned. This is a very valuable function to have when dealing with using CSS transforms in JavaScript.

Listing 12.5   **Getting the Vendor Extension**

```
// get the proper transform extension
function getTransformExtension(element) {

    "use strict";

    // create a static array of known extensions
    var properties = [
        "transform", // normal
        "WebkitTransform", // Safari and Chrome
        "msTransform", // Internet Explorer
        "MozTransform", // Firefox
        "OTransform" // Opera
    ];

    // get array count for looping
    var count = properties.length,
        i;

    // loop through the array
    for (i = 0; i < count; i = i + 1) {

        // save the property in context to a variable
        var property = properties[i];
```

```
          // pass the property through the element's style object and check if it's
➥defined
        if (typeof element.style[property] !== "undefined") {

                // when you get something that's not undefined, return it
                return property;

        } // end if
    } // end loop
} // end function

// anonymous function to contain the variables
(function(){

    var body = document.getElementsByTagName("body")[0];

    // alert the vendor extension
    alert(getTransformProperty(body));



})();
```

When executing the function in Listing 12.5, you can see that it is being attached to the body element (it doesn't really matter which element you use) and alerting the return value. This value will be applied to each transform so we can use the same syntax and assure that it will work in all appropriate browsers.

To effectively show this example, we will be taking the basic HTML for a block and scaling it based on the zoom level reported back from a pinch (gesturechange) event.

Listing 12.5.1 shows the HTML we will be using along with the accompanying CSS snippet to set the dimensions of the block. Note the two extra properties at the end of the <style> block: transform-origin and transition. These will need CSS vendor extensions to work properly.

Listing 12.5.1   **HTML for Vendor Extension Example**

```
<!doctype html>
<html lang="en">
<head>
        <title>Chapter 12</title>
        <meta charset="utf-8">

    <style>
        #block {
            height: 125px;
            width: 200px;
```

```
            background: cyan;
            margin: 50px auto;
            transform-origin: center 0; /* add css vendor extension */
            transition: all linear .15s; /* add css vendor extension */
        }
    </style>

</head>
<body>

<div id="block"></div><!--/#block-->

<script src="js/transforms.js"></script>

</body>
</html>
```

Using the HTML from Listing 12.5.1, we will first apply a normal transform through JavaScript to illustrate the syntax and usage of the getTransformExtension function we built.

Listing 12.5.2 shows how to apply a CSS transform to the block object in our HTML. This transform will rotate, move, and scale the object on load of the document. To apply the extension, you will pass the function return value through the style object; from there it's normal CSS syntax.

Listing 12.5.2   Using the Vendor Extension

```
// anonymous function to contain the variables
(function(){

    "use strict";

    var body = document.getElementsByTagName("body")[0],
        block = document.getElementById("block"),
        extension = getTransformExtension(body);

    // rotate, scale and translate the block
    block.style[extension] = "rotate(45deg) translate(300px, 50px) scale(1.5)";

})();
```

The second step is to make the scaling respond to user input. Scaling and zooming is linked to gesture events in JavaScript. We will be working with the gesturechange and gestureend events. gesturechange is triggered when a pinch value begins to change (scaling starts), and a gestureend event is triggered when the two fingers leave the surface of the screen.

Because gesture events are directly related to pinching and zooming of an object, they return a scale value that you can access and manually apply to an object. In this example of scaling the HTML `block` with a pinch-zoom, we will be utilizing the `getTransformExtension` function combined with the returned scale value from the gesture event to apply the `scale` transform to our object.

In Listing 12.5.3, you can see an event listener set up to capture the gesture change event, prevent the default behavior of zooming the entire document, and apply the scale value inside the transform.

Listing 12.5.3   **Scaling a Block**

```
// anonymous function to contain the variables
(function(){

    "use strict";

    var body = document.getElementsByTagName("body")[0],
        block = document.getElementById("block"),
        extension = getTransformExtension(body);

    // rotate the block 10 degrees
    block.style[extension] = "rotate(10deg)";

    // when the scale value changes, apply the scale value to the block
    block.addEventListener("gesturechange", function(e) {

        e.preventDefault();

        block.style[extension] = "scale("+ e.scale +")";

    }, false);

    // when the pinch is over, check the scale value
    block.addEventListener("gestureend", function(e) {

        // if the scale is over 1.5, scale to 3, otherwise return to original state
        if(e.scale > 1.5){
            block.style[extension] = "scale(3)";
        } else {
            block.style[extension] = "scale(1) rotate(10deg)";
        }
    }, false);

})();
```

Listing 12.5.3 also has an event listener for when the pinch is completed. This listener checks the scale value and if it is less than 1.5, the block is returned to its original scale level of 1. If the ending scale value is greater than 1.5, it is zoomed to a level of 3.

Because we added a linear transition to the #block element in the CSS, this action of completing the zoom to either 1 or 3 should appear to animate. This is an example of how to use CSS and JavaScript together to create a seamless interaction and apply a dynamic CSS transform to an object that responds to touch events.

Interacting from the Desktop

As a designer, you are focused on creating the best interaction and visual experience possible to the user. Sometimes this includes working desktop interactions. Uploading files is currently one of the more clunky aspects of dealing with Web interaction. Most of the time the interactions we build are restricted to the browser, and we leave system-level browser behaviors alone. However, as a next-level interface designer, you want to do whatever you can to create a natural experience in all aspects of an application.

Normally, the desktop is the desktop and the browser is the browser, but when uploading files from your local machine there can be some overlapping. This overlapping allows us to hook into the File API to create a desktop-to-browser drag-and-drop file interaction. This is where your designs begin to break out of the browser.

In this section we will be going through a somewhat advanced demo on how to create a system where the user can drag a file from the desktop and drop it into the browser while we render the image and file information that can be used to create a file upload system.

Creating a Desktop-to-Browser Drag-and-Drop Interface

In Listing 12.6 you can see a basic HTML document containing a div element with an ID value of drop-zone (where the image will be dropped), CSS to give some light styling to the drop zone, and a class set up to give the user some feedback (we'll get to that).

Listing 12.6   **HTML Document with Drop Zone for Image Upload**

```
<!doctype html>
<html lang="en">
<head>
        <title>Chapter 12</title>
        <meta charset="utf-8">

    <style>

        #drop-zone {
            min-height:300px;
            max-width:300px;
```

```
                padding:15px;
                border:4px dashed #999; }

            #drop-zone img {
                max-width:100%;
                display:block;
            }

            .over {
                border-color:#333;
                background:#ddd;
            }

        </style>

    </head>
    <body>

    <div id="drop-zone"></div><!--/#drop-zone-->

    <script src="js/filedrop.js"></script>

    </body>
    </html>
```

If you were to load the basic HTML document in a browser and drag an image to it, it would load the graphic in the browser window per its default behavior. This is something we will need to prevent because we want the image to be embedded into the document.

This example will be using a combination of the File API, which allows us to grab file information such as name, type, and file size. We will also be using the Drag and Drop API to handle drag-and-drop events. The primary events we will be using are `dragover` and `drop`. The `dragover` event will tell us when a file is being dragged over the drop zone, and the `drop` event will tell us when the file has been dropped into the zone.

After the file has been dropped, we can use the File API to grab information, output it, and render a preview of the image in the browser. Listing 12.6.1 illustrates the two events set up to create this effect.

The `dragover` event listener is set up to add a class of over to the drop zone. This is to provide the user with some feedback about what they're doing. It also ties back to the CSS we wrote.

When the file is dropping into the zone, we trigger the file API through the event, which contains a `dateTransfer` object. Inside that object you will find an array of all the files being dropped, along with information about each. We are looping through that object and outputting the name, file size, and file type into the drop zone.

Listing 12.6.1   **Getting the File Data**

```javascript
// Anonymous function to contain the variables
(function(){

    "use strict";

    // define the drop zone
    var dropZone = document.getElementById("drop-zone");

    // add a drag over event to the zone
    dropZone.addEventListener("dragover", function(e) {

        e.preventDefault();

        // add a hover class so you can see it's working
        dropZone.setAttribute("class","over");

    }, false);

    // on file drop grab all available image information
    dropZone.addEventListener("drop", function(e) {

        "use strict";

        e.preventDefault();

        // get all the files being dropped
        var files = e.dataTransfer.files,
            fileCount = files.length,
            i;

        if(fileCount > 0) {

            // loop through all the files and output the data
            for (i = 0; i < fileCount; i = i + 1) {

                var file = files[i],
                    name = file.name,
                    size = file.size,
                    type = file.type;

                // remove the hover class
                dropZone.removeAttribute("class");
```

```
                // output the image data
                dropZone.innerHTML += "<div>name: " + name + "<br>type: " + size +
➥" bytes<br>size: " + type + "<br><br></div>";


            }
        }

    }, false);


})(); // end anonymous function
```

Creating a File Preview

After running the code from Listing 12.6.1 in the browser, you should be able to drop a file into the browser and see the information render inside the drop zone. From here, the next step is to set up a system to preview the file. For this, JavaScript provided a `FileReader` object that needs to be initialized to render the image in the browser.

In Listing 12.6.2, you can see that the preview code block has been modified inside the loop. After initializing the `FileReader` object, we are setting an `onload` event handler that will wait until the image is entirely loaded into the browser. This will return the `src` attribute of the image into the form of a `dataURL`.

Listing 12.6.2   **Previewing the File**

```
// on file drop grab all available image information
dropZone.addEventListener("drop", function(e) {

    "use strict";

    e.preventDefault();

    // get all the files being dropped
    var files = e.dataTransfer.files,
        fileCount = files.length,
        i;

    if(fileCount > 0) {

        // loop through all the files and output the data
        for (i = 0; i < fileCount; i = i + 1) {

            var file = files[i],
                name = file.name,
                size = file.size,
                type = file.type,
                reader = new FileReader(); // initialize the FileReader Object
```

```
        // remove the hover class
        dropZone.removeAttribute("class");

        reader.onload = function(e) {
                dropZone.innerHTML += '<div><img src="' +
➥e.target.result + '"><br>'+ name +', '+ type +', '+ size +' bytes</div></div>';
        };

        // render the image as a data URL
        reader.readAsDataURL(file);

    } // end loop
  } // end count check

}, false);
```

After the file is loaded into the browser, it cannot be directly rendered; we can use the returned `dataURL` and a `readAsDataURL` method within the `FileReader` object to preview the file inside the browser.

This example can be a lot to take in. We mentioned a lot of new concepts with the Drag and Drop API, the File API and the `FileReader` object. As you step forward as a JavaScript designer, you will come across times where you need to dive pretty heavily into code like this to create your desired interface. When that happens, it is important to take your time and step through the processes piece by piece, like we did here. Knowing that these events exist is half the battle in creating the interface you want. Keeping abreast of the newer additions to JavaScript will make sure that you create the best possible interface while always keeping the user in mind.

JavaScript for Developers

Just as there are JavaScript designers who design the interfaces we all love, there are also JavaScript developers who spend time behind the scenes architecting the inner workings of the JavaScript rendering and design libraries and systems in which designers find themselves working.

In this section, we step away from the interface design level of JavaScript we have been talking about so far in this chapter and move to a more developer-focused model. Let's face it, the only goal that developers share with designers is providing a top-notch user experience. They come from completely different angles to arrive at the same place, but they both have that overarching goal in mind.

This section is your introduction to JavaScript for developers. When you're moving forward and learning more about the language as a developer, you will probably be focusing on things like how to properly structure a codebase for the best efficiency. You'll be going through object-oriented models, event-driven models, and even some of the more back-end focused model-view control methodologies to find out which provides the most flexibility on any particular project.

One such area you might explore that is gaining a lot of traction right now is the concept of using JavaScript as a layout engine to structure a document that is being built from a data feed. This is called using JavaScript templates.

JavaScript Templates

JavaScript templates are used to process and structure data inside an HTML document. They function in a very similar way to the view level of an MVC framework (back-end code stuff). JavaScript templates are blocks of HTML with special hooks built in, wrapped in a `<script>` element inside the HTML document. The intention of JavaScript templates is to parse through imported data, whether it's loaded in through an Ajax call or data embedded into an object in the main scripting file.

Throughout the book you have read about progressive enhancement and learned how important it is to keep the three layers separated. At the same time, you have seen us write HTML in our JavaScript file while looping through data and outputting it to the DOM. This creates a little bit of a conflict with the methodology when the layers get intertwined like that. JavaScript templates address that issue in a very direct way.

One of the major problems with parsing large amounts of data is that you end up with a JavaScript file containing a disproportionate amount of HTML snippets that are used to output the data into the DOM. You experienced this issue in the autocomplete search form we built when we were looping through and outputting the data. Listing 12.7 shows the JavaScript snippet we built displaying the HTML code that is embedded into the data loop.

Listing 12.7   **HTML in JavaScript (Snippet from autocomplete Search Form)**

```
if(count > 0 && searchValue !== ""){

    // loop through the contacts
    for(i = 0; i < count; i = i + 1) {

        // look through the name value to see if it contains the searchterm string
        var obj = addrBook[i],
            isItFound = obj.name.indexOf(searchValue);

        // anything other than -1 means we found a match
        if(isItFound !== -1) {
            target.innerHTML += '<p>' + obj.name + ', <a href="mailto:' + obj.email +
➡'">'+ obj.email +'</a><p>';
        } // end if

    } // end for loop

} // end count check
```

Removing the HTML snippet from inside the data loop in Listing 12.7 will create a more fluid JavaScript document. By moving it into the HTML and rendering it with JavaScript templates, we can also keep document structure where it belongs, in the HTML. I'm leading you into a potential issue, as you might have guessed.

There are many popular JavaScript templating libraries available today, and trying to cover them all wouldn't do you any favors. Even though each library contains slightly different syntax models, the overall concept of embedding a template in HTML and parsing it with JavaScript combined with JSON data still reigns true, no matter which library you choose to pursue. For our purposes we will be looking into the Mustache library for our JavaScript templating needs.

Learning Mustache

Mustache is a JavaScript templating library that holds the principle of rendering document structure in HTML better than many other libraries available. Because Mustache is a library, it needs to be downloaded and included in the document the same way we included jQuery into the document in Chapter 10, "Making JavaScript Easier with Libraries."

Including a Templating Library

Because the best way to illustrate the functionality of a JavaScript template is to take a look at them, let's examine Listing 12.7.1 and see exactly how a document is prepared to accept JavaScript templates.

The first glaring change that you may notice at the bottom of the document is the inclusion of the mustache.js file. This is the library, the same way we included jquery.js. The other addition that you may not recognize is the <script> element. This is where we will come back to add in the structure for our JavaScript templates.

Listing 12.7.1   **HTML Structure in Preparation for Mustache Templates**

```
<!doctype html>
<html lang="en">
<head>
        <title>Chapter 12 — JS Templates</title>
        <meta charset="utf-8">
</head>
<body>

<form action="" method="get" id="search-form">

    <div>
        <label for="q">Search address book</label>
        <input type="search" id="q" name="q" required placeholder="type a name"
➥autocomplete="off">
    </div>
```

```html
    <div class="button-group">
        <button type="submit" id="search-btn">search</button>
        <button type="button" id="get-all">get all contacts</button>
    </div><!--/.button-group-->

</form>

<div id="output" aria-atomic="true" aria-live="polite"></div>

<script type="text/x-mustache-tmpl" id="mustache-template">

    // special mustache templates go here

</script>

<!--js-->
<script src="js/mustache.js"></script>
<script src="js/addressbook.js"></script>

</body>
</html>
```

You might notice that the `<script>` element has an id of `mustache-template`. This can be whatever you want, and it's just a normal `id` value for a DOM hook in the JavaScript file. The `type` attribute is also semi-arbitrary; if omitted, the template will render just fine, but there are issues in other libraries, which can clash with JavaScript templates embedded in `<script>` elements if you don't provide a `type` attribute. Using a unique attribute such as `x-text/mustache-tmpl` will ensure that the value will never clash in the future and also create a semi-human-readable description of the element's contents. It will also make sure that some browsers don't attempt to execute the contents of the `<script>` element as normal JavaScript, which can cause the browser to throw errors in some cases.

Now that our HTML document is prepared to include the Mustache-style templates, let's jump over to the main JavaScript file where that HTML snippet used to live. We will be replacing it with a call to an object in the Mustache library that converts the contents of the `<script>` block into HTML.

Integrating a Templating System into Your JavaScript

The first step to rendering the Mustache template is to target the `<script>` element. Even though this isn't a normal element we target with JavaScript, it's still an HTML element in the DOM, so it can get saved to a variable. After it's saved to a variable, you need to save all the contents; this is how you bring the template into JavaScript to be processed. In Listing 12.7.2 you can see the variable block containing a reference to the `<script>` element in our HTML and how we are storing all the contents with `innerHTML`, being saved to the template variable. We'll be passing this variable into the Mustache rendering method to parse the content.

After we are inside the Ajax call, you can access the `Mustache` object and the `to_html` method, which takes two arguments. The first is the template variable we previously stored, and the second is the JSON object (`data`) that was returned through the Ajax call.

Listing 12.7.2   **`addr.getAllContacts` Method Modified to Use Mustache Templates**

```
//wrap everything in an anonymous function to contain the variables
(function(){

    //define the DOM elements and common variables you'll need
    var getAllButton = document.getElementById("get-all");

    //define address book methods
    var addr = {

        getAllContacts : function () {

            // set the output element
            var output = document.getElementById("output"),
                mustacheTemplate = document.getElementById("mustache-template"),
                template = mustacheTemplate.innerHTML;

            // start Ajax call
            ajaxCall('data/contacts.json', output, function (data) {

                // render the mustache template by combining the HTML with the JSON
➥data that was returned
                var renderedContent = Mustache.to_html(template, data);

                // put the rendered template into the DOM
                output.innerHTML = renderedContent;

            }); // end ajax call
        }

    } // end addr object

    // get all contacts when you click the button
    getAllButton.addEventListener("click", addr.getAllContacts, false);

})(); // end anonymous function
```

After using Mustache's `to_html` method to convert the template into more useable HTML, it's inserted into the DOM as usual, by using `innerHTML` and passing it the `renderedContent` object.

Creating a JavaScript Template Within the DOM

Now that all the JavaScript is set up, let's jump back into the HTML document from Listing 12.7, and by using Mustache's special template syntax, we'll add some actual content into the `<script>` element we previously left blank.

Whether you're using Mustache or one of the many other JavaScript templating systems, you will inevitably encounter slight differences in the syntax of the templating language, but the concepts are all the same. Mustache uses double curly braces: `{{object}}` to signify an object that needs to be parsed. Listing 12.7.3 shows you the simple Mustache template you would use to output a list of names from the `addressBook` JSON object that was returned in the Ajax call. If you were to run this program, you should see the same output created from the examples in Chapter 8, "Communicating with the Server Through Ajax," but now rendered as a mustache template.

Listing 12.7.3   **Mustache Templates to Be Added to the HTML**

```
<script type="text/x-mustache-tmpl" id="mustache-template">
    <ul>
    {{#addressBook}}
        <li><a href="mailto:{{email}}">{{name}}</a></li>
    {{/addressBook}}
    </ul>
</script>
```

Mustache will parse the information inside the `<script>` element as a template and then pair each `{{object}}` with its counterpart in the JSON data we called in (the second argument in the `to_html` method). You probably noticed that `{{addressBook}}`, `{{email}}`, and `{{name}}` are the same objects used in `contacts.json`. This is no coincidence. The objects in your JavaScript template need to match the objects in your data source. The data source doesn't need to be an external file brought in through an Ajax call; it can also be embedded right in the main JavaScript file, but using JavaScript templates with Ajax is one of the most common use cases.

In Listing 12.7.4, you can see the contents of `contacts.json` and how each object in the JavaScript template also exists in the JSON data.

Listing 12.7.4   **Mapping Mustache Template to the Data**

```
{
"addressBook" : [
    {
        "name": "hillisha",
        "email": "hill@example.com"
    },
    {
        "name": "paul",
```

```
        "email": "cleveland@example.com"
    },
    {

        "name": "vishaal",
        "email": "vish@example.com"
    },
    {

        "name": "mike",
        "email": "grady@example.com"
    },
    {

        "name": "jamie",
        "email": "dusted@example.com"
    }
]
}
```

Benefits of JavaScript Templates

There are many benefits of using a system of JavaScript templating. For those who very much dislike having HTML content inside a JavaScript file, they are a great way to abstract structure out of your behavior layer and put it back into the HTML where it belongs, but in a slightly different, more dynamic way.

There's always the debate over putting behavior in your CSS file with animations, and now there's another debate to be had about putting part of the structure layer into your JavaScript. Although using JavaScript templates that render content on the client don't align with the concepts of progressive enhancement in the way that you must always have content available, in other ways using these templates creates a harder line for the structure layer because it's not JavaScript in the normal sense. I don't think there are any developers in the world who can honestly say that the first time they saw a JavaScript template they said, "Oh, yea, that's definitely JavaScript." It doesn't look or act like JavaScript. The only way you can really tell is that it's wrapped in a `<script>` element, and if you turn off JavaScript, it breaks.

Having your content break without JavaScript is a big deal; I won't lie. It's an issue where you would need to poll your audience to see if any number of them turns off JavaScript. If your audience has 100% JavaScript usage, the risk of rendered content not appearing is extremely low. These are decisions you will have to make as a developer. At times they can be difficult calls to make, such as when to drop support for a certain browser, but with the right amount of analytics data you can be assured you'll make the right decision for your users.

JavaScript on the Server with NodeJS

NodeJS is a server-side implementation of JavaScript, but it goes much further than that. The goal of NodeJS is to provide a platform to create incredibly fast network applications. It's more than just JavaScript running on a server though; the server itself is written in JavaScript. With

Node, a back-end library is provided that includes modules to help you easily write your own Node server. That probably sounds really complicated, but in a little while I'll show you how easy it is to write your own server running Node JavaScript on the server.

The Web browser is considered to be a context in which you can run JavaScript. JavaScript in the browser runs on the client and is susceptible to rendering errors, browser problems, security holes, and server communication bottlenecks. You may not be thrilled to hear negative things being said about a language after you're almost finished reading an entire book about it. But it's no secret that JavaScript has had its problems in the past, many of which we're still paying for in the form of endless support checks and conditional statements. However, JavaScript is still a very powerful programming language. It's generally pretty easy to use, it makes sense, and it is widely adopted and gaining momentum in the industry at a rate that few other languages have experienced. For this reason, JavaScript is testing out its sea legs and trying to break free of the browser. The server is now another "context" in which we can run JavaScript. This is the Node project.

As I mentioned earlier, the Node platform is somewhat of a library because it provides you with a set of predefined functions and methods you can access, but they're much more powerful and they use a loading model called the Asynchronous Module Definition API (AMD). The AMD loading model is also applied to a lot of front-end JavaScript libraries as a way to manage resources. Think of it like a PHP include. In Node there are a bunch of modules available for use, but to use them, you don't want to have to load the entire codebase. The AMD loading model allows you to load only the modules that you're going to be using.

In this section, we jump straight into the fire with Node and go over installation and how to set up an http server in a surprisingly small number of steps.

Installing Node

The first step to using Node is installing it. Installation packages for both Windows and Mac can be found at nodejs.org. After you have NodeJS installed, we can start putting together the server.

As a developer, you will probably find yourself spending a fair amount of time on the command line. If you're a designer, you probably hate it with a passion. Running a server of any kind requires a little time on the command line, and Node is no different. However, to start off, let's create a directory called "node" and put a file called `server.js` inside it. It doesn't matter where the directory lives, but be sure you can easily access it from the command line for when we start to run the server. As long as you have Node successfully installed, you'll be fine.

Next we're going to open up `server.js` and get to work. NodeJS contains a module specifically for creating a server, called `http`, and, you guessed it, it's for creating an http server. Using the AMD loading model we can include that module and save it to a variable we will reference later. Listing 12.8 shows code to include the http module inside of `server.js`.

Listing 12.8 **Contents of `server.js,` Including the http Module**

```
// include the http module you need
var http = require("http");
```

If the http module were a library by itself, using the `require()` method would be the equivalent of adding a reference `http.js` to the bottom of your HTML document. Any methods, objects, or functions stored in Node within the `http` object can now be used in your application.

Writing the Server

After the http module is included, you need to access the `createServer()` method inside the `http` object to begin building the server.

Inside this method you will start the `response`, set the content type (`text/plain` for us), and then pass any data into the server that you would like outputted. This very basic example of writing an `http` server with NodeJS is illustrated in Listing 12.8.1.

Listing 12.8.1 **Contents of `server.js`**

```
// include the http module you need
var http = require("http");
// access the createServer method in the http object
 http.createServer(function(request, response) {

    // tell the server what kind of file is coming at it
    response.writeHead(200, {"Content-Type": "text/plain"});

    // make the server output a message
    response.write("Welcome to the future of JavaScript.");

    // End the server interaction
    response.end();

}).listen(3000); // listening on port 3000
```

After the server is created, you need to set a port for it to listen on. This port is how you will access the server contents through a browser window. In Listing 12.8.1, toward the end of the server setup function, you can see that we are telling the server to listen on port 3000. This means that after you start running the server, you can visit http://localhost:3000 in a Web browser and see the output message of "Welcome to the future of JavaScript."

So far, you have installed NodeJS, included the http module in a server file, wrote the server itself, and set it to listen on port 3000. (You can set the port to anything you'd like.) The last step in the process is to actually run the server. Whether you're using IIS, Apache, Node, or something else, there is an on and off switch for a server. To run the Node http server you just wrote, you will have to make a visit to the command line.

From the command line, find the directory in which you created `server.js` (or drag the folder into the command line window). When you're there, type `node server.js` (still in the command line) to run the file. Typing `node server.js` will turn on your Node server. Now, open up your favorite Web browser at the port you specified (http://localhost:3000 in the examples), sit back, and enjoy your future with JavaScript.

Summary

In this chapter, we took a short step back to review some of the higher-level topics we went over through the course of this book in hopes of jogging your memory and connecting the dots from chapter to chapter, exposing the path you took to get to this point. We went over progressive enhancement, manipulating the DOM, all the ways you learned how to store data in JavaScript, and server communication models like Ajax and Web workers.

This chapter was also broken down in to two major components: JavaScript for designers and JavaScript for developers to illustrate the two very different paths you can take, however you choose to continue in learning the language.

The designer path discussed a future of advanced interface design and creating rich applications that not only function cross-device but also target and enhance features of each in unique ways. We talked about how to capture both touch and mouse events to create a single interface that can work without having to refactor feature-specific code. We also got into applying dynamic styles with CSS transforms in JavaScript and how to make an object respond to touch interactions.

From there, JavaScript for designers broke out of the browser and onto the desktop by creating a drag-and-drop interface that interacted with a combination of new APIs available in JavaScript.

The developers learned about creating document structure with JavaScript templates. We went over a new method of creating and laying out dynamic content with a templating system called Mustache. We learned about the pluses and minuses of this type of system and how it all relates back to progressive enhancement.

Finally, like the designers, the developers also broke out of the browser, but in a very different way. We introduced a new JavaScript platform for running the language outside the context of the browser on its own server. We talked about NodeJS and went through a simple implementation example of creating and running a server that is based off of NodeJS and written in JavaScript.

Exercises

1. What are the mouse-event counterparts of `touchstart`, `touchmove`, and `touchend`?

2. What are the four types of events that can be created by the `createEvent()` method?

3. What are JavaScript templates used for?

A

Answers

Chapter 1

1. Structure, presentation, and behavior
2. Content
3. Progressive enhancement ensures that you are using the proper amount of code in the correct places, which promotes strong caching of the technologies in the browser.

Chapter 2

1. The behavior layer
2. JavaScript at the bottom allows the entire document to load before JavaScript blocks the download of subsequent objects on the page.
3. Cookies

Chapter 3

1. A function that is declared as it runs and has no assigned name
2. When it is called by another function
3. Through events

Chapter 4

1. Document, Element, Text, Attribute
2. The DOM is a standardized outline of an HTML document that creates access points or "hooks" in the form of nodes by which JavaScript can enter.
3. The attribute node will be created automatically and then set as normal.

Chapter 5

1. Number, String, Boolean

2. An associative array is a normal array that uses strings as index values instead of numbers.

3. An array that contains other arrays

Chapter 6

1. Variables cache in JavaScript, so it's best to cache them all at once for better referencing.

2. Reserved words are references to terms that already exist in the JavaScript language. Therefore, using them in your code would create unwanted collisions and errors.

3. Anonymous functions execute immediately and have no label or name assigned to them.

Chapter 7

1. With event handlers, you can attach only a single function to a specific event of a DOM node. This limitation does not exist with event listeners.

2. `attachEvent()`

3. The `preventDefault()` method is used to stop the default browser behavior of a given event, such as stopping the browser from executing an `href` or a form submit.

Chapter 8

1. `method`, `file/url`, `asynchronous` `username`, `password`. `username` and `password` are optional.

2. Ajax doesn't stand for anything; it is simply a combination of technologies meant for server communication from the client.

3. `setInterval()`

Chapter 9

1. The four things are

   Get the code to work.

   Get the code to work well.

   Make the code easy to follow.

   Make the code as reusable as possible.

2. In other languages an underscore signifies privacy, which doesn't exist in JavaScript.

3. When you want to use a block of code only once

Chapter 10

1. A JavaScript library is a collection of functions and methods presented in a reusable format.

2. A plug-in is a built-in way to extend the functionality of a library.

3. A content delivery network is a large distributed collection of servers that deliver content based on a user's geographical location.

Chapter 11

1. Landmark, document structure, abstract, and widget

2. Information from the battery API includes Level, Charging (true or false), chargingTime, and dischargingTime.

3. The network information API returns the following connection types: 2G, 3G, WIFI, ETHERNET, and UNKNOWN.

Chapter 12

1. mousedown, mousemove, and mouseup/click

2. UIEvents, MouseEvents, MutationEvents, and HTMLEvents

3. JavaScript templates are used to process and structure data inside an HTML document.

Index

M

Try Safari Books Online FREE for 15 days

Get online access to Thousands of Books and Videos

Safari Books Online   FREE 15-DAY TRIAL + 15% OFF*
informit.com/safaritrial

> ## Feed your brain
> Gain unlimited access to thousands of books and videos about technology,
> digital media and professional development from O'Reilly Media,
> Addison-Wesley, Microsoft Press, Cisco Press, McGraw Hill, Wiley, WROX,
> Prentice Hall, Que, Sams, Apress, Adobe Press and other top publishers.

> ## See it, believe it
> Watch hundreds of expert-led instructional videos on today's hottest topics.

WAIT, THERE'S MORE!

> ## Gain a competitive edge
> Be first to learn about the newest technologies and subjects with Rough Cuts
> pre-published manuscripts and new technology overviews in Short Cuts.

> ## Accelerate your project
> Copy and paste code, create smart searches that let you know when new
> books about your favorite topics are available, and customize your library
> with favorites, highlights, tags, notes, mash-ups and more.

* Available to new subscribers only. Discount applies to the Safari Library and is valid for first
12 consecutive monthly billing cycles. Safari Library is not available in all countries.

Addison Wesley

REGISTER

THIS PRODUCT

informit.com/register

Register the Addison-Wesley, Exam Cram, Prentice Hall, Que, and Sams products you own to unlock great benefits.

To begin the registration process, simply go to **informit.com/register** to sign in or create an account. You will then be prompted to enter the 10- or 13-digit ISBN that appears on the back cover of your product.

Registering your products can unlock the following benefits:

- Access to supplemental content, including bonus chapters, source code, or project files.
- A coupon to be used on your next purchase.

Registration benefits vary by product. Benefits will be listed on your Account page under Registered Products.

About InformIT — **THE TRUSTED TECHNOLOGY LEARNING SOURCE**

INFORMIT IS HOME TO THE LEADING TECHNOLOGY PUBLISHING IMPRINTS Addison-Wesley Professional, Cisco Press, Exam Cram, IBM Press, Prentice Hall Professional, Que, and Sams. Here you will gain access to quality and trusted content and resources from the authors, creators, innovators, and leaders of technology. Whether you're looking for a book on a new technology, a helpful article, timely newsletters, or access to the Safari Books Online digital library, InformIT has a solution for you.

informIT.com

THE TRUSTED TECHNOLOGY LEARNING SOURCE

Addison-Wesley | Cisco Press | Exam Cram
IBM Press | Que | Prentice Hall | Sams

SAFARI BOOKS ONLINE

informIT.com
THE TRUSTED TECHNOLOGY LEARNING SOURCE

 InformIT is a brand of Pearson and the online presence for the world's leading technology publishers. It's your source for reliable and qualified content and knowledge, providing access to the top brands, authors, and contributors from the tech community.

Addison-Wesley   **Cisco Press**   EXAM/**CRAM**   **IBM** Press.   **que**   **PRENTICE HALL**   **SAMS** | Safari

LearnIT at InformIT

Looking for a book, eBook, or training video on a new technology? Seeking timely and relevant information and tutorials? Looking for expert opinions, advice, and tips? **InformIT has the solution.**

- Learn about new releases and special promotions by subscribing to a wide variety of newsletters.
  Visit **informit.com/newsletters**.

- Access FREE podcasts from experts at **informit.com/podcasts**.

- Read the latest author articles and sample chapters at **informit.com/articles**.

- Access thousands of books and videos in the Safari Books Online digital library at **safari.informit.com**.

- Get tips from expert blogs at **informit.com/blogs**.

Visit **informit.com/learn** to discover all the ways you can access the hottest technology content.

Are You Part of the **IT** Crowd?

Connect with Pearson authors and editors via RSS feeds, Facebook, Twitter, YouTube, and more! Visit **informit.com/socialconnect**.

informIT.com THE TRUSTED TECHNOLOGY LEARNING SOURCE   PEARSON

Addison-Wesley   **Cisco Press**   EXAM/**CRAM**   **IBM** Press.   **que**   **PRENTICE HALL**   **SAMS** | Safari

Safari
Books Online

FREE
Online Edition

Your purchase of *Learning JavaScript* includes access to a free online edition for 45 days through the **Safari Books Online** subscription service. Nearly every Addison-Wesley Professional book is available online through **Safari Books Online**, along with over thousands of books and videos from publishers such as Cisco Press, Exam Cram, IBM Press, O'Reilly Media, Prentice Hall, Que, Sams, and VMware Press.

Safari Books Online is a digital library providing searchable, on-demand access to thousands of technology, digital media, and professional development books and videos from leading publishers. With one monthly or yearly subscription price, you get unlimited access to learning tools and information on topics including mobile app and software development, tips and tricks on using your favorite gadgets, networking, project management, graphic design, and much more.

Activate your FREE Online Edition at
informit.com/safarifree

STEP 1:   Enter the coupon code: IROZQZG.

STEP 2:   New Safari users, complete the brief registration form.
            Safari subscribers, just log in.

If you have difficulty registering on Safari or accessing the online edition,
please e-mail customer-service@safaribooksonline.com

 Addison Wesley Adobe Press ALPHA Cisco Press FT Press FINANCIAL TIMES IBM Press Microsoft Press New Riders O'REILLY

 Peachpit Press PRENTICE HALL Que Redbooks SAMS SAS Publishing  vmware PRESS WILEY WROX